Mark 947

Mark 947

✦

A Life Shaped by God, Gender and Force of Will

Calpernia Sarah Addams

Writers Club Press

New York Lincoln Shanghai

Mark 947
A Life Shaped by God, Gender and Force of Will

Writers Club Press
an imprint of iUniverse, Inc.

For information address:
iUniverse, Inc.
2021 Pine Lake Road, Suite 100
Lincoln, NE 68512
www.iuniverse.com

ISBN: 0-595-26376-3

Printed in the United States of America

To the ones who gave me everything.

I would like to thank Andrea James and my Southern sisters in crime, members in good standing of the Southern Baptist Girls Society.

Also, Chyna, my second mother, and the Snake Pit and everyone there who taught me new ways to survive.

And let's not forget my family, Mom, Dad, Ginger and Jerm.

And finally, all the incredible women I know who inspire me by just getting out of bed in the morning.

Contents

Mark 9:47 xi

Foreword xiii

CHAPTER 1   In the Beginning 1

CHAPTER 2   Dad 34

CHAPTER 3   Church Camp 53

CHAPTER 4   Kamala 65

CHAPTER 5   School 75

CHAPTER 6   Camping 88

CHAPTER 7   The Fall 96

CHAPTER 8   "Graduation" 99

CHAPTER 9   Leaving Home 107

CHAPTER 10   Boot Camp 109

CHAPTER 11   Desert Storm 125

CHAPTER 12   Adak 132

CHAPTER 13   Confrontation 139

CHAPTER 14   Showgirl 143

CHAPTER 15   Brigitte Carmichael 162

CHAPTER 16   Murderous Friends 167

CHAPTER 17   Learning 177

CHAPTER 18   Barry.............................. 181

CHAPTER 19   Visit to Chicago 200

CHAPTER 20   Relationship 204

CHAPTER 21   Pageant............................... 214

CHAPTER 22   The Trial 229

CHAPTER 23   Epilogue 234

Mark 9:47

⁴³ And if thy hand offend thee, cut it off: it is better for thee to enter into life maimed, than having two hands to go into hell, into the fire that never shall be quenched:

⁴⁴ Where their worm dieth not, and the fire is not quenched.

⁴⁵ And if thy foot offend thee, cut it off: it is better for thee to enter halt into life, than having two feet to be cast into hell, into the fire that never shall be quenched:

⁴⁶ Where their worm dieth not, and the fire is not quenched.

⁴⁷ And if thine eye offend thee, pluck it out: it is better for thee to enter into the kingdom of God with one eye, than having two eyes to be cast into hell fire:

⁴⁸ Where their worm dieth not, and the fire is not quenched.

The Bible, King James Version

Foreword

o o o o o o o o o o o o o o o o o o o o o o o o o o o o o o o o

*And if thine eye offend thee, pluck it out: it is better for thee to
enter into the kingdom of God with one eye, than having two
eyes to be cast into hell fire.*

—*Mark 9:47*

To the faithful who believe a religious text is a direct message from the
divine, you are committing a special sort of blasphemy when you quote
from their text to defend actions and feelings they deem indefensible.
An utter transgression! An unholy perversion!

Yet if these revered words are the weapons used against us from earliest memory to instill fear, shame, and self-hatred, then we must come
back to them if we survive to be old enough and strong enough to
wield these words ourselves. We must see these words as what they are,
and expose them to others as what they are.

Can this passage be right? Does going through this life self-muti-
lated offer hope for avoiding sin and reaching salvation? What does this
mean for transsexual women? Are these words to be taken *that* literally?

Is one form of genital modification a symbol of the Lord's covenant,
and another a sign of unspeakable depravity? Aren't the differences
between circumcision and sex change really just a matter of degree?
And what of that sinful eye Jesus tells us to pluck out? Where does holy
modification end, and unholy mutilation begin?

I grew up a few years earlier and a few hours north of Calpernia, my
childhood also steeped in a mingling of rural and suburban sensibilities
from the American heartland. The softened and sanitized version of
Christianity to which I was exposed did not instill a crippling fear of an

imminent hell, or make me feel my desires rendered me an abomination. Still, I always felt strangely baffled that an arcane book rife with contradictions and condemnations held those I love under its spell. Perhaps that is the gift of the outsider looking in: a blessing of perspective to offset the curse of being so different.

How do you drive out fear and hatred that others have confused as love? Do you wield the words they hold holy, using them to defend yourself? Do you counter with I Samuel 16:7, or shield yourself with Galatians 3:28? Can doing this reach those who have hardened their hearts? Or must light be used to drive out darkness?

Here in front of you is one answer to the words used to maim us, and even kill us. We can set down our own words. We can open a door to let light and fresh air into the dank cells of imprisoned minds. We can show what love looks like from our perspective, in hopes that scales will fall from blinded eyes. Perhaps in time, people will stop hating, especially while calling it love. After all, that is the most vile of obscenities, and the true blasphemy.

The painful yet beautiful story set down here is a journey upriver, traveling back up a lifelong flow of memories and emotions. It traces them to the headwaters where familial memories first mingle and pool and start to swirl together, later blending with memories of friends and foes who ebb and flow as time rolls ever-onward.

In that place of early memory where earth, air, and water blur together into mist and marsh, love has always floated in the air soft as a quiet fog, gentle as cleansing rain or silent snowfall. Fear and hatred have always flowed here, too, silent and powerful poison springs forced to the surface from dark places below. We taste both when we drink from these still waters.

The words set down here are a message born of love, a beautiful snowflake or cool raindrop cast into the mingling waters. With enough of these, we can dilute the hot poisons of hatred flowing up from below, and perhaps a day will come when the waters from which we all drink will flow clean and pure, dark and cool.

Andrea James
Chicago, 2002

1

In the Beginning

I used to dream of a black ship, wrecked amidst the cast up debris of an unsettled sea. The end of the rain faded into spray at my feet, and dark waters uncoiled to drown the uncovered moon's reflection in shifting, secret surfaces. As thick sheets of cloud melted above and ran to slip into the smoldering red crack between ocean and sky, ripples dissolved across shrinking steel-colored pools at my feet, distorting the stranded creatures that writhed in death beneath. I had been left behind with this ship. It was dark and rotten with absorbed seawater. "I am not supposed to be here," I said to the sky, but there was no answer. It was easy to lie down, eroded by the exhalation of waves and the soft, tearing fingers of the wind on my back. There was no one here. No will. No harm.

My first awareness was the aroma of fresh coffee. I followed it back through the mists and opium light to a warm place under covers on a twin mattress in my room. Next the door would open, allowing in bright light and household sounds familiar as an old song. Mom would pick me up, trailing blanket and pillow, and deposit me on the couch to fall back asleep while Daddy finished breakfast. There was the smell of his oily jumpsuit. The tinkling of the metal fixtures on his workman's lunchbox as it received a thermos and sandwiches.

"And then what?" Her voice was like antique silver.

"I'll try to pick up another shift or two this week."

"Honey, we need at least half by next Friday, or we're gonna hafta…"

"I know, Beverly."

I pressed my face against the cushion and tried to ignore them, but the distraction of my dreams had faded. On the television a man in a rowboat with the sun for a head paddled down his cartoon river as a helium voice sang, "Funshine Saturday on A-B-C!!!"

Dad rolled me up in my red blanket like a burrito and carried me outside to the car. The screen door snapped shut behind us and my slow inhalations drew cold, damp predawn air. I wriggled closer to the stiff fabric across his chest, to the warmth. Moving through space in the side-lit fog of dawn, carried in Daddy's arms barely awake, and then into the warmth. I was lying on the seat in the back, feeling its still-cold plastic through cotton. Fuzzy morning-talk, two doors slamming shut, and the mesmerizing rush of heated air from vents in the front seat. Familiar voices of old men I had never seen reading farm reports between songs by Loretta Lynn and Patsy Cline. The music of gravel and grooves in the road played up through the tires and into my bones, dissolving me into nothingness again. Each time I emerged from sleep it was a bleary-eyed underwater awakening into the warmth, murky windows pressed in on all sides by fog, up and down the hilly roads of Tennessee.

"Go back to sleep, honey."

"Will you get me donuts? The little kind?" I was gone before the answer came.

I have never seen my mother wear the slightest hint of makeup. It didn't seem odd to me as a child. There was nothing to compare it with. She worked with the natural graces and flaws that God had given her in a seemingly unconcerned way, so that few indications of fashion and era could be picked out in photos taken from different decades. I never imagined an earring dangling from her ear, a bracelet on her wrist. I never questioned why. I never had to.

"First Timothy says 'In like manner also, that women adorn themselves in modest apparel, with shamefacedness and sobriety'" Her tone was reverent, and the ancient words came out softened by her sleepy country accent. They were a gift, a special secret she wanted to give to me. "Not with braided hair, or gold, or pearls, or costly array," and my mother's hands, to this day, remain free of even a wedding ring. Vanities. She moved through them like air and they were nothing to her.

I had her eyes, green, unlike the blue of my father and siblings, and her hair was thick and brown to her shoulders. "Momma, Grandaddy used to pay you twenny five cents to pluck out his gray hairs." An old story.

"Yes, honey."

"I could do you too."

"What does Proverbs say?"

"Every gray hair is a crown." Sung tiredly.

"Gray hair is a crown of splendor...It is attained by a righteous life." Only in this way did she display her abundance of jewels. Today her skin is fresh, her eyes are bright and beautifully worn from caring. Bangles and paint would look obscene on her.

In 1973, when I was only two, a Church of God of Prophecy missionary came to visit us and murdered the unsaved parents I would never know. That day they died in the Lord and were washed in the blood of Christ, born again as servants of God. I remember a home movie projected onto a sheet at my aunt's house, a jittering grainy image of my mother dancing with a cocktail in hand. Her young face was open and excited, flushed with the drink and effort. Filmed ages ago, it was a source of comedy for my less devout relatives and the cause of nervous laughter for my parents. Seeing her wantonness terrified me then, because I had never known her without God. Even when I lost my own faith years later, I did not wish for her to follow me. I have lived my life in a certain way because I had to, but I still do not know what will be the result. Fire or bliss or nothing at all, but I would take no one else down this path. Yet watching her dance I wished I could know that person. What would have happened if she had been my mother? Who would I have become?

It was called the East Nashville Church of God of Prophecy. I was too young to know that 'East Nashville' meant bad neighborhood. Too young to know that 'of Prophecy' meant goodbye to things of the world, like Disney and Star Wars, dancing and popular music, or basically most everything anyone else was doing. Every Sunday morning and night, every Wednesday night, and all week during Revival was the unrelenting, inescapable ritual of church.

In the beginning we were like any of the church's other babies. They started as tightly wrapped newborns rocked through interminable sermons and then matured into glassy-eyed toddlers enviably corralled into activity rooms during the preaching. As soon as a child developed enough sentience to obey commands, the first step towards adulthood was made. From then on they were expected to sit quietly and listen to the preaching. A knowledgeable observer could, at this point, watch for the slow apparition of horror to appear in their faces as their first sermon dragged on and they realized that there were to be no coloring books. No juice. No glitter and glue.

The bad neighborhoods in Nashville are different from their big-city counterparts. Instead of crowded, dirty streets blocked in by tall buildings, they are the leftover communities of an earlier era. Large decaying houses, once home to calm suburban families, had been divided into apartments by the disenchanted children and rented out to be managed from newer, finer neighborhoods.

When I was about five years old, just before we moved into our permanent home on McAlpine, we spent a year in one of these old houses on Lischey Avenue in East Nashville, not terribly far from the church building. Directly across the street was an incongruous Cantrell's Barbeque in our otherwise entirely residential area, and the ice cream truck that patrolled the streets also carried firecrackers and little toys. We left there after a fugitive tried to force his way in past my sleepy mother, who had foolishly answered the door late one night, but during our short time in this house I grew up just enough to reach the Age of Reasoning. It was at this point our church believed one became responsible for sins and could finally face Hell as a real consequence after death.

I lay in bed unable to sleep in the fat silence of our cavernous house, which was only occasionally broken by a click or groan of settling foundations. Sometimes I thought I could hear whispering in the corners of the high ceiling and fell asleep feeling watched. The supernatural was very real to me, as it went hand in hand with the teachings of our church.

It was winter, and I had placed a red balloon on the black metal heating vent chopped into the floor. The warm air blowing up forced the balloon to hover, suspended in the current, spinning and bouncing but somehow never falling off the column of air. I watched this balloon turning in the heat, barely visible in the dim streetlights filtered through my curtains, and began to imagine what it would be like when I went to Hell. I had already learned about the burning lake of fire, the immortal worms that ate the flesh of the damned. I mostly thought about the burning, how it would be like when I got a whipping and had to lie across the bed. No matter how I danced and screamed, the stinging belt kept coming. But whippings always ended quickly with a stern hug and no permanent damage done. Hell was forever. I had no words for my sin, but I knew without ever forming the intellectual conclusion that something was wrong with me. I was bound for fire.

I began to cry, imagining myself alone in red caverns with monsters behind every turn. I imagined my mother's tears tinged with shame, and I felt helpless knowing that she must harden her heart and accept God's will on the matter. Mom and Dad were the only people I had completely on my side, and God controlled even them. Soon my sobs and weeping were beyond restraint and I felt the blankets pull tight against my body with my mother's weight on the bed. Her hair was mussed from sleep, Dad silhouetted in the door.

"What's the matter, honey?" her voice was high with concern, a delicate hand brushing hair from my hot forehead.

"I don't want to go to Hell," I sobbed, choking on tears and snot, the last word coming out countrified as "Hay-ull." I was ashamed to admit it, but rendered powerless by despair. My mother blinked, unable to fathom why I would be concerned about this, much less in the middle of the night. Dad came over to kneel beside the bed and stroked my arm.

"He's just havin a bad dream, Beverly."

"Oh honey," Mom drew back the blanket and gathered me to her. "You don't have to worry about that. God only sends kids to heaven." She rocked me against her chest, but despite the comfort it offered I knew that God wouldn't take me to heaven. I just didn't say anything. Mom held me away so that she could look into my eyes and said, "Let's pray to Jesus that he will take care of you and watch over you, and everything will beOk."

My crying had diminished and I desperately clung to this new hope as I climbed out of bed and we all knelt in the dark with elbows resting on the quilt.

"Dennis, you pray..." Mom said. Dad was a little unsteady as he knelt.

"Oh Lord Jesus," my father began, "Please protect our son and help him feel your love. We pray you will hold him to your heart and help him walk the path of righteousness."

"Dear God," my mother took up the prayer, voice beseeching with fearful conviction, "Please show us your love and accept our praises. Oh Jesus, help Scotty let you into his heart forever and ever."

It was my turn, and I said the prayer I said every time we bowed our heads in church. "Jesus, forgive me for my sins, in Jesus' name, Amen." They told us in Children's Church if you didn't say "In Jesus' name" at the end, God didn't hear the prayer. It was like stamping the envelope, a necessary last step. Mom hugged me and Dad said goodnight, but when they closed the door behind them I saw the red balloon still jumping in the corner of the room. I knew that God knew I was messed up. It was between him and me and nothing had changed. I pulled myself together with a deep breath and the tears stopped of their own accord, leaving me to fall into dark dreams with a grim acceptance of my fate.

I was the oldest. My sister Ginger had been born four years later, and then Jeremy one year after her. Ginger was a thin, pixyish girl with a shy smile, close-mouthed to hide her crooked teeth. Her hair was golden brown like clean molasses and hung straight down her back, a blunt line of bangs cut above her eyes. When she was very young the girls at church passed her from lap to lap, quietly playing with her hair as if she were a doll, but as she grew she went out of fashion. In these fallen years she had no secret confidants and was left to sit forlornly next to Mom. Braces would come and go for me, music and friends and a missionary trip to Europe with the church. Ginger passed that time with bad teeth, drawing pictures of jug-headed ballerinas and rock stars with little ponytails, singing tonelessly into the mirror alone in her room. Many difficult years would pass before she became the self-sufficient, successful woman I know today.

Jeremy, or 'Jerm' as I called him, was bony and small. He was the only one of us to inherit Dad's perfect smile. Blonde as a baby, he now had the same brown 70's cut I wore throughout the early 80's, the only difference being that his hair laid straight while mine poked up in cowlicks. As soon as he could walk I latched onto him as my inseparable sidekick.

Then, life was measured in games of 'king of the hill' on the knoll in front of the church and time spent collecting fallen pinecones from the impossibly high trees in its lot, while other children watched cable television at home and retrieved cold beers for their relaxing parents. The building was made of red brick and wood. It cut into the side of a steep hill, banded by a creek in the back just distant enough that we could

sometimes plausibly ignore worried shouts like "Y'all c'mon and get
outta there, it's time for church!"

When we were little we sat patiently beside Mom and Dad in the
second pew, right side. Dad was on the aisle, always in his good overalls and pressed dress-shirt. The left strap was twisted once on purpose,
to protect from lightning. Considering Dad's sense of humor, this pre-
caution was probably wise. Mom usually wore a simple print dress and
listened with contented calm, focused on the preacher and his message.

On the back of the right front pew there should still be two small
crescent-shaped tooth marks. Sometimes to keep from nodding off I
leaned forward to rest my head there and rocked my buck teeth side to
side in the soft wood. Our preacher, Brother Goins, was a round,
beseeching, owlish old man never seen out of a suit and glasses. He
could sweat on command and made copious display of this talent to
accent his sermons. When he became particularly excited, usually an
hour or two into things, he began to shout and speak in tongues. The
air in our small church grew close with heat and sweat. He was pacing
to and fro, up and down the aisle, and I could smell what I thought
was mucus in the air from his choked vehemence. It was boring and
frightening at the same time. My eyes wandered from the attendance
board wavering between 43 and 57 to the 1950's light fixtures above
the center aisle that looked like dusty alien flowers glowing against the
evening sky outside the windows.

Before church everyone greeted the preacher in the foyer, and this
tiny room's faux paneled walls were hung with black wire racks displaying various tracts, all written and published at our church's headquar-
ters in Cleveland, Tennessee. When I was old enough to read, I
grabbed several on my way into the sermon, anything to take my mind
away from the hours of droning lecture and sweaty admonitions. My
favorite tract was the story of a boy who died without being 'right with
God.' It was embellished with a tiny woodcut of a winding country
path leading up to a covered bridge, which had nothing to do with the
story. The cramped black print gave a vague account of his wicked

ways, leading up to a prodigal return to his parents because of illness. In the end he lay on his deathbed and cried out to his grief-stricken mother:

"Pull me up, Momma. My feet are burning!" They pulled him up, but a few moments later he screamed and said, "Momma, pull my feet out of the fire, I can't stand the burning!" They pulled him up further until he was sitting. Finally he twisted and moaned and no amount of water dipped from the well could make him feel cool again. His entire body was burning in agony. As his eyes closed for the last time, the fires of Hell could be seen gleaming from within and he whispered, "It burns, Momma…it burns…" It was like the country ghost stories my Uncle told me, and I found the end scary and satisfying at the same time.

I was not allowed to read any real books in church. We could not talk. The hours passed, nights and seasons and years, and somewhere inside I absorbed from these rantings that this church did not love me. They wanted to, that much was clear. But they could only love me if the game was played their way, and I couldn't seem to do it, no matter how I wanted to. I tried to feel inside the way I was supposed to and it never ever came. Not even once. I knew something was wrong with me, something that drew the flames of damnation like an open door's draft, and as soon as it became clear I would be destroyed. Around this burning knowledge a smooth pearl of hatred began to form, and my heart was very quickly lost to God altogether.

It did not take many years for me to absorb the basic premise of the church's doctrine and recognize that it made integration with my peers impossible. I was to live among them, but completely apart. From that realization grew an ever increasing frustration with the hours of ranting from the pulpit, and this soon festered into hatred of the foolish, uneducated people who ran my life from that tiny brick building on a hill.

By 1980 we were quite accustomed to our life in Christ. Just as con-
victs invented games to pass long imprisonment, my nine-year-old
mind sought escape while seated on a hard wooden bench for hours at
a time. Jeremy sat close next to me so that we could reach our outside
arms around behind our backs and secretly thumb wrestle or pinch. As
long as we didn't get too out of hand we were left alone. Church literature in various shapes and colors was deposited weekly in holders on
the back of the pews, and Jerm and I became experts in origami, building miniature tableaux of people, animals and houses. The faces of the
apostles appeared in the folds of donkeys or the bows of Chinese fishing boats. Occasional red-lettered pronouncements direct from Jesus'
mouth became labels for the boxes and pyramids that housed our characters. Mom would sometimes look away from the sermon to find a
complex diorama of creatures and buildings had sprung up at her side.
"Y'all put that up now and listen."
If I could I might slip a penny under one of his buildings and hiss:
"Money-changer in the Temple! Jesus hates you!" before crushing it.
Discouraged from speaking out loud during the message, we created
our own systems of silent communication. The most versatile was
adapted from sign language learned during summers in church camp.
It quickly grew complex enough to communicate a developed lexicon
of sarcasm, frustration and ever-present boredom. Jerm surveyed my
little paper village built on the tilting landscape of blonde wood pew
and, with his eyes, selected my temple for his disparaging hand gesture.
A helplessly falling letter "S" signified the hissing of a punctured balloon, as if to say the temple was so disappointing it entirely deflated
him. For particular emphasis, the sign was accompanied by a slump
and dead-face expression. Sensing movement in his peripheral vision,
Dad sometimes lightly caught a wrist in mid-sign and with a look
ended our fun for a few minutes. I kept my eyes forward and face blank
as I discretely spelled out "Hee" in sign language. According to our
weird imaginations, this was the resonant, tuning-fork sound made by
a mocking angelic grin. Or it would be, if such grins made sounds.

One Saturday the house was empty and we had nothing to do. Dad was working, as usual, and Mom had decided to clean out the basement since it was such a nice sunny day. All the doors and windows were open and each breeze carried in humid scents of sprinkler-wet pavement and grass. I was in the front yard banging geodes with a hammer. White sunlight fell hot on my shoulders but the constant gusting wind played in the trees and bushes, drying any sweat before it could bead. Somehow in spite of the warmth, the thick patches of clover felt cold as iced pennies under my bare feet.

A zing of icy water shot into my ear. I screamed and pushed Jerm down before I even realized what was happening. He was laughing and did not even try to get back up, instead continuing to crush his dish-soap bottle as hard as he could. He directed a constant stream at my face as I tried to reach past his defensively deployed legs and take the weapon.

"STOP! QUIDDIT! STOP!" But I was laughing too. He quickly ran out of water pressure and I tackled, securing him helplessly against the ground with my legs and snatching the bottle to hold it over his face. There was plenty left for a final squirt.

"Say I'm your master."

He only scrunched his face and turned it to the side, struggling against my weight. I tipped the bottle and let a drip fall. He screamed with tortured laughter and managed to slip out from under me. The screen door was locked before I had a chance.

"That's my squirt bottle." He said gravely from behind the screen.

"Well you're not gettin it." I slung the last gasp of water at the screen.

"Momma, Scotty's squirting water in the house." Jeremy said it just quietly enough that I knew it was a ruse. Mom was in the basement.

"Jerm go get me one and we can draw on Mr. Norman's."

Sometimes when it was hot outside we played a game on our neighbor's crescent driveway. Our squirt bottles were perfect for drawing a bird's-eye view of scenes around ourselves on the pavement. Mom's empty contact-solution bottles gave the most precise stream, but anything with a small opening would do. Our enmity dissolved and I went past the magically unlocked door to follow him into the kitchen. Ginger was on the couch watching television. Her white t-shirt had a crude appliqué of a pink daisy.

"Can I come?" In my memory her voice is always pleading, frightened of dismissal. I hate myself for that.

"We're gonna play squirt bottles on Mr. Norman's driveway." This meant yes and she scrambled off the couch to find herself one as well.

I drew the deck of an enormous boat under myself, leaving Ginger to create the wavy circle of an island around her feet with a pirouette. Jerm made a fish to ride on, which was initially met with skepticism as viable transport until his addition of cool fins and teeth won us over. We hopped back and forth from ship to shark to island, screaming at close calls with the deadly ocean and using precious squirts of water to punish the unwary. A minute or less after we had drawn them, details began to fade and the outlined scene would evaporate under our bare feet. As Ginger's island disappeared, she had to leap to the safety of my ship or else Jerm and I would yell, "You're DEAD!" When the sun lost its heat and passed into evening, our lines of water took longer and longer to fade, instead expanding into messy looking caricatures of whatever we had drawn. We left off our game and I went back to my geodes.

Each strike with the hammer caused sparks and grit to fly from the rock. I found them in certain parts of the cow-field at my grandmother's farm. This one looked like a stone potato, now covered with white scars from my attempts to open it, and would yield coarse crystals which I collected in glass Coke-bottles. I liked to imagine that they were magic. I got a sense of the structure from each hit, building a mental picture of the inside until a final well-placed bang burst it open, spilling bright gems into the grass.

"Scott, can I play with your BB gun?" Ginger had reappeared in the front door, cringing. She knew I would say no. Her hair moved slightly as the house inhaled another breath of summer air.

"No."

"Pleeeeeze…I'll be careful."

"If you go get Jer'my, I'll take y'all on a picnic." Distraction was key, or else she would cry to Mom and I would have to share. I didn't want her playing with my things, but sometimes an unexpected guilt seized me and I tried to make up for being a bad brother. Ginger disappeared back inside and I put the pieces of the geode by the porch, to be dealt with later.

Dan Mills elementary school was a small campus folded neatly into the residential landscape, easy to miss if you didn't know it was there. All three of us would eventually pass through it on our way to troubled teen-age years in junior high and high school. Out behind it a dusty plain rimmed in trees served as the baseball field, and a small playground with some hoops sat desperately resisting entropy and rust on one side. The area was usually deserted in the summer unless a few kids wandered in to play basketball on the blacktop. A Boy Scout meeting-house sat on its other side. I felt a twinge of the old resentment whenever I saw it. I could never join because my parents didn't want me exposed to the looser version of Christianity practiced by the people involved. But Mom and Dad felt safe allowing us to walk the two blocks to the school and play in its fringe of trees on pleasant summery days.

At home Ginger and Jeremy began preparations for our picnic. A cooler was excavated from the catch-all laundry room and packed with three white-bread baloney and cheese sandwiches, a thermos of ice tea and three Little Debbies. I folded a threadbare red cotton blanket in on top and Ginger found a portable radio from Mom's stash of 70's relics. She wore pink jelly flip-flops and a headband, her small face intently focused on her actions. She wanted to get everything right because I didn't show this much attention often.

We began walking side-by-side down our empty street. I carried the cooler and held Ginger's hand, feeling a bit inflated with responsibility. The neighborhood was empty, evacuated in the hot afternoon. Jerm skipped alongside carrying the old radio. Unintelligible music hissed out from its single waffled speaker, now near and then distant in his swinging arms. None of us seemed inclined to speak, enjoying the motion and sunlight. So much was just understood, anyway. Sometimes it seemed to me that our quarrels and whines and chatty exclamations were all performed to prove we were normal to outsiders. I was glad to be doing something on our own away from any restriction or observation.

The embankment where we set up our meal overlooked the baseball field by a few feet. One time I had sat there with Mom during Jellybean Field Day, a school event where the kids ran around completing mini-hurdles for jellybeans. This funny looking black girl I knew came up and said Hi to Mom and me. Her name was Emaryion, and she had one eye that looked off in its own direction trapped behind super-thick glasses. Her hair was wooly and separated into two twisted pigtails tied with real red yarn. One time in a school talent show she had amazed everyone by singing an incredible version of "Why do fools fall in love?" and despite her pariah status I had held her in awe ever since. It was strange to have her meet my mom. Two entirely separated worlds converging.

Ginger spread the red blanket and began taking out sandwiches. Jerm had set the radio to classical music, I'm sure because he knew I liked it, and as afternoon tilted into evening our former trance melted away leaving us finally able to talk. Away from the vigilant ears of home, we laid out our cares and concerns to be examined in the angled sunlight.

"I'm gonna be a singer." Ginger said. Her sandwich was impossibly white and she took a bite without looking up at either of us. The ice rattled in her glass when she gulped some tea to wash it down.

"You can't sing." Jerm said. He had opened his Little Debbie already. It was one of the Swiss cake rolls, and he carefully removed its chocolate coating in a single curved sheet. It cracked and half fell onto the blanket.

"You're not supposed to eat that yet!" Ginger screamed. "Scott! He's eating the Little Debbie first!" The 'can't sing' comment had stung. I decided to ignore Jeremy. If she wanted to sing…well, then…I began trying to think of how that could work.

"You can sing in church," I suggested. "Pass me the tea."

"I want to really sing. Good music. And I'm going to, I've already been practicing." She pointedly took the thermos of tea from Jeremy's part of the blanket and gave it to me. I saw her jug-headed, pin-legged drawings of girl singers in my mind.

"Mom and Dad won't let you sing music like's on the radio." He was unrolling the cake part to reveal the thin layer of white 'cream' inside. He licked at it like a little monkey.

"She can sing if she wants to. We can do anything we want to. Why not?"

"Well, if you want to sing what's on the radio, I won't tell." He ate the dissected cake in three bites and it was gone.

"And I won't either."

Ginger thought this over for a second. "Well, thank you. I won't tell on you either if you want to do stuff."

I guiltily thought back on the times that Jerm and I had made fun of her. When she first started her habit of clutching a pillow to her chest and rocking, she did it anywhere including the living room couch. We always rushed to sit on either side and match her pace. With each slap of our backs against the couch we droned, "GIN-ger is a DUM-dum, GIN-ger is a DUM-dum," until she jumped up and stomped past us to her room. Eventually she only rocked there, alone. The cruelties between Jerm and me were more subtle, more intimate, the kinds of things you had to know a person very well even to understand enough to ridicule. Once when we were riding home from Church I reached up into the front seat to take some gum from Mom. Jerm looked at me and announced, "Scott has hair under his arms!" Everyone in the car was silent for a moment. This was not earth-shattering news, although probably a bit unexpected as a conversational topic. In my heart of hearts the early appearance of these changes had revolted me, and with that comment he had instantly mortified me far beyond what I would have thought was possible. My face turned scarlet and I prickled all over with shame. Ginger giggled and somehow Mom sensed my embarrassment, although I can't imagine she understood its depth or reason.

"Jer'my, leave him alone. You don't need to worry about that."

Jerm fell back into the seat, silent, but I knew that he knew he had scored a victory over his big brother without even understanding exactly what had happened. He didn't hate me. We didn't hate Ginger. It was just that way things were. A constant testing of the balance of powers.

In the field behind our school a truce settled, and we relaxed into a natural human kindness only seen when we were alone together. Ginger poured the tea, Jerm complimented the sandwiches, and I didn't try to boss anyone around. The tensions of home had evaporated in the sunlight, and now as afternoon fled into the orange horizon beyond our trees, we felt clear enough to pack up and make our way back.

Walking home we held hands, and as the coming darkness met our steps it found no fear or division.

Every year our little church celebrated the day it was founded with "Homecoming." According to what we learned in Sunday school, a man named AJ Thomlinson experienced a vision in the woods in the 1940s describing a new church based on the "whole Bible, rightly divided." On the anniversary of this revelation we had a big dinner lasting from morning till night. Mom started cooking days beforehand. There were always stashes of relics from the sixties throughout the house, chunky things colored in earth tones and bigger than they needed to be. The kitchen's stockpile consisted of a chipped green electric skillet large enough to make fried baloney for four and a heavy brown crock-pot embellished with partially scratched off flowers. The bulky removable power cords for these appliances were probably irreplaceable. Usual items on the menu were fried pork chops in gravy, baby green peas or glazed carrots, and shiny buttered yeast rolls that released a hot breath of steam with the first bite. In leaner times we had big skillets of milk gravy poured over white bread sprinkled with pepper, sweet tea in ice-filled mason jars laid out beside each mismatched plate. Mom collected our dishes and silverware from yard sales, and we hardly knew that sets were even supposed to match. Vanity over material possessions was beneath us; perversely we learned to have pride in the plainness of things.

Although the pleasures of conventional vanity were discouraged, we did enjoy eating. For celebrations like Homecoming there was no limit to the amount and complexity of country cooking the women of the church prepared. Our busy house filled with promises of simmering peppered green beans seasoned with ham and sweet cornbread baked in a black iron skillet rimmed with butter. A Tupperware bowl of bubbling Velveeta cheese was carefully brought from the microwave and poured into a pot filled with drained macaroni. My sister and I begged for the privilege of stirring them together, creamy orange cheese thick and fragrant and delicious when licked off the long-handled wooden spoon. Salt flowed liberally from Mom's prized shakers, bought at an old woman's yard sale. "They're just like from a 50's diner!"

"You and Jer'my get your instruments, I want y'all to play in church today." She was pouring the macaroni into a casserole dish, getting everything ready for travel.

"Ok Momma." Jerm and I ran to get our cases and tune up. I had started playing before him, but his musical talent was more natural and easy. He waited patiently for me to tune my fiddle and give him an E, from which he quickly developed a crystal clear chord. Neither of us had ever had a lesson.

"What do you wanna play?" My bow was poised. Jerm seemed tiny with the huge guitar hanging from its strap across his shoulders. He looked up toward the ceiling for a moment, all business. Then he started to fingerpick a bluegrassy version of *At the Cross*. I jumped in, sliding up and down on the notes and playing double-stops where I could. It was so bright and fun, making music out of nothing, and as we played it was as if our two minds were holding hands and running across a giant field of October wheat. At least that's how I imagined it. Mom sang from the kitchen as she put everything together.

"At the cross, at the cross, where I first saw the light…"

"And the burden of my heart rolled away…" That verse was plaintive and she always sounded honestly touched, even now just singing it while cooking.

One of her favorite cooking devices was a steel pressure cooker. She set it on the back burner and carefully turned the handle away from her.

"Always turn the handles away from the edge so y'all don't accidentally pull the pot down and get burnt," Mom used to say.

The pressure cooker had a small, heavy metal cylinder that rested on top of a spigot, and it jiggled like a mad rattlesnake, releasing bits of steam as pressure built. Faint traces of bean shrapnel still show in the plaster above the stove, a reminder of the only time Mom didn't fasten the lid tightly. Massive forces built up in the cooker, softening the cheapest, toughest meat into tender succulence. Onions, carrots and potatoes absorbed the salty brown gravy and the meat separated easily into juicy slivers.

Everything for the Homecoming was ready to be carried still warm in our laps to church in the back seat of the car. I sat in the middle, a position I usually jockeyed to avoid because even while holding tricky dishes of food my siblings could not resist a performance of our ritual:

"You're in BETWEEN!" They sang in a whisper, carefully but forcefully slamming me from both sides with their shoulders, "You know what I MEAN!" Slam! Slam! "It's the saddest thing that I have ever SEEN!" Slam! Slam!

"Don't step on the pie, Jer'my," Momma cautioned, concerned for a buttermilk pie on the floor between my brother's feet, the only bit of room left after three kids and two parents crammed into our small car. A short drive past slightly rundown houses and we arrived at the green tree-spotted oasis of our church's property. Jerm hopped out with the macaroni.

"I'm first!" he proclaimed. Ginger rolled her eyes, performing a moving impression of adult weariness as she maneuvered her dish of roast out of the other side. Her white dress was spotless. Mom and Dad opened their doors, placing foil-covered plates of deviled eggs and celery with cream cheese on the roof of the car. I scooted over with my bowl of sloshy boiled peas and stepped immediately into the center of the pie.

"Scotty Mark Lawson!" Mom struggled to control the stunned annoyance in her voice. My stomach fell about a hundred miles. No pie!

"I'm sorry, Momma." My expectations of a shortened sermon and then hours of food and playing with the other kids were suddenly overshadowed by dread. Warm sunlight and the buzzing of cicadas from the creek filled the air, the only sound as I awaited Mom's scolding.

She paused for an instant, trying to be angry, and then lifted my paralyzed foot out of the pie. "Come on, I was afraid one of 'em would get messed up, that's why I made two." My parents' eyes met with beleaguered smiles and she said to my father, "Dennis, hand me the other one. We coulda ate this one at home." She had carried a fudge pie up front under her own feet, which Dad retrieved.

"That was your son, Beverly" he said.

"Don't try and blame that on me..." She laughed as they disappeared into the basement entrance.

Mom's dishes joined the spread laid out on the large basement table made from plywood laid across sawhorses. Once church had started, the only way to slip out of the sermon and peek at the feast was to go to the bathroom downstairs. Around the corner I could secretly watch the church women dodge each other's elbows and ample behinds in the small kitchen area, placing related foods together and warming rolls in an old black gas oven. The sermon went on above them as they worked, and although the exact words could not be made out, a tone of particular conviction caused the women to close their eyes for a second and shout 'Yes, Lord! A-men!' I jumped at their outburst and ran back upstairs.

The smell of the food came up through the floor vents and I awaited the magic words prefacing the closing prayer more desperately than usual: 'Let's all stand.' Instead of relief they had come to trigger a heightened tension…would he pray, or would he continue preaching? Sometimes Brother Goins faked us out, saying the words but then being led to speak a little more. When my escape was arbitrarily blocked I danced in frustration, filled with the clean, pure hatred of a child. But usually on Homecoming, with the scent of hot rolls and chicken filling the church, the prayer was said without delay.

After dismissal the adults crowded back through the foyer and down the narrow stairway to the basement, along the way trying to shake as many hands as possible. Jerm had a game he played in which he ran to shake certain members' hands we had singled out during the sermon. Running back, eyes fixed on me while smelling his hand, he would say "Mmm! Cherries!" or "Mmm! Soap!" Somehow our assessment of them based on hand-smell left us feeling superior, and we found this wildly funny. I awaited his reports and we laughed, passing time until we could go down and get in line.

Once all the adults went through and seated themselves at folding tables, we kids were free to fill our paper plates with all the food we could eat. I always selected my Mom's contributions first, already sure that I liked them, and then branched out with a few samples from other kitchens. I knew Sister Beasley made good desserts. Sister Creasy made delicious green-bean casserole, with cream of mushroom soup in it and crackly crumbs on top. I looked for the bits of masking tape on each container identifying its owner and chose accordingly. Jerm and I exchanged knowing looks of disgust over the platters labeled 'Sis. Jenkins,' containing colorless macaroni and damp fried chicken. Jerm lightly crushed my foot and indicated her dish with his gaze. Ever since I had told him the story about Ben Franklin's dad slapping him silly to imprint the experience of seeing a salamander in the fireplace, Jerm employed similar techniques for wordless emphasis. A glance was exchanged communicating our scorn and the macaroni was left to its gelid decomposition. We were ever mindful of perils that faced the incautious in church, and happily merged our way into the dessert line.

Soon I was carrying one plate of heavy food and a smaller dish of Bundt cake with pudding on it to sit next to Mom and Dad. The concrete room was full with chatter and the clatter and scrape of aluminum folding chairs. They were deeply engrossed in conversation with Brother and Sister Michaels, a young couple moving to Alabama to take care of her mother. She was our church's regular piano player, and there was some question as to what we would do after they left. I hoped we would not go back to using a boom box and cassettes as we had during her first absence. Not wanting to be distracted from my eating I led Jerm off to find Ginger in the Sunday school classrooms and sit with the other kids. It would be a contentedly quiet ride home that afternoon.

Sometimes Mom would take a few of her old records and lift a square plastic dome to stack them on the turntable of our ancient stereo. She loved old things, things that had some memory associated, and this heavy receiver was like the one her family owned when she was a child. We never locked our front door, and in the summer Mom opened it to the breeze while she cleaned the house. The chugging guitar of America's "Horse with no name" paced Mom's broom across the wooden floors. She loved horses, and would draw them for me if I asked. Her pencil moved easily with this surprising skill, sketching out a squarish nose and round cheek in profile before the intelligent eye and ear were placed, all with a minimum of lines. I watched her sweeping now and imagined us riding a horse across the cleanest gold sand, like in "The Black Stallion." Mom used to have long hair, framing her smile in my baby pictures. Now it was shorter and she had a church lady come over every once in awhile to snap in little plastic rods and perm it into no-fuss curls. I thought it would be prettier the old way, and asked, "Why don't you grow your hair back long, Momma?"

She continued sweeping, probably wondering where that question had come from. "Honey, long hair's not as flatterin on me until I lose some weight."

I peeked at her body while she remained intent on the floor. As she passed in and out of the white sunlight coming through open windows, her form was alternately visible and then brilliantly silhouetted in broken patterns. She didn't look big to me. Just normal. I remembered one time when she was putting up groceries she had started to lift a twenty-pound bag of potatoes into the cabinet, but she paused.

"I am this much overweight." She said sadly, thinking out loud. She put them away and resumed her labors.

I still wished she had long hair, but we were never encouraged to argue about anything. It went without saying, and upon later reflection I couldn't even remember when the impetus to argue had died in me, or what it felt like. Besides, the music playing was so nice, and it was just me and her downstairs.

I always felt like there was something more to know about Mom, some secret that might slip out if only the circumstances were right. I knew life was different for her and Dad before I was born, but I wasn't sure exactly how. What if they had been bank robbers? Hippies? Satanists? When my mind was idle it played with these invented mysteries, expanding them in fantastic directions.

The first record finished and Linda Ronstadt dropped into place. I fell asleep on the couch with the comforting sound of dishes in the sink and the hum of a lawnmower filling the breeze with the delicious scent of cut grass.

On nice days we were ordered outside to play in our enormous back yard, and generally we did not mind. Its ruined wire fences were perilous tightropes I could walk with the others following behind, supported on elastic saplings grown sheltered from the mower's blade. The trees bled supposedly poison milk when I plucked their velvet leaves and higher up their branches split like distant roots thirsting for the clouds. The bark peeled away easily and I could lay bare a damp twig with a few quick cuts of my Swiss-Army knife. It felt cool to my tender fingers, smooth as if already polished, and once dried out it had the appearance of a perfect pale bone.

With these wands I directed the breeze. I imagined I could call it to me in the stillness of a humid Tennessee summer and somehow it seemed to come, playful enough that I could never completely believe its allegiance. A gentle gust, a sigh through leaves like the memory of rain, touched my hair on its way to lay down the grass and weeds. Sometimes it came strong, pulling me up towards the blue for a thrilling second before losing interest. I had many dreams of being carried away by the wind, like Dorothy without her house, but instead of Oz I usually saw below the churning maelstrom of an ocean at war with the sky. I felt so bright against that darkness. When it stormed at home, the air swept through so clean that all of a sudden I wondered how we were even breathing before, thickened up like a murky fish tank and we hadn't even noticed it. My mundane surroundings were charged with menace unconnected to the Devil or any human wrongdoing and I loved it. I felt so alive I had to jump up and try to fly.

"Momma, where's those big bags Daddy got from work?" Mom had opened the front door so we could watch the show, foretold by the agitated hissing of trees.

"They're in the laundry room, but wait till I see what kinda storm this is before y'all get out in it." She was setting up some baby-food jar candles we had crafted in children's church, just in case. "And take off your watch." I had gotten a watch that played the theme from the Twilight Zone whenever a certain button was pressed, and it had a knock-off version of the video game Space Invaders built in. Right there on my wrist. It was one of the coolest Christmas presents I had ever gotten and one of the only reasons I had ever felt even close to cool at school. When I first brought it in, everyone wanted to see it, to play it, and whenever something happened that our young minds found unusual I was called upon to press the button and cause the tinny little song to play. This watch was a talisman of cool, and I loved it completely.

"I will."

The laundry room had briefly served as our great-grandfather's sickroom, until he went on to a retirement home, and it still had his curtain for a door. A roll of clear plastic leaned against the wall inside, almost as tall as I was. I set it down and pulled off a huge sheet. These were industrial trash bags, but to me they looked like giant sandwich baggies. Jerm pushed aside the curtain and a thrill of shock prickled across my face before I recognized he was just wearing some scary glasses Daddy had rigged up. Dad had taken a pair of thick black safety frames and put two red light-emitting diodes where the eyeballs would be, winding black electrical tape around the wires and down the side to a nine-volt battery. The effect was shocking despite their simplicity: a pair of glowing, beady red eyes. Just like in *The Exorcist*, I thought. One of the few movies secretly watched on cable at my grandmother's house.

"What are you doing?"

"Let's get in this baggie and walk through the storm."

Outside the sky was the color of wet newspaper. The streetlights had come on prematurely, tricked by the altered light that made our neighborhood look like a tinted photograph. Thunder exploded, distant and invisible, and then the rain came almost all at once from down the street. It slashed past our house, eating up the dryness of the road like a quick-lit fuse. The familiar picture framed by our front door was now staticky black and white, crackling in the downpour. Dad was stretched out in his recliner, a damp cloth and ice pack over his eyes to chill another headache. Mom appeared from the kitchen to refill his mason jar with generic cola and then took a seat in her rocking chair to listen.

The sound was like a drug, and as she stared at the clock and then at the wooden floors I noticed her eyes flutter before refocusing. In the rushing exhalation of the rain, which was like a kind of silence, I heard the thin creak of her chair and noticed that with one toe she rocked herself slowly, once, then twice. I wondered where the birds went when it rained, and the flies. I looked at her face, tranquil and unguarded.

"Momma, can we go outside?"

"Go on."

I went back to the laundry room and gathered the plastic bag into the tightest ball I could make, so that it wouldn't rustle too much when I took it past Daddy. "Jer'my? Come on." I called upstairs.

"Comin." He was wearing cutoff blue jean shorts, his shirt depicting some character from an unseen movie. We walked past mom and onto the little front porch. Every smell was amplified in the dampness. We stepped into the curtain of rain at our doorstep and immediately gave muted squeals when the cold water touched us everywhere at once. We unrolled the bag and desperately searched for its open end, finally managing to pull it over our heads. The yard drank in water and breathed with elemental satisfaction outside our suddenly close world inside the bag. We stepped forward like characters walking on the moon and tried to stay synchronized enough not to trip as we rounded the house towards the back yard.

The grass was swollen and suspended in the transient layer of water that had not yet soaked into the dirt. It felt plush under my bare feet. The sound of the falling water was amplified and pitched higher inside the plastic, so that Jerm and I could barely talk. Without words we knew our simple goal was to walk the length of the yard, all the way to the back. It was a passage into an enchanted wood. A magical quest. A challenge. The wind had greater purchase against the broad sail we made and gusts threatened to knock us over or steal away the bag, causing us to scream and clutch at the slippery inside. At the end of the yard, surrounded by flailing trees and standing on soggy leaves freshly dislodged by the storm, I looked into the face of my brother and saw a connection more trustworthy than love. We were of the same heart and mind, even bound by blood, and together we held up our transparent barrier against the raging of the storm. No one understood me as he did, I thought. He smiled back at me. More than words.

Later that summer I heard a loud commotion at the front door and rushed out of my room to see Dad and one of his work buddies wrestling in a dark upright piano.

"Daddy got you a piano!" I said redundantly.

Dad was strong, but knowing his back I cringed to see him lifting anything heavy. At the same time I dreaded being asked to help with manual labor, so as Mom scooted furniture out of the way I rushed to clear rugs and lamps. I always felt intimidated by the rough guys Dad worked with. They reminded me of the coaches and gym teachers who I imagined could see right through me and who, if unconstrained by adult rules, would have savaged me relentlessly.

"Where did you want it, Beverly?" Mom plinked a few notes and directed them to roll it against a wall. I followed Dad outside to watch him carry in a bench. Jerm stood in the truck bed, where I was sure he had been right in the way during the move. Ginger made a rare appearance from her room/crypt and was already reaching past Mom to tentatively press keys when I came back inside.

"I can't believe you came out for something besides the phone!" I said, trying the sarcasm I would wear thin as I grew older.

"Shut up." She looked directly at me and hit two more keys.

"Rebellion is as the sin of witchcraft. First Samuel fifteen twenty-three. Thou shalt not suffer a witch to live. Exodus twenty-two eighteen. The Bible says I can kill you."

Mom closed the keyboard cover and a fleeting look of weariness crossed her face. "Those are separate verses, honey. The Bible does not say you can kill." Three other verses detailing God-directed slaughter involuntarily sprang to mind. Perhaps Mom was herself thinking of Psalm 137:9. "Ginger, you can play this in a minute, but y'all move out of the way 'till we're done."

"Fifteen, Twenty-Three, Twenty-Two, Eighteen..." I whispered, making a slicing motion across my throat with a finger. She moved so quickly I hardly saw her hand before it had withdrawn and tracks of stinging scratch marks were left behind. I was furious but immediately covered the wounds with my hand. Mom would cut off her fingernails if she saw her scratching and I preferred to keep it between us.

Mom went back to directing the movement of furniture, making excited note of the turned columns and carving on the front of the piano. In our family it was very important to compliment something about any gift, to show appreciation. The new piano looked majestic against the living room wall.

"Well praise the Lord!" Mom was radiant. Seeing her so excited made me feel happy for her. It was rare that she or Dad got anything big for themselves. I guessed that this was really for the church, but I hoped she would get some fun out of it, too. For a second I wondered what it would be like to have parents who enjoyed modern-day music. Or at least followed some popular form of entertainment. Dad had an old banjo he played when it wasn't pawned to pay some bill or other, and sometimes Mom listened to oldies stations, but these occasional indulgences only seemed sad because of their infrequency. I knew other parents outside the church went dancing, saw movies, or in some normal way had fun. I wished mine did too, but I saw the church as a big roadblock that wouldn't let them. They never seemed to mind, but our differences made me so angry when I really thought about them. I felt like I was missing out on everything fun in the whole world.

Warm summery air swept in when Dad opened the door to trundle his borrowed dolly back outside. Mom and Ginger were all over the new piano. I wanted desperately to tell her to stop and let Mom enjoy it for a second, but Ginger never had responded to any of my silent signals like Jerm did. I spent this lovely moment standing across the room trying to think of some way to boss her without getting in trouble.

In the country there are certain thoughts about the way children and parents should relate. Biblical edicts such as "spare the rod, spoil the child" were mixed in with old country philosophies into an unbreakable class system. Children were at the lowest level, ruled from an unassailable Olympian perspective by God-fearing parents. No talkback, no eye contact during lectures, no insolence. I was never one of the rebellious kind who flouted such things openly. Panicked feelings of horror and dread seized me when in the presence of other kids who dared to question some order from a parent. I was literally stunned when I first heard the occasional bit of smart-mouth my outside-world acquaintances let slip. I certainly had my own ideas about what was right and wrong, but I could only imagine them taking form in my life if it was away from my family. I had often dreamed of escape, fantasizing about institutional settings like orphanages or mental hospitals. In such an environment I would find help for the unnamed thing wrong with me, comfortably low expectations, and it would be unlikely that the damaged losers there would reject me. Once there perhaps I'd take up a bad habit, like cussing. Profanity really wasn't me, but even saying "darn" was annoyingly forbidden. "Everyone knows that's just another way of saying d-a-m-n, and if it's in your heart, the sin is just as bad as if you had actually done it." My missionary Uncle had told us this once, and I wearily accepted it as another law against me. There were plenty of sins in my heart. I never left, though. The church was undeniably horrible, but I began to wonder if the rotten odor that destroyed my comfort was really from there. Outside the church there was only love at home. I soon decided that the only truly terrible thing I had to escape from was somewhere within myself.

I remember playing after the girls on the monkey bars in grade school, mimicking 'routines' of drops and flips they devised. I envied them, talking in closed groups away from the boys. I always stood somewhere in between, not accepted in the bragging, aggressive bonding of the boys and too afraid to attempt joining the girls because I knew I would be ridiculed and rejected. So instead I hung listlessly on the chain link swings reading a smuggled copy of any tiny book I could find, the easier to hide until the P.E. teacher confiscated it. I would then be consigned to grudging inclusion in whichever activity involved the most boys. I was a quiet child, never rude or outrageous, not effeminate so much as gentle. But from the earliest time I can remember, I knew I had something to hide, something I couldn't pin down, and I spent so much effort concealing it that I simply came out as a blank. One afternoon at that same school, I remember clearly leaving down the side stairway to begin my short walk home and a kid talking to me called someone a faggot. I had heard the word before, and asked him what it meant.

"It's somebody who gets fucked up the butt." he said casually, both of us parting without a backward glance. Somehow a scattering of facts crystallized into the overwhelming realization that, sexual experience not withstanding, the word was somehow me. I looked back at the school, at the faded construction paper flowers taped to windows slicked in brilliant glare from the afternoon sun. There was nothing for me there, I now realized, despite the struggling hope carrying me through each day that I might join in their normal world. They wouldn't want me if they knew. I walked home filled with a weighty dread, as if I had just awoken to find my fingers wrapped around a bloody knife and a fresh corpse in my lap. Faggot was me. I'm a faggot. If Mom and Dad found out...it was too horrible to imagine. That night I dutifully consumed pot roast and vegetables washed down with sweet tea, secretly went outside to vomit it back up and bury it, and went to bed early.

Within days, Mom came home with *The Peaceful Easy Feelin*songbook. If the radio was ever turned on in our house it was mostly older music providing a background for her housecleaning. Many of these tunes were written out in the chunky volume, including some I recognized like 'Rhiannon' and 'Horse with No Name.' She also purchased a smaller technical book filled with charts showing hundreds of chord formations. With these two books she began a daily practice squeezed in between housework and cooking. Tentative repetition of simple chords progressed in complexity over the weeks, the basic three-fingered structure unfolding in depth and richness as she focused intently on the music. It was fun to watch her study since we were usually the ones with homework, and without having to be asked we left her alone during practice. I watched her teach herself and never doubted that she would soon be playing as well as anyone.

Without ever a lesson, by the 'grace of God' she quickly developed a style that was a little bit bluegrass, a little bit ragtime and consisted mostly of bouncy chords with occasional notes of the melody sprinkled in. Although her goal was to be the next church piano player, she often put aside the practice of our familiar hymns and from upstairs I heard her laboriously picking out "Desperado" or some other selection from her songbook. After losing patience with the sheet music, she simply followed the guitar chords written above the measures and the music became graceful, her soft alto voice carrying the melody. In these moments after laundry, dinner hours away and the other kids playing outside, she made music from nothing and I felt a sort of amazed pride and love for this woman who had also created me.

When Sister Michaels left, Mom took over as our piano player. The main function of her music was to back up the singing portion of the service, but it also called the congregation to order at the start and counterpointed Brother Goins' altar call at the end. Sometimes, as a final closure to the evening's preaching, a girl around my age named Sheila would sing a "special song." It was always arranged beforehand, and the slow, loose background Mom had been improvising over the altar call would coalesce into an intro for Sheila's song as the preacher wound down.

Brother Goins introduced her, mopping his shiny age-speckled forehead with an old-fashioned handkerchief. "And I say unto you, come unto me as a little child, for theirs is the kingdom of heaven. Little Sheila Hollister is gonna bless us with a song to close us out this evenin.'"

"Ooooh Lord!" The old ladies moaned softly, clutching their sufferin rags and praying with hands raised above their heads. The boldest Christians prayed with arms up, visibly supplicant, and it was a mark of difference between the teens who were wholly converted and those who where too image-conscious to be so showy. I was usually too embarrassed.

Sheila, who had been sitting on the front row in readiness for her performance, stood and made her way up to the pulpit. She looked sad, moved by the spirit almost to tears before she had even begun to sing. She stood on a booster kept in the hollowed out lectern and Mom struck the solid beginnings of accompaniment. Her voice was choked with emotion as she belted out the morbid tune, detailing persecution leading up to a fateful death. The chorus climbed up an octave in slow repeating notes, each precarious step up the scale causing a palpable tension in the congregation as they anticipated her faltering. "Its SUCH A," she climbed up two notes, "SWEET RE—," climbing two more, "—WAAARD!!!" She plateaued shakily but successfully then dived back into the verse.

"Ooooh Lord! Hallelujah!" The ladies fanned themselves with leaflets and staunched tears with their rags.

Dad had gone home early with a headache. Free of close supervision, I was overwhelmed by barely held-back giggles and Jerm's expert eye caught this. He began moving his flattened palm up and down in synch with Sheila's voice, mimicking Fran Powell, a pubic television singing teacher we watched in school. With each rise in tone, his small hand went up hidden from Sheila by the pew in front of us; with each dip it fell. Our visible upper bodies were motionless. Ginger rolled her eyes and scooted away. Mom watched us from her bench at the piano, sensing mischief. As Sheila approached the final chorus I could tell her untrained voice was tiring. The wavering, sepulchral moans of particularly moved members of the congregation clamored at the threshold of the music. My eyes were tightly shut against the sight of Jerm's mockery, so he snaked his other hand into my armpit and tickled me, fingers desperately, gleefully searching out just the right chink in my armor that would unleash the flood of laughter.

By now Mom had noticed my hunched posture. Jeremy was fully absorbed in torturing me. She struck the final chords while glaring at us from the front of the church.

"ITS SUCH A—," Sheila clawed her way up two more notes, "SWEET RE—" Jerm reached up in a desperate final ploy to make me laugh and pried open my eye with his fingers, just in time for me to see his fluidly note-following hand implode into gnarled fingers and fall dead as Sheila's voice raggedly leapt at the last "WARD!!!" and missed, splatting with a screeching note so satisfyingly flat it elicited a collective gasp from the old ladies and caused my mother to falter on the last chord. In the uprising of Hallelujahs that came to cover the horror of that final syllable, I let loose a pent-up laugh so hard that I banged my head on the pew in front of me. I struggled to catch my breath between spasms, covering my forehead and continuing to laugh in spite of the pain. I was completely vulnerable, all self-control lost, and Jerm relished his moment of superiority. These victories were wordless, as subtle as the power exchanges between jungle animals. None of the congregation paid attention to our little display. They were standing to shout their closing prayers over Mom's loud final music, arms raised and bodies swaying. Amidst this chaos Jerm and I were in our own world, sitting hunched behind the pew in front of us. I tenderly explored the red blotch forming on my forehead.

Close to my ear Jerm whispered smugly, "That's your punishment."

2

Dad

Daddy had terrible headaches. He labored through the pain, weeks without a day off, always coming home late with one eye in a red-veined squint and his mouth drawn into a frown behind the mustache. We rushed to unlace his boots for him as soon as he collapsed into his recliner. Dad's Duckhead overalls smelled like machine oil and felt stiff with it when we hugged him. Mom poured a Mason jar full of Coke over ice that popped and whistled, setting the glass and can on his little chair-side table. After dinner in the recliner he shuffled off to bed, his room as dark and cold as Mom could make it. If it were a really bad one he might moan a little, an awful sound that sent a shiver through my stomach.

A light fell across my face, bringing me out of my dreams. Mom's voice came with it, into the dark.

"Honey, come on, we're gonna have prayer for your Dad."

I heard a murmur of men's voices from the living room and knew that some members of the church must have come by. Half-awake, I dreaded seeing them here in my home.

"O.K., Momma. Just a minute." I took a deep breath and got out of bed to dress myself. My bedroom was off the kitchen, and when I stepped out I was immediately confronted by the unwelcome sight of Brother Freddy and Brother Thomas, talking over coffee Mom must have made for everyone. Brother Freddy loathed me. I understood this from the way he spoke to me in a slightly raised voice, as if struggling to reign in self-righteous anger at the impudence of my existence. As a young teenager I had begun to settle into a sullen coldness at church, obviously ignoring the sermons and reading books I smuggled past the exhausted vigilance of my parents. I stopped standing for singing and prayers. I had no control over my attendance, but no one could command enthusiasm. I often looked over at Brother Freddy when the rest of the church stood for some tiresome thing or other. I sensed his outraged glances like clattering arrows against the walls of my impenetrable fortress.

"Howdy, Brother Freddy. Brother Thomas."

"Hello, Scotty." He sounded like a disappointed principal, I thought. "Your dad's not doin too well."

"I know. He's out of his medicine." It was medicine he needed. Not you.

Brother Thomas chimed in: "Praise Jesus, there's no greater medicine than our Lord."

Cool. Whip us up a batch, won't ya? So many thoughts, so little courage. Brother Goins appeared and called us to begin prayer in the living room. All impertinence left me when I saw Dad sitting in his chair.

His face was screwed up in agony and he was crushing a limp rubber ice bag against the side of his head. Condensation from it ran down his face, mingling with cold sweat, to collect in a towel Mom had rolled and put around his neck. His faded blue denim workshirt was open at the top. The men of the church gathered round him and I felt a confusing anger as I looked at them. If there was a God, then I hated him for allowing my Dad to suffer like this. If there wasn't, then I hated these church people for wasting our lives and hopes on nothing. Brother Goins shook a bottle of oil against his finger with a practiced flick of the wrist, not even looking at it, and anointed Dad's forehead. His wrinkly, rough looking hand stayed there as he began to pray and I watched it tremble against Dad's skin. I moved forward and prayed too, loath to touch any of these men in their church suits and communicate even in this serious moment any confluence with them. I prayed and felt embarrassed for doing so, because all I could think about was the gloating sense of security it gave them to see me assimilated. I pinned a cold look onto my face to show I was not enjoying my prayer one bit and said silently to the Lord, "Dear Jesus, please help my Dad feel better. Please take away this pain you gave him. Please stop the headaches." Even as I thought it I knew my tone was too challenging to warrant anything but damnation. Why did He give the bad things and then make us ask to take them away? I couldn't begin to think of anything else to say and abandoned the attempt, feeling empty and cheated on some cosmic scale. The voices of the men were loud and beseeching, free of any self-consciousness. I looked past their closed eyes and outstretched arms to Dad's face, still contorted with pain, and hoped this was helping him. Maybe the distraction, or the positive mental energy. Something. I was sleepy. I hated having these men shouting up to Jesus in the same room where I watched television. I couldn't wait for them to go.

In addition to constant prayer, Dad went through a lot of pain medications, depending on availability and cost. Amber-colored prescription bottles in uncommonly giant sizes rattled in his lunch cooler when he brought it home, the only thing left in there besides empty Tupperware after a double shift. He went to so many doctors that he stopped talking about them hopefully and I only knew he had been to a different one by the appearance of a new kind of pill in the medicine chest. Eventually only injections of Imitrex took away the pain, which he saved for the very worst because it was so expensive. We watched tensely as he drew up a small syringe of the fluid from an ampoule, knowing what it cost and how bad Dad must be hurting to use it. One shot and off to bed, until time to get up for work.

In the fall of most years we went out to my uncle's farm in the country to kill hogs. Mom loved any chance to go see her mother there. It was a short drive, about thirty minutes, in which we left behind suburban homes and swung around the edge of the city into forests and farms. The trees bound everything together. They were everywhere, scattered in the city, shading our homes and thick into blackness in the country outposts along the edges of the woods. The city had barely faded from the rearview mirror when we began to see little country stores selling Stuckey's Pecan Logs and bait, and the occasional possum running across the road. Hints of wood smoke from hidden hearths came in with the air-conditioning and we all said, "Mmm..." without even thinking about it.

"Mom, when our first house burned down in the country, was it from a fireplace or wood-burning stove?" We always told family stories when we drove.

"It was an old iron potbelly stove, honey. That wasn't our first house, but it's probably the first one you remember. I guess some creosote got built up in the flue and caught fire."

"And when we got home from church..."

"On Christmas mornin!" Ginger added.

"You weren't even born then."

"Yes she was, Scotty. Jer'my wasn't born yet, though."

"When we got home, all that was left was a tin roof on the ground, right? And all our Christmas presents were burned up."

"Yes, the only thing left standing was the outhouse and the stove and a metal shelf with some beans on it, out in the middle of all those trees." Mom laughed, watching the road. It was a dark laugh, at a dark day. "Your Daddy went up to that shelf and said, 'Look Beverly, at least we got something left,' and that can of beans exploded right at that exact moment..." She was really laughing then, a little high-pitched squeaking sound. Her laugh always made us laugh harder.

"Y'all used an outhouse?" Jeremy was up on the back of my seat, almost in the front with me now. He already knew all this.

"We had plumbing inside, honey. Sit back. The outhouse was just always there, from before."

"And my new Viewmaster with Peter Pan got burned up, and my frog toybox, that I had just got that mornin, and what else?"

Right then mom sneezed, one of her huge sneezes that sounded like a scream. It took her a moment to recover. As she wiped her eyes she said, "Oh lord, I don't know honey. Everything. We lost everything but a bag of dirty diapers and a mattress. It's a good thing we were in church."

The best part about going to Uncle Peach's farm was that my grandmother lived in a little trailer on one side near the cow field. Uncle Peach and 'Aint' Alma (as we pronounced 'aunt') lived in a huge, comfortable farmhouse next door, but Sissy's trailer was the focus of my visits. Everything was clean and well kept. There were no plastic flamingos or crocheted plant holders, no cars up on blocks or any of the other props outsiders love to garnish their demeaning fantasies of Southern life with. Sissy got her nickname from the younger siblings she pretty much raised her herself, and somehow we came to call her that too, instead of grandma. She was a tiny, vivacious, beautiful woman, one-fourth Cherokee, with high cheekbones and little cherub lips. If I look like anyone today, it is her. Old picture albums showed her as a young bride with Betty Boop hair in a black dress and red lipstick next to her Army husband in the fifties. Other photos showed daring black wigs and eye makeup in the sixties. She had run a women's auxiliary in Tripoli, Libya, a honky-tonk nightclub in Nashville and dated rich men with big cars even into her senior years. When she stepped out of the damp, frigid air of her open trailer door to run up and hug us I was always struck with her elegance, her beauty and the love she expressed with cool, soft hands.

"Well y'all come on in, I made some macaroni salad in there, and there's some ice cream." Sissy hugged Ginger especially tight. "Well baby you look so pretty today…you're not gonna get out there and get dirty with all those hogs are you?"

"I wanna stay with you, Sissy."

Inside it was dark and cold and comfortable. Heavy curtains obscured most of the sunlight and the view of smoky blue tree-covered hills outside every window. All of the furniture was covered in throws and blankets and coverlets, worn to softness and sweet with Downy fabric softener. She had photographs of us and Mom and her son covering over the wood paneled walls, and I could see more on the walls of her sumptuously decorated room through its open door. Satin and ruffles and a vanity table with neatly arranged bottles of real Chanel number five, moisturizer and Coty air-spun face powder.

My cousin David knocked on the screen door.

"Scotty, come on…they're gettin out the guns!"

David was stocky and blond and as country as they came. I thought he was the cutest ever. The door banged behind me and we kicked up fallen leaves as we ran past chicken coops and through a fence to where people had gathered near the hog pen. Killing and dressing hogs was easier if several neighboring farmers combined their work in one place. David and I stayed on the fence, watching as a single animal was led into a narrow chute and a gate closed behind it. A grim, leathery man in a cloth cap and denim raised a shotgun to his shoulder and dropped it with a single bullet to the head.

"Man!" David was mesmerized.

I had flinched and was glad he hadn't seen me. I always felt a little distanced from the country, living in the burbs and going to a city school. I felt a bit like a cultural tourist here, family ties being my only ticket in. They dragged the carcass up to a homemade scaffold and hung it by its hind legs. Uncle Peach was talking to his friends, laughing at something around a cigarette. He casually positioned a tin bucket under the hog, adjusted it after some eyeballing and then slit the animal's throat with a deep slice of his knife. A cataract of blood followed the stroke, opening into a black sheet of liquid revealing the knife's path. Next came a wet vomiting sound as organs and intestines fell out in a huge gelatinous clump.

"Damn, that was a good cut." David looked at me. "I wish I could try it."

Just then my watch beeped the hour.

"Look, my watch has space invaders on it." I held up my wrist to show off the chunky silver watch. It had two buttons beneath its thick quartz display and I pressed them to make the theme to the Twilight Zone play and tiny LCD aliens line up for destruction.

"Oh man, can I play it?"

I snapped it off and handed the whole watch to him. "The left button moves the gun and the right one shoots it..."

"I know..."

"There's no way you could know, I just handed it to you..." We were walking away from the distraction of blood and smoke towards the metal grid where they would skin the hogs after scalding the bristles off of them. It was just high enough to sit on. David stood with one leg up on its edge, bouncing a little as he pressed the buttons and tried to kill my little aliens.

"I get to play next."

"Yeah, but just one more game after this, I'm just now gettin it..." Another rifle blast cracked behind us, and a squeal. David jumped and said, "Shit!" The watch fell from his hands and in an instant of silence the clink of glass on metal shot directly into my heart.

"Oh shit..." David repeated. We stooped over to pick up the watch. I snatched it from his hands. There was a half-inch crack like a jag of lightning coming up from the bottom of the crystal and little black LCD aliens were visible everywhere, motionless. Tears and anger pressed behind my eyes.

"This was my only thing..." was all I could say. How could I make him understand?

"I'm sorry, Scotty...Gosh, I'm sorry."

"Nevermind. I'm goin inside. See you later." I held the watch like an injured bird and went back to Sissy's trailer. I didn't tell anyone. It was best to keep it between us, I thought. I lay down on the couch to watch television until it was time to go.

"Scott, let's go out in the woods." Jerm was already bored.

"Ok." I put the watch in my jeans pocket and as we went out the door Sissy called behind us, "Y'all be careful where they're shootin…"

"We will…" Jerm called back.

Outside the day was fading and the crisp woody air was scented with cedar smoke and rendering lard from a cauldron out by the hog carcasses. We avoided everyone entirely and squeezed through a wire fence out behind the tractor shed, into the cow field. Our goal was the gray-blue treeline at its edge. Jerm and I wore the same jeans and flannel, his two sizes smaller than mine. We were both skinny and pale and healthy and I thought in those moments it was the most wonderful thing in the world to have a brother.

"Mom and Dad know you been reading Dungeons and Dragons." We crossed the field easily, walking on flat limestone and soil. The cows had departed to a safer distance from the slaughter. My heart felt tired.

"How? It's not hurting anything. I just like 'em."

"After you messed up that Bible, they've been keepin an eye on you. I heard Dad on the phone with Brother Goins." I had gotten a really nice Bible for Christmas, with my name on it in gold letters. It cost almost a hundred dollars. I always fell asleep with a stack of books in bed with me and that night I had my new Bible to one side and was reading a borrowed Dungeon Master's manual. I must have fallen asleep, because the next thing I remember was a tingling sense of danger. I woke up to the horror of Mom slipping the banned book from my fingers and then she made a miserable sound that I didn't immediately understand. The air conditioner next to my bed had a huge black bucket underneath that was full of dripped condensation, and there floating on the surface of the dark water was my new Bible. Swollen like a waterlogged corpse, it rained stale smelling liquid from its ruined pages when she fished it out. She took both books without saying a word and I listened to her creak back down the stairs. It was an accident, but I knew no one would believe my innocence. I laid awake, agonizing, for hours after that.

"I wish I hadn't messed up that Bible." The trees were around us. I loved the brittle, colored leaves. Antique yellow and rust. Once inside them it was cooler and damp. Every breath was rich with scent.

"If I could have a wish, I would wish for a motorcycle."

"Well if we're wishin, I would wish that I could go to a big college and get away from all this junk."

"And do what?"

"I can write my own books, or be famous. I can play music or be an actor like on Fame."

"We already do our own books." He grabbed a grape vine and tugged on it. They didn't really have grapes on them, big bark-covered vines as thick as rope, but that's what we called them. Satisfied it would support his weight, Jerm tugged it back and swung past me.

"Not our cartoon books. Readin ones."

"If wishes were horses, then beggars would ride." Jerm laughed, swinging slower and slower until he was almost stopped. Mom and Dad always said that when they caught themselves coveting after something. I pulled him down and set him behind me. The vine was mine.

"I'm not gonna be a pipe-fitter like Daddy."

"There's nothin wrong with it. I like helping when he lets us go."

"I know. I do too. I just want to do somethin else is all." It was fun to swing in the open space between trees. It felt good.

"You can do whatever you want, just don't tell Mom and Dad."

"Ain't that the truth." I let go of the vine. Another rifle shot split the air outside the trees. It was beginning to get dark. "We better get back in, Sissy's gonna be goin crazy by now."

"My motorcycle would be red."

As we walked back I stared into the dark space among the trunks and brush where we had just been and was afraid. It had been so gradual I had not realized the coming of night. Sissy's windows were the color of candle flames out across the field, beyond a wire fence and the glowing smoke of people making lard and dirty jokes. I knew Mom was inside, she and Sissy and Ginger, and I loved them. Jerm and I ran like ghosts in the wind until we reached the light gasping for breath. We ran up the steps into laughing and fresh rice crispy squares and air conditioned comfort.

"Beverly, did you see where they think they found where Noah's ark washed up?" Mom and Dad came back from the big yearly General Assemblies with thick reference tomes and paperback dissections of particular Biblical books. In his free time Dad pursued these interests, studying with an honest, earnest desire to understand everything. We discussed the stories and information they contained over nightly family dinners or the drive to church.

"Well they know where Mount Ararat is. Its about time they figured that out."

"Mom, pass me the tea please." If anything about the church was interesting to me, it was the finding of such relics. I wasn't sure if I wanted substantiation of the realness of Bible stories or not, but I secretly took these books down and read them anyway when no one was around. I had to figure out for myself if things were true, so that I could plan accordingly.

He usually read before bed in the flickering light of the television, never too engrossed to miss changing the channel at any exposure of flesh or bad language. He and Mom bounced ideas off of each other in the semi-dark about what the gemstone layers in the floor of the city in Revelations symbolized, and what manna might have tasted like. I liked to listen in the dark, only a pair of ears floating in the dimness.

"...And, behold, a throne was set in heaven, and one sat on the throne. And he that sat was to look upon like a jasper and a sardine stone. And there was a rainbow round about the throne, in sight like unto an emerald." The television cast an inconstant blue light and I was forgotten, laying on the wooden floor next to the heat vent. With my eyes at this level I could imagine I was as tiny as a bug, and I looked up to the seated forms limned in color and shadow.

"And out of the throne proceeded lightnings and thunderings and voices…And before the throne there was a sea of glass like unto crystal: and in the midst of the throne, and round about the throne, were four beasts full of eyes before and behind…And the four beasts had each of them six wings about him; and they were full of eyes within: and they rest not day and night, saying, Holy, holy, holy, LORD God Almighty, which was, and is, and is to come." I imagined walking on the vast shining floor, past the creatures made of wings and eyes whose movements sent breezes across its surface and chilled my skin. With these things in mind I often fell into weird dreams that ended with me being carried half-conscious to bed.

Sanitized and distilled into intellectualism, I could almost find our religion interesting, although I would not have dared to offer any opinion aloud. But however these little games helped me pass the individual hours, my thoughts always returned to the reality of an assured fate. While the winged people danced across crystal floors, I would be far below, burning in Hell. Forever.

For members of our church, receiving 'The Call to Preach' was a momentous and celebrated occasion. I watched with an ever-maturing sense of scorn as various young men of the congregation blurted that they had 'received the call' in trembly voices. These announcements were met with rapturous wailing from the congregation and meetings with the pastor afterwards. They went on to lead a few Bible Study groups or perhaps deliver a Wednesday night sermon. As they progressed further into their young adult-hood with barely supported wives and babies, the 'call' was put on hold. Nearing forty, Dad had long ago established his family. When he felt his calling he moved with the same practical dedication he had in his other interests. After some soul-searching, he had a long talk with our preacher and one night as I settled into bed she told me the news.

"Honey, your Daddy has been called to preach." Her voice was soft and distracted from considering what this meant for our family. I looked away, thinking about what I should say.

"Is he gonna quit workin at the plant?"

"No, it'll take him a long time to learn everything he needs to know before we get our own church." She sat on the corner of my bed, a comforting weight.

"O.K. then." Satisfied he still had a job, I turned away to sleep. I don't know what response she had been expecting. She got up silently and left me to fall into my dark dreams alone.

In the weeks to follow Mom acquired a lovely mahogany desk from a yard sale and Dad set up his own little study area. Decades later, I would sit in my own home writing this book at the very same desk where my father learned to become a preacher, but it had many purposes to fulfill before coming to be with me. Dad began purchasing enormous study books whenever he had any extra money and stacked them up along the back of the desk. There were his several concordances, which indexed the Bible by word and by verse, Bible dictionaries, and texts that tried to integrate Bible stories with known history. Dad received study guides in the mail from our church's publishing house in Cleveland, Tennessee, and slowly the wall above the desk accumulated framed certificates for each course he completed.

I wondered if the men he worked with knew that after every dirty, exhausting shift Dad came home, showered, and sat in his ratty blue bathrobe at that desk. It must have been so important to him. I knew there was a lot about the Bible Dad really didn't understand at all. There was a lot that no one understood. I had heard him ask difficult questions in Home Bible-study when it was our family's time to host it. He was searching for answers in his life, too. What a comfort it must have been to have the confidence that they really were there, all in that book.

Going to a movie theater had been out of the question for so long it seemed too distant and exotic to even contemplate. Something other people did, crass and cheap, like tattoos or dyed hair. It would have been easier to ask if we could pierce our lips with bone-plates. We did not even speak about it and suffered in silence, pretending to know what classmates were talking about when each new film came out and wondering desperately what it was like inside the forbidden buildings. Sometimes the buzz was too great and continued social interaction became impossible without a working knowledge of a particular movie.

"Where are you goin?" Ginger watched me from the door.

"To the Tenneco."

"What for?"

"To get something."

"Scotty can I go please I've got some money and I need to get something too..." Talking fast.

"No, just stay here." I started walking. A sound, a mixture of anger and some weak breaking in her voice made me stop. She was stranded at the edge of our yard, desperate, and I hated myself looking at her. The thrifty clothes that did not seem so out of place on Jerm and me looked uncomfortable on her small body. Her hair hung limp as corn-silk from a side-knotted ponytail, attempted emulation of someone she had seen somewhere that I never looked. A thought flashed, her asking for stirrup pants and being denied. I had been angry at her then, for vanity, but today I saw something I hadn't wanted to think about before. She was trying. I had always been hiding.

"Come on."

She made a feint toward the house, thought better of it and ran to my side. We began our walk in silence. It was only a half mile down the street and across to the gas station market, past old-people houses with quiet yards.

"So what have you been up to?" I felt funny asking her this, but I really didn't know what she did with herself most of the time.

"When?"

"Just whenever."

"Me and Kim are making jean jackets with gems on 'em."

A hardness swept over me…Kim was her trashy little friend from a bad family two houses down. Kim's dad drank beer and I had seen her mom step on a roach with her bare foot. I swallowed everything down as best I could. "Neat."

At the Tenneco I went straight for the magazine rack and found what I was looking for. Seventy five cents, cheap. Cheaper if I read it in the store. Mad magazine's parodies gave me just enough information to extrapolate backwards and extract the nuggets of truth behind the jokes. I then pieced together what must have been the main themes and characters and faked my way through the craze for movies like Star Wars, E.T., and many forgettable others.

I finished my mission and found Ginger outside in the sun. She had a large can of Aquanet hairspray in her hand and chucked it into a paper bag when she saw me come out. Contraband. I closed my eyes and jerked my head towards the road, then looked her in the eye. I didn't smile, but I didn't frown. She crumbled the top of the bag closed and we turned back into the tree shaded sidewalk that led home.

Access to the four channels on television was fairly liberal, although as programming expanded and UHF channels were added we were given mandates as to which programs we had to avoid. If a woman in a bikini entered the picture, the channel was changed, so that often watching a good show was fraught with tension as to what the next scene or commercial might contain. Shows like 'The Smurfs' and 'Bewitched' were outright forbidden due to their promotion of magic, while confusingly 'I Dream of Jeannie' was permitted. There were very few visual entertainments we could pursue without stress or guilt, but every weekend we watched the Three Stooges, the Little Rascals and Looney Tunes in peace. We would all sit together after church, snuggled on the couch and on blankets in the floor, and laugh until we could not breathe at the pie fights and ridiculous inventions. It was one of the few things we all did together that was almost pure pleasure.

"Dad, why can't we go out to eat tonight?" Ginger asked one evening after the last Stooges short went off. It's funny to me now that the pre-assumption was that we couldn't.

"Well, we can go to my favorite restaurant..." he began.

"Where, Daddy!" Jerm chimed in.

Dad paused a second, savoring the moment. "Well, I thought we could all go to Lawson's Kitchen tonight."

"Daddy! No!" we groaned.

"When I was little,"

"NOOO, Daddy! No!" We were a wailing chorus of despair.

"When I was little we had to put a piece of pork-fat on a fishhook and hang it from the ceiling over a barrel."

We had heard this story a million times and clung to Dad, supplicating. "Noooooo," we moaned like tortured souls, trying to drown out the story that was his funny, drawn-out version of "not this time." Daddy continued: "When we were hungry, we all took turns gettin up on the barrel and chewin on it. If anybody tried to swallow, my Daddy KICKED the barrel out from under em!" On the word 'kicked' Dad jerked his leg and mimed a fishhook yanking into his cheek with a sooty finger.

"Nuh-Uh...Daddy! Reeeeeally, can we go to Morrison's Cafeteria? Pleeeeze!" At this point we were limp and tragic, resigned to playing the scene to its finish.

"Beverly..." Daddy called out over our moans. "Bring me the fishhook!"

Once, in a rare confiding moment, Mom told me that one of the main reasons she fell in love with Dad was his sense of humor. "Your Daddy didn't used to have to suffer like this," she said, at that moment indicating his sleeping headache-slain body behind their bedroom door. She seemed to be wistful, remembering some particular moment. "He made me laugh all the time."

From scrounged artifacts in attic boxes and rare bits of history various family members had let slip I attempted to piece together a pre-conversion description of my parents. Although raised in the church, I theorized that Dad must have strayed from the path by the time he and mom had their fateful missionary encounter. In their early twenties, they were living in Colorado following the available work he found as a pipefitter. I was just learning to walk and talk. Mom once told me the Northerners were concerned by my thick Southern accent when I chirped out my early words and they asked her, "Are you going to let him keep that accent?" Mom said, "Well, I don't have much to say about it, seein as where he gets it from."

I was desperately fascinated by the idea that once my parents had been normal, perhaps even wanton. I'm told that during the missionary's witnessing to my young parents I became frustrated by something and, right in front of everyone, looked up and said "SHIT!" An embarrassed slap followed, and to this day it was probably the only time I used that word outside of a literary context. Considering the impact that missionary had on the rest of my life, I think it was also one of the most appropriate moments to use it I will ever encounter.

Whenever the opportunity presented itself I went through my parent's drawers and closets looking for clues. Summer was the best time to explore and think about the data I collected. We were home alone for hours at a time while Dad slaved away at the steam plant and Mom ran errands. As each summer arrived, I gathered more information and processed it with the newly gained perspective of the latest year.

In one of my archeological explorations of the boxes in our attic I found some oil paintings Dad had done before we kids were born. In the hot prickly air among the rafters and pink insulation I ran my fingers over the bumpy paint laid by his brushstrokes and felt sad that all he seemed to have now was greasy work with metal and fire. Again I wondered what kind of person I would have come to be if they had not found the church. This was my vital fantasy: What would it be like to live outside the church? To be normal? I didn't know details, exactly, but I imagined that I would go to movies and get to spend the night with friends on a Saturday. Everybody had their spend-the-night parties on Saturday night, but I couldn't go because I would miss church the next morning. Missing a party was a weak argument to bring up to Mom and Dad, but the resulting alienation built subtly over time. I saw kids at school and had one or two casual friends, but generally once I left class it was back to the isolation of our church. No Saturday nights, no roller-skating, no dance music, or dancing. No movies, no parties, and always censored television. There in the attic I clicked through my familiar rosary of sufferings. "Rosaries are not in the Bible." I heard Brother Goins say in my head. "Idolatrous ritualism."

Stacks of never-played records provided a soundtrack to my parents' prior life. Led Zeppelin, Edgar Winter, and The Eagles leaned frozen in lurid cover art against one another in our small record cabinet. These were not the ones Mom played when she cleaned house and I wondered why my parents even kept them.

One summer Saturday I found it impossible to go outside due to an outbreak of gypsy moth larvae. This manifested as thousands of translucent green worms suspended on invisible silk from the walnut trees around our house. The worms seemed to float in midair, each breath of wind swinging them in lazy waves. I knew if I felt the airy touch of a thread on my skin, too slight to reveal its exact location, it would mean the worm was freely roaming my surface somewhere. Unendurable.

Mom had taken a part time job at "Expressway Hand-burgers," a tiny drive-thru next to my junior high with an inexplicably gruesome name. Dad worked right through the weekends whenever he could, and today we were alone in the house until Mom came back in time to make supper.

Ginger liked to blast her radio and sit on the bed rocking to the forbidden popular music. Spying on her, I saw her sitting Indian-style and clutching a pillow to her chest. She rocked with the beat, eyes closed. At the time I felt disgust. Why did she have to listen to that music? She knew she wasn't supposed to. I wanted to listen to stuff, I argued with her in my mind, but I was strong enough not to do it. Despite my growing hatred of the Church itself, old ways of thinking still controlled my sense of right and wrong. Sometimes I saw her disobeying and a choking hatred bubbled up inside my chest, especially when she made insolent sighs and cut her eyes behind Mom's back. Later I would feel painfully guilty for being such a bad brother. It was so confusing, deciding what was right and what was wrong in the blinding presence of what I was coming to see as a false beacon. Sorting through the counterfeit truths was worse than having no guidance at all. Open rebellion was not an option, but if one of us was particularly down about missing a skating party or movie, I tried to soften the frustration with a picnic in the back yard or some game. As loving as Mom and Dad were, a chillingly disappointed "No" always came down in response to any infrequent, hopeless request to do something forbidden. Year after year of potential friends sailed away together, doing all the things that encouraged bonds and relationships to form, and we watched them go without a word. I was left torn between justifying the rules to make sense of them and finding some way to make up for them when I could not. Ginger continued rocking on her bed, unaware of my presence. I wish I had ever asked her what was wrong.

Downstairs was silent except for the reverberations of Ginger's music. Jerm must have braved the worms to walk to his one friend's house. As part of my investigations, I went for the stereo and slid out record after record, looking for a cover that seemed like it had something to tell me. Then I would carefully take out the large disk and play it, skipping the needle from track to track looking for whatever I wasn't supposed to hear. I didn't consider this the same as Ginger's sinful enthrallment to Debbie Gibson. I was only looking for answers, I thought. I wasn't enjoying anything. I seized upon "Witchy Woman" by the Eagles, because it was so obvious.

Mom's stereo was a large wooden box raised up on little legs a few inches high. The whole base was a speaker, faced with gold netting, and the top was the record player and a big tuner lit at one end by a bulb so old it shone orange. I kept the volume as low as I could. I could sit on the floor and put my ear right next to the big speaker, eyes closed, and imagine the vision of the song as it played. There were no music videos at the time that I had seen, but Jerm and I always played the game of telling the story of songs. One Christmas we had both gotten identical Walkman radios, and at night in our bunk beds we tuned them to WPLN, Nashville's classical station. With the same music playing in both our headphones, it was like we were in an invisible room together. We took turns telling what we thought was happening.

"This part is where they are ridin a horse through the woods." Jerm might say, his voice coming up through the dark to my top bunk.

"Yeah, and now they are comin into a cave."

"With all these little lights are around 'em, like ghosts."

"And now something bad's fixin to happen."

The story I imagined to Witchy Woman was this cemetery, with the witch in front of a big stone grave-angel. "Raven hair and ruby lips, sparks fly from her fingertips…" the song said, and all I could see was the night sky, far away and so blue it was black. The music was slow. It made me feel hot and relaxed, like falling asleep next to the fireplace. Sparks. She could fly, and even higher than her the stars were scattered like glowing pearls across an inverted ocean floor. Later in the song it said she slept in the Devil's bed, and I knew this was about sex. At this part, the big stone angel cracked open and down inside it was a red pit, down into the grave and the Devil with black horns like my Uncle's goats, horns that curled up out of hot red skin. I felt electrified when I saw these images, like I was understanding the real stuff behind everything else. Magic and sex and the Devil, all covered over and hidden away in a little cabinet right in our living room.

3

Church Camp

Church Camp was a summer event every year beginning at age nine. Every year I managed to forget its more horrible aspects, and the end of school found me looking forward to getting out of the house and mixing with kids who were required by the Bible to be nice to me. It was held at Fall Creek Falls deep in the Tennessee wilderness, in a group of small, thin-walled wooden 'cabins' surrounding a log and concrete meeting hall and similar cafeteria. Usually about two hundred kids from congregations around the state attended, kids I only ever saw outside of camp at the yearly General Assembly in Cleveland, Tennessee. Each session lasted one week, divisions made by age, so that the younger kids went first, then the middle kids, and the last week was for teens. The kids in my everyday life generally had no idea about the way I lived, since I only encountered them at school. When we all went home, they were returning to cable TV and parents who drank beer. My home routine was quite different. Although Church Camp was more of the same religion, it was a relief to be with kids who didn't ask questions like, "Which did you like better: *E.T.* or *Close Encounters?*" Those pressures were lifted, and though it seems impossible, there in the woods I felt very free.

We had a blue Samsonite suitcase that I excitedly packed with my no-name jeans and flannel shirts, toothpaste in a Ziplock baggie, and a 99 cent box of Little Debbies. Anything I might need in a week of relgious-themed camping was stuffed inside and everything was packed into our Fairmont, which had air-conditioning. Mom absolutely lived for air-conditioning and would not have been able to drive the three hours without it.

When our car arrived, the tires were rimmed with chalky white from traveling the newly poured gravel road into the woods. The maddening grind of the stones beneath our wheels crunched to a stop and Mom shifted the car into park, leaning back in the seat with a tired sigh.

"Well praise the Lord, that's over."

I was immediately out and running across the common area to the church office so that I could get my cabin assignment. My chest was tight with worry over the possibility of not getting into a good cabin, but this year a new anxiety suffused my usual jumble of emotions. Being in a cool cabin was essential, but I wouldn't really know until I had met the other guys and my counselor.

This year, more than wanting a funny counselor or winning cabin awards, I desperately hoped that I would be placed with some cute guys. In the past, my urges to peep at the occasionally available revelations of male flesh that occurred in my secluded life were handled by cutting my eyes away. I had certainly seen things, but always at the edge of a redirected, guilty glance. I knew without being told that I was not supposed to look. I had struggled with the issue while daydreaming in school and concluded that this year I would allow myself to look. This decision in my favor sat like a present on my inner horizon, approaching as Church Camp drew nearer. I was going to look. Discretion was unquestionably necessary, but now I consciously chose to replace guilt with a more empowered concept: stealth. Boys in underwear, Boys with no shirts, Boys coming back from the shower smelling like Irish Spring soap and toothpaste, in noisy flip-flops and ratty towels with bare chests exposed. My hyper-rationalizing brain easily excused this invasion. Every incidence of locker room talk I had ever heard was hauled to the surface, detailing what the very boys I desired would do if they ever got into a position of power or confidence with a girl. My secret peeking was nothing compared to the antics of male fantasy I overheard. Feeling justified, I had packed for Church Camp with great anticipation. All I wanted was to see skin. I could not wait.

Brother Cooper and his wife stood outside talking with parents. Mom and Dad made their way across the scorched grass, greeting old friends from other Tennessee churches. The Church of God of Prophecy was a fairly small religion, and most people in our state knew each other to some degree.

Brother Cooper was enormously fat. He was the pastor and director for our camp and he always carried a white cotton handkerchief with which he swabbed away quivering droplets of sweat as he moved from one brown building to the next in the dull summer heat. He was everything an enormously fat man might be expected to be: florid, jolly, easily winded, but in the nightly sermons he spoke powerfully. The extra work his lungs were forced to do in carrying him around paid off in a trumpet-like voice that delivered his convictions across the pulpit and directly into our young souls. Older people in our church had a way of speaking, a wavering tonality in their voices when reading from the Bible that could send a chill of doom through my body. He had mastered this, and it carried over into everything said as a sort of deathly concern for my status in eternity. I pictured my soul as a raw, immortal nerve quivering wetly in some dark space, waiting to feel burning immersion in the lake of fire. The way Brother Cooper rained sweat, I wondered if he would simply douse any Hellfire or if perhaps he might be standing too close to it for comfort.

Assignments were made, kisses were distributed and we all tried to respectfully conceal anxiousness for our parents to hurry up and leave. The younger group that was here a week before had probably shed a few tears at parting time, but our worldly teens were ready for a change in supervision. At this stage, most of us were veterans of the system and quickly set to unpacking and claiming our stakes in the cabins.

Each one was just big enough to hold four squeaky bunk-beds and some shelving along one wall. Once I had seen a tiny black scorpion crawl from out of one of these shelves when I touched it, something so completely unexpected in a Tennessee woods that felt like it was a sign from the Devil himself. Usually the cabins were connected in pairs by a concrete bathroom in the center, with standard humiliating communal shower, a row of sinks, and thankfully, partitioned toilets. My counselor, Brother Freeman, was probably twenty years old. He was sweeping the concrete floor when I came in and handed me a poorly xeroxed 'get to know you' bio sheet. I had immediately noticed the two other boys already filling out their forms. One was ugly, with black hair sprouting above a doughy face slapped on both sides with freckles. The other singularly fulfilled my hopes by being uncommonly gorgeous.

Peter, as he introduced himself, wore a yellow t-shirt bearing the plastic iron-on photo of a racecar. Not the toy kind, but a real, particular driver and his car. It was the kind of image that eventually faded and peeled off after it had been washed too many times, but evidently Peter's Mom had purchased this shirt for him to wear on the first day of camp. When I wore a t-shirt, it draped my meatless body as if it were still on the hanger. On Peter, it clung without being tight to suggest a naturally athletic physique. Wider shoulders, thicker arms than I saw on most fourteen-year-old boys at school, and the suggestion of pectoral development. His hair was curly and the color of oatmeal, a hearty dark blond. Peter's eyes were light hazel and they barely saw me when he gave his name before going back to the paper. He was absolutely dreamy, I thought, still present enough to mock my head-spinningly forbidden lust.

Most of the first day was spent settling in, but soon the afternoon had burned off and twilight began to spread up from the treeline and cover the sky. Bits of conversation among the boys of my now-full cabin sounded loud and raucous in the close quarters as we prepared for supper in the cafeteria. There was no clothing emblazoned with blatantly prideful logos, but somehow certain boys seemed to look more stylish than others. Judgment based on appearance was going to occur no matter what any parent said, and without access to augmentations like nice clothing or makeup for the girls, we were left to the most unfair standard of all: the unadorned looks God had given us. I was powerless.

Besides Ugly-boy and Peter, there were two other boys in my group. Mark was deep-woods country, somewhat raw and bewildered seeming. I guessed his daily routine must include slopping some sort of animal and reading fishing magazines. Terry was a junior criminal in the making, a type strict religions seemed to manufacture reliably, and I knew he was probably popular at his school. He would seamlessly backslide into normal society once old enough to be out on his own. He had already made friends with my Petey. Argh!

We went in groups from our cabins into the evening, converging on the large cafeteria. The air had cooled rapidly from uncomfortable to refreshing and carried a moist perfume of pine trees and earth. Inside, fragrant acres of church-lady prepared food lay spread in spotless aluminum steam-trays along the serving line. In later years, after I stopped going to camp, Mom volunteered as a camp cook and told me how they happily slaved for hours preparing the food from scratch. It was absolutely delicious.

I had a few friends from previous years at camp, our relationships perennial summer blossoms that opened in this week and faded dead at its close. I sat with one, turning about to see where Peter was whenever I could.

"What are you looking at?" Danny Evans, another preacher's kid, asked me. He sounded annoyed.

"What? What did you say?"

"I said you better get your elbows off…"

Suddenly a chorus of rhythmic claps and voices filled the room, shouting a toneless chant directed entirely at me:

"MABEL MABEL STRONG AND ABLE,
GET YOUR ELBOWS OFF THE TABLE!
ROUND THE TABLE YOU MUST GO, YOU MUST GO,
YOU MUST GO, ROUND THE TABLE YOU MUST GO,
MABEL MABEL!!!"

I reflexively snatched my elbows back from the table the instant the song started, but it was too late. By camp tradition another table could start the chant if anyone was caught, which the entire cafeteria would then take up. It ended with a gleefully shouted "GO! GO! GO! GO!" until the guilty party, in this case me, got up and ran around the table. Danny had joined in, pounding the table along with everyone else as he said, "GO! GO!" I wearily got up from my stool and ran listlessly around the rectangular table to stinging applause. Conversations were resumed and we finished eating without incident. This ritual was not malicious. Just another tiresome hoop to jump through I had accepted as part of my world.

After supper we had a little time to digest and pray before the evening sermon. The boys usually showered and slapped on some Old-Spice borrowed from their Dads to get ready for church. I watched with envy as they knowledgably applied mousse or gel to their hair. I was afraid to attempt such enhancements, so simply wetted mine and combed it to one side. When it was almost time for the service to start, the sound of the organist warming up could be heard outside blaring into the camp and a twilight migration centered on our giant meeting hall.

I took a seat near the back on a hard folding chair, trying to be discreet with a drawing pad balanced on my lap. People who sat all the way in the back were universally recognized as sinners and backsliders, so my position had to be carefully calculated. As far as I could tell, I was close enough to the front to be Saved, but not quite at Holy. After some warm-up singing and announcements, the main sermon began. The continuous drone of Brother Cooper's preaching was punctuated with emotional outbursts seemingly designed to shock us out of complacency. Pulled from my writing, I thought about the video of a religious prisoner we had been shown one year. His head was dunked in icy water whenever a particular point of his brainwashing was to be made. I accompanied each outburst from Brother Cooper with a sarcastic "ker-splash" in my head.

"What are you writing?" Brother Freeman had scooted to sit next to me and I hadn't even noticed. He was a friendly young guy who would have been a little-league coach if he weren't spending summers guiding boys like myself along the path of righteousness. I looked up at his sincere eyes framed by unfashionable glasses and a short masculine haircut considered attractive in our church. The page I had written seemed to hum with forbidden occult energy in my lap, and I was desperate to flip it over, but I couldn't move too quickly. I wrote everything in a substitution alphabet of runic characters I had pieced together from various books and I knew that anything looking "mystical" would be grounds for prayer. I casually turned the page to a blank sheet and called upon the classic response:

"Nothin."

"What is that? Some kind of foreign language?"

My skin prickled and the preaching echoed from the amplifiers at either side of the stage. I couldn't believe Brother Freeman was talking to me during church. I glanced up towards the covey of youth ministers and counselors sitting in front and was horrified to make eye contact. Their attention confirmed that he was here talking to me with their knowledge. Perhaps I was a topic of conversation at their nightly meetings…The earnest young men's voices raised in sweaty prayer, legions of night-flying insects crashing into the illuminated screen windows of their plywood shanty office. I would die if I thought they were all praying for me by name. Brother Freeman was still looking at my notepad. To actively conceal it would be admitting wrongdoing. In a way I was proud of my little language and wanted to show it off, but I knew it would appear to be evil to anyone in the church.

"Can I see? What does it say?" Could he possibly appreciate the coolness of my runes? He had an easy self-assurance that normal looking, athletic guys who weren't impossibly messed up in the head like me came to so naturally. For a brief instant I wished it were that simple for me, and I wanted him to like me. I wanted someone to look at my page of carefully formed characters and really, honestly think they were interesting. Then I saw his pathetically grasping eyes and the spell was broken. His ignorance was loathsome to me. Moronic. They would never understand the things I understood, the deep layers of concept that my mind swam through when it wasn't interrupted by their blundering communication. My sense of self-importance was inflamed and swollen by this irritation. I felt vastly intelligent and from the vantage of my arcane scholarship Brother Freeman appeared harmless.

There is no way he could read this, I thought. I turned the page back to the one covered in angular characters and passed it to him. "Well, it's a Celtic alphabet they used thousands of years ago. I just write in it because it's faster than English." I actually wrote in it to conceal my evil thoughts and because it looked cool, but there was no need to burden him with complex issues. I looked for signs that he was impressed, but he only said, "Hmmm." I think he felt sad for me, I could hear it in his voice, and I was so embarrassed all at once that a hot wave of self-loathing limned my entire body. So stupid! How dare he pity me. I wanted to snatch the pad back and I imagined myself immolated in punishing, protecting flames. I was so weak! Weak!

"Here, guy. Look, if you need to talk later, you know where I am." I could tell he thought I was toying with dark forces by the sadness in his voice. He handed me the pad and scooted back to sit with another counselor. My head throbbed and I could not wait for the sermon to end. It seemed I spent so much of my time waiting for people I could not stand to just shut up.

Just as it did at home, the sermons in Church Camp finished with an altar call. Instead of my mother, an old lady with white hair was the musical siren that lured us to crash upon the altar and spill out our guts for all to see. The false-sounding music of her synthesized organ came back empty from the high vaulted ceiling of our meeting hall, and soon the migration began. Brother Cooper pleaded with God on our behalf, begging Him to enter our hearts and guide us to his arms. It was late at night by the time this portion of the service hit, and after a long day of sports and classes in the summer heat-soaked woods I felt woozy, vulnerable. My confidence had been eroded by Brother Freeman's pity. The music was so loud, and the voice in the loudspeaker cried and cried, a grown man crying in front of all of us kids, begging God not to let us fall into the hands of the Devil.

As the crowd evaporated, praying bodies rising like zombies to stumble up onto the stage and fall in abject surrender at the altar, I felt more and more conspicuous. The air was filled with cries and ululations, children literally begging for their souls and speaking in tongues like saints consumed by the fire of the Holy Ghost. I looked around at awkward teenage girls who did not go to the mall, at boys who had never been kissed, and they were all crying their eyes out because they felt unworthy of God. Some had gotten down on their knees facing a chair and prayed leaning across the seat. I copied this, relieved to be in a new position. I closed my eyes and let my head rest on top of folded hands, feeling desperate. If the noise didn't stop I thought I might scream too, but then they would think they had won. The thought of them seeing me cry, watching me break, made me so angry. I imagined their relieved, smug faces gloating over my assimilation and the fury that welled up allowed me to squeeze my soul down so small and hard that they could never crack it. I looked across the room and outside the screen doors of the chapel and felt centered by the elemental deep-wood darkness I saw. Inside myself, imagining the fire all around me, I promised that I would slash my wrists before I ever gave in to them.

After the final altar call, if no one presented any demons to be cast out or other time-consuming problems, people made their way back to the now-cold folding chairs and the service was dismissed. Everyone seemed to feel cleansed after a night of sweaty prayer and screaming. Emerging into the dewy cold midnight air, the kids broke up into universal social groups themed by beauty and charisma. Everyone was chatty and bright with the weight of the world lifted from their souls. Our destination was the refreshment stand at the other end of camp. There we could have an old church-lady punch tiny dollar amounts out of the perimeter of Xeroxed cards our parents had purchased for us. Our selections were made from a moth-battered sign lit by speckled bulbs the color of dirty moonlight. My favorite was a "suicide," a drink so named because it was the dangerous combination of every drink on the menu. Mountain Dew, Coke, Seven-Up, Dr. Pepper, all gunned into a wax-paper cup by the bored church-lady.

"I can guess what you want!" she said knowingly. I always got the same thing. "A suicide and a Hershey bar, right?"

"Exactly." She punched my ticket and the exchange was made. I swirled the exposed end of my candy bar in the fluid to watch it fizz and then swigged the concoction with Socratic dignity as I walked away.

In the course of the week, our cabin had managed to bring home a few awards for cleanliness and other meaningless superlatives. We were pitted against other groups in volleyball and kickball, and went swimming in same-sex rotation. I couldn't swim at all. I was not allowed to go to public pools in normal life because they allowed mixed-sex swimming, and no one I knew had a private pool, so I had just never learned. Peter and Terry were horsing around one day on the hard cement around the camp pool when Terry got tackled and sprained his arm. I was floating in the shallow end of the pool in a t-shirt and shorts, enjoying the feeling of bouncing on my toes in the cool near-weightlessness when Peter and Terry crashed to the ground right beside me. Peter made a thick, organic sound when he hit the concrete and I was close enough to hear him whisper, "Crap!" Both boys had their shirts off and Peter's body was all the same color, like he went half-naked a lot. My body was about the same as any other boys I had seen, but I was impossibly embarrassed by it. I could not bear to be exposed to anyone and desperately envied the unconscious way other boys displayed such comfort in their own skins. A little trickle of blood showed from a scrape along Peter's shoulder when he got up, and the adults rushed over to examine him. Peter was wincing with pain, saying "I'm alright," and carried his arm close against his naked chest as he was escorted back toward camp. A quick-thinking counselor threw a towel over his shoulders before they got out of the pool's enclosure.

That night in the cabin, we were all preparing for bed after a long sermon. It had been a hot, busy day and everyone was damp and clean from their showers except Peter. I had waited until the other boys were done with showering by pretending to write a letter, and gathered my towel and soap when I saw everyone was back in the room. Peter was unable to shower because his new bandage could not get wet, and he looked absolutely dashing sitting on his bunk in nothing but a pair of green shorts and the bandage. In the dimly lit room his skin appeared even darker, more golden, and he was working a wet washrag over his torso with his awkward left hand in an attempt to wipe off the sweaty grime of the day. I hesitated, unsure that the focus of my eyes was not apparent in the dark recess of my bottom bunk.

"Hey, uh, can somebody get my back?" Peter seemed a little embarrassed to ask. While I doubted any of them understood anything about the reality, every adolescent boy I knew lived in terror of being branded "gay." Anything with even the appearance of gayness was anathema.

"I will." I said it way too quickly, the words out of my mouth and in the air before I could stop them. As the resident skinny introvert, I was ripe for some further-stigmatizing label, and this would be the perfect moment to earn "gay." But I was getting up, moving confidently and displaying a nonchalance I hoped would put off any suspicion.

"Well...Ok," Peter looked up at me for an instant. I had always been good at reading people, and I could tell he was rethinking his request, but he gave me the rag. I carefully swiped it over the surface of his back, across the shoulders and down the narrow channel along his spine. I tried not to wash like I was 'enjoying it,' although I did not know what that might look like enough to avoid it. Honestly it was more of an exploration than a seduction. There were no thoughts of sex, directly. For what must have been the first time in my life, I was touching a guy's naked flesh. I had wanted to know what it was like, and here it was, separated from my fingers by a millimeter of wet cloth. It was wonderful.

"OK, that's enough. It feels clean now."

"Here's your rag."

"Thanks."

I went to the painted cinderblock showers alone and stepped into the hot water. The fear that someone might walk in and 'see me' was ever-present at the fringes of my consciousness, but I felt mostly numb on the surface. By now it was probably past midnight, and I knew that the dark woods were directly on the other side of the white wall, separated from my naked form by a bit of whitewashed concrete. The only sound was of the water falling, louder and softer as I moved around in its stream. There were always bugs in the drain that had slipped inside the room and drowned. This time a tiny frog startled me by hopping against the wall, probably drawn in by the moisture and now trapped. I finished my shower watching it in my peripheral vision. When I was done I scooped it up and carried it, both of us completely naked, to the door leading outside.

4

Kamala

The Inglewood Branch Library was a medium bike-ride away from home. A solo flight down quiet neighborhood streets playing out elaborate fantasies in my head. What if magic was real? What if I could fly? What if I could change into someone else? There was a dim idea of another person, one glimpsed in the motion of turning away. One of the thousands of books I read had a protagonist named Amber, a male, but the name had always been associated with girls for me. He was a magician, the kind of thing that excited me then, and as time went on I assigned the name to my own fantasy persona. Whenever I found an eyelash to wish on, or a four-leaf clover, it was always the same. So many times, until it became a reflex, I said in my mind, "I wish I am Amber." And blew the lash away to carry my wish to God. "I wish I am Amber." And pressed the clover in a book. "I wish I am Amber."

Tennessee is all hills, on large and small scales. A little pedaling was rewarded with a lot of coasting. On the slopes I rested on the pedals, one up one down, sailing forward without effort. The library was small, staffed by a quiet old Asian woman and a blond young man, both of whom seemed individually out of place. The atmosphere inside was always cold and the smell of books immediate, like a pheromone that calmed me and displaced daily concerns. Here I had painlessly learned about adolescence, sex and most any forbidden thing I cared to look up. Before the Internet this was done in the real world, and each book was like a box, small and physical, that I could open or carry with me.

If I had no particular subject in mind, I would just wander through, pulling out books that looked interesting. I had a powerful fascination with the occult, since it was the exotic flipside to my own horrible religion. I claimed the church as my own even though I hated it, like one might claim cancer or some congenital birth defect. While my church was a dreary list of forbiddances, magic seemed like possibilities to me. If I could just learn to *"Develop your E.S.P!"* or delve the secrets of *"Earth Magic"* I could have some kind of control, some kind of adventure. I could get away...although from what exactly I didn't know. I loved my family, and was loved. We were not poor. I was not beaten or ridiculed. Aside from being smothered in the insular world of our religion, things were pretty good. But in a jumble of nebulously identified ways I just did not feel like things were as they should be.

In one book about weird and supernatural "things," basically a hodgepodge of whatever stories were leftover from other such books, I remember coming across a section on "feral children." First was the story of the wild boy of Aveyron. In the 1800's, it told me, a "feral child" was discovered who was believed to have been raised by wolves, and this sparked interest among the philosophers of the time. They wondered what qualities were innate to humanity, and which ones were a product of environment. "Victor," as the boy would come to be called, was a perfect blank slate with which to study this, since he had not been exposed to any kind of human influence. Raised by animals, he knew nothing of his true nature as a human being.

More recent was the story of a girl from India in the 1920's. Supposedly it was not unheard of for wolves to carry off children there, left at the edge of a field by a working mother. This was the story of Kamala. She and a younger human sister were discovered living in a hole by accident, and a hunting party was gathered to rescue them. The hunters killed the wolf-mother and dragged the girls from their den. The younger sister died in the following captivity, but for some reason Kamala survived. She became the pet project of a Reverend Singh, who managed to clean her up and made attempts to socialize her, but fully overcoming the years of living as an animal was impossible with his limited resources. What fascinated me most was the fact that although she was really a girl, she didn't even know it. She had been raised to be a dirty, snarling wolf. She tried to approximate her given role with limited success because it was all she knew, but nonetheless she was still a girl.

The thrill of identification passing over me was a realization that I, too, might be something more than I thought I was. That just because everyone around me treated me as one thing, it didn't mean that I might not be another. The wolves were only doing their best for Kamala, doing what they knew how to do. Kamala was only doing *her* best in the life she was given. It took an outside influence, an event to break into her world and show her that there was more than living in a hole and eating rotten meat. I had always fantasized about finding the door to another world, out into a different life where I was not the boring, sad person I seemed to be unable to change. Maybe I didn't need a magical fairy-land. Maybe the world I wanted was right here, and all I needed to see it was a change in perspective.

There are many types of girl. Some in my situation are bold, reaching after the things they learn early on that symbolize what they recognize in themselves: lipstick, high heels, frills. Then there was me. In my world womanhood was a state of being, defined more by roles and interactions than by accoutrements and accessories. I could not yet admit to myself the core fact that I wished I was a girl, but I knew absolutely that I wanted all the corollaries: the attention of boys, the consideration, the free indulgence in a mindset that came so naturally to me. But I did my best to march forward, head down, intuitively avoiding the unacceptable. I muted out these needs before they ever had a chance to bother anyone or cause a ripple. I look back at those years and see a child, silent and desperate and ignorant, laboring to live a life for which there was no heart. Sterile years in echoing halls of the mind, the whispered question: What is wrong with me?

Mom's look was decidedly unglamorous. Without movies or television to show me the extravagant excess on which many future queens and transsexuals thrive as inspiration, my ideas of what it meant to be a woman evolved simply. Thus I did not have the seminal experiences of dressing up in my mother's clothes or playing in my sister's makeup. Vain interest in my appearance was completely discouraged, so that only enough room was left for sad self-loathing with no way to fix whatever was wrong. My clothing was practical. A daily uniform of jeans and flannel was easy and painless, invisible in Nashville. I wore thrift and 'stole' my father's old shirts because I was comforted by their associated memories. Most of my clothing became tailored security blankets, ragged reminders of events and people more than adornment.

The mirror was my greatest source of self-flagellation. Sometimes I was unable to look directly at a reflective surface, and others I steeled myself to spend ages studying my face from every angle as if it were a horrible insect I had managed to trap behind the glass. I tried to figure out what made me so "ugly," searching to pin down my flaws so I could some day have them corrected by plastic surgery. I traced pictures of my face and erased jaw lines, redrew cheekbones and turned my eyes up at the corners. If I could just figure out exactly which part was off…I still did not realize that what was wrong in the mirror was my gender, so I was tortured by an elusive truth that hid just on the tip of my brain, maddeningly almost seen. The early onset of acne and a thin, unathletic body did not help. I filled entire notebooks with write-offs of 'I hate myself' and 'I wish I was dead' in my secret languages so that no one could discover them and realize I was crazy. Longing fantasies of suicide rode on tides of depression that engulfed me for months at a time, uncertain fear of Hell the only thing that kept me from acting. It was so easy for the people who preached against homosexuality, I thought. They were already hardwired to like the opposite sex, and built to attract its attention. All they had to do was connect the dots, color inside the lines, and they were heaven-bound. I hadn't even been given any crayons. I felt such an anger and hatred towards God during my adolescence because I never asked to be involved in his plan. I was made by him outside his parameters of acceptability, yet still forced to play the same game as everyone else. My soul filled with bile when I was told how merciful God was in holding out the chance to renounce the Devil and the world, the chance to serve him in bliss. I did not see a legitimate choice when the options were 'serve or burn.' It was like holding a gun to my head and forcing me to choose: say Uncle or be shot. Was that any kind of choice to be thankful for? I wanted no part of it, I simply wanted to end when I died, and if I had felt assured of that straightforward fate I would have killed myself at the first opportunity.

Instead, not yet ready to cast myself into the impossible machine of His judgment as a soul, I continued living. I adapted to the sparse social and artistic environment I had at hand, learning to play folk music on an old violin, escaping through the difficult-to-monitor activity of reading, and spending as much of my time as possible in the woods or walking nighttime streets of the neighborhood.

My one friend throughout Junior high was Jerry. He was a fairly normal kid, longish hair in the back, KISS posters in his bedroom. He worshiped his older brother, who had an edgy, thin cool due to being deathly sick with cystic fibrosis. The brother would light a cigarette and take a few puffs before flicking it away as if it wasn't worthy of being smoked. Really I guess it just made it too hard for him to breathe. Jerry's mother was divorced, worked outside the home and also smoked cigarettes, which made her exotically interesting even though I reflexively condemned her as wicked. I rode my bike the long distance to Jerry's house at every opportunity, spending the night whenever allowed so I could watch cable TV and draw comics.

When I was younger my dad and I played a drawing game in which he made some random shape on a sheet of paper. I had to make the shape into something. A wiggly line became a snake, a loop was the nose on a cartoony face. I had an intense absorption with drawing and tried to make surprising images from shapes Dad drew to challenge me. I began drawing paneled cartoons mocking the people around me at school and sharing them with Jerry, portraying his Dungeons and Dragons characters as fumbling fools and mine as their gloating superiors. We passed them in class and at lunch, me leaning over his shoulder to watch him read my scathing jibes and sputter "Aww man! Naw! *You're* the one who's *clumsy!*" or whatever the particular insults were. He could hardly wait to sit down and line out a sheet of notebook paper to frame his rebuttal. I neglected class work, odorous stacks of mimeographed assignments from lazy teachers hiding my cartoons whenever I was watched.

As graduation from Junior high approached, Jerry received an application to a magnet school downtown called Hume-Fogg. When he showed it to me, excitedly explaining how it would involve college level classes and elbow-rubbing with more creative kids, I immediately struggled to hide my jealousy. I had desperately watched other kids leave class to attend special programs for gifted students during earlier grades, later feigning disinterest while straining to hear them tell friends of fascinating experiments with miniature hover cars and pea plants. I knew I was as smart as they were, if not smarter. But my teachers returned homework assignments with low grades, bearing statements like "I know you can do better than this" written in sad red at the bottom. I knew I could, too. My mind was always racing ahead of the topics at hand, quickly extracting what I considered the pertinent information and moving on, too bored to complete repetitious assignments and homework.

With Hume-Fogg I saw a chance to finally enter the sacred company of 'real' human beings. I chafed at the thought of languishing in the obscurity of 'normal' Stratford High. I asked Jerry if I could borrow his application to copy it. I rode my bicycle as quick as I could all the way to the library, trembling with fear and excitement and fantasies of intellectual utopia, and pushed into the air-conditioned foyer all out of breath. A quick dig for change and I walked to the copying machine, nervous that somehow the Asian lady would guess that I was perpetrating espionage of the highest level and stop me. I made one copy for ten cents, borrowed some whiteout to erase Jerry's name, and sat down at the public typewriter to delicately position the page so as to seamlessly add in mine. Then it was up and back to the machine and its brilliant light spilling from the edges, another dime purchasing a ticket into a new world entirely.

I cannot believe it worked, but it did.

The best times of my life have been in the fall. The cold seemed to calm my brain, thicken the fluids and slow the sparks that floated up like crackling embers into the dark. In the fall of 1985 I began high school at Hume-Fogg Magnet School, an old structure for Nashville's relatively small city. It was made of pale gray stone, shaped fantastically like a castle with two towers crowned by tooth-like merlins.

The halls were aromatic with a mix of industrial cleaners and hundreds of adolescents in close quarters. Variegated layers flaked off the antique radiators revealing a dozen shades of painted-over institution gray. We sat on boards across their tops in the mornings to gossip while penetrating heat soaked through and into the seats of our jeans and gypsy skirts. The school had high ceilings, concrete walls painted over and wood trim around every large doorway and window. It had been built ages ago for many more students, but in its current incarnation as a school for 'the gifted' we only used three floors. The basement was an echoing labyrinth, the top floor mostly empty and sparsely maintained.

The year I started, it was graduating its first class of magnet school seniors. I walked the echoing passageways past rows of black frames, each stacked with a honeycomb pattern of gray oval portraits: students reaching back into the city's earliest history. Among them were Bettie Page and, not pictured, Dad. He had taken some vocational classes here during one of the school's other incarnations. The atmosphere was Bohemian and earthy, different from the junior professionals I see marching down its front steps now. There was no internet to speak of; computers were slow and stupid. There were no Columbine gunslingers. These were the children of people who had gone to college in the 60's. I encountered my first vegetarians, punks and proto-Goths. Kids using words new to me like Pagan and Nihilism to elicit interest and unity among other drifting, gentle rebels who were secretly optimistic and operating under Christian paradigms. There were type-A hard core study-fiends and pre-grunge slackers, Dr. Who fanatics and classical instrumentalists. The common ground here was intellect, which everyone had to some degree and which manifested in an overwhelming display of personality.

Jerry and I found a table in the small lunchroom on our first full day and I laid out the first cartoon of the year. I opened my paper bag lunch as Jerry read and was glad to have a chunky peanut-butter and apple jelly sandwich. This main course, which was essentially a dessert, would be followed by a Little Debbie Swiss Cake Roll. Milk was the drink of choice.

"What's this?" Jerry asked.

"That's your arms and legs being chopped off."

"I know, but these other lines…"

"That's where you're falling onto the conveyor belt. Those are to show you're falling, stupid."

Just then two girls came and sat at the other side of our table. This did not seem to be unusual in the small cafeteria, as the normal segregation of castes by seating had not had time to really solidify. We exchanged hello-looks and went back to our conversation. I couldn't help noticing that the girl with wavy hair had given the girl with straight hair a wrapped gift. The straight-haired girl was petite and fine boned. She made me think of a Bronte heroine and her fluty voice had a bit of waver to it, as if she were constantly in a state of nervous bemusement. A slightly drunk Victorian girl kidnapped by the circus, I thought.

"What is this, Crystalline?" She stared directly into the other's eyes as she shook the box next to her ear, looking ready to leap away like an insolent child searching for secrets in a Christmas present. Crystalline reached for the box.

"Don't break it! Its what I *owe* you, according to you." She had a heart-shaped face and thick, wild eyebrows. Her hair was all the colors of Autumn leaves, red and gold and brown. "Just open it."

"But what is it?" She leaned away from Crystalline and shook it again, on purpose. Crystalline snatched again and the girl held it out of reach.

"Travis! Give it *here!*"

"No, it's *my Precious!* Don't touch it! Don't touch *my Precious!*" She laughed, a sort of asthmatic gasping broken by a musical chuckle. Jerry and I were completely caught up in this exchange. Crystalline was all over her trying to get the bright box, and their game escalated into a quick brawl with chirpy laughing noises between gasps. They became suddenly unbalanced and managed a unified theatrical scream as they fell backwards onto the floor. A few people stared.

I stood up a little and asked if they wereOk. Crystalline regained her seat with the box in hand, ignoring the other girl completely. "Yeah, yeah, sorry. I was *not* going to let her break this."

"*My Precious!*" She said from the floor. Travis, as she was apparently called, quickly regained her composure and sat back down. Crystalline ripped the paper off the box and put it in front of her.

"Here." It was a G.I. Joe fighter vehicle.

"*Ohh! Thank you!*" Travis hugged her neck. Jerry and I stared at the toy. I did not quite know what to think of a girl who bought G.I. Joe stuff. Of girls named Travis.

"I'm Crystalline," she introduced herself.

"Hey, I'm Travis."

Jerry and I introduced ourselves casually. Two best friends meeting two best friends. An instant of awkward silence followed and then Crystalline asked, "What is that?" She indicated my cartoon. I noticed for the first time that her earrings seemed to be one-cent Queen Victoria stamps pasted back to back over loops of wire.

"You draw cartoons?" Travis said.

"Yeah, me and Jerry do." I pulled it closer, instinctively protective.

"Oh, Let her see it." Jerry scooted it over to the girls and I tensed as they hunched together to read it. The G.I. Joe vehicle sat forgotten beside them. I had to go over to their side to explain who was who and what was going on. Pretty soon they were smiling at the on-purpose megalomania and calculated insults to dignity. There were no limits to degradation or self aggrandizement in my comics…that's what made them funny to me. I only drew the line at cursing and sexual content. It sounds prudish until the gore and mockery are taken into account.

"Hey, some people are coming to my house this Friday night. My Mom is making snacks and stuff. You guys should come. You can bring more cartoons." Crystalline was inviting me to a party—Why? A sick feeling bubbled up in my stomach and I knew I would make an idiot of myself somehow. Jerry answered for us.

"We'll be there. He just has to ask his Mommy." There, it had been done for me. High-school is full of little deaths.

5

School

"Hey, why did you go off on that bum today?"

"He asked me for money. It makes me sick when some piece of human garbage invades my space like that. After all I do to get every dollar, and he wants me to hand it to him?"

"That's a dangerous way of thinking, Scots. Garbage is something you throw away. That's the way Hitler saw people. Every person has some value to them, you can't judge."

"Its Pavlovian, idn't it? Somebody questions a person's inherent worth as an organism and 'Hitler' pops out. No, that's the big problem with all this PC stuff. You try to control people's language but you're really tryin to control how they *think...*"

"Well, that's the idea, isn't it? To change ways of thinking that don't respect people's humanity?"

"No, what it does is discount the faculty of discernment itself. Words like 'judgment' and 'discrimination' are so off-limits now that the entire concepts are forbidden. People *need* to judge and discriminate in certain situations."

"It freaks me out when you try to be intellectual in that farmhouse drawl. Like what situations?" Ouch.

"Is this tuna-fish too old to eat? Will this girl make a trustworthy babysitter? It's like anything else...when attempted by morons it goes wrong, but judgment itself is not a bad thing."

"If I thought you were talking about a tuna-fish sandwich I wouldn't really care, but you're saying that human beings are garbage because they aren't as rich as you. That's bull!"

"I don't know then. Because I know I'd never lift a finger to hurt any one of 'em, but at the same time I feel like they contribute nothin to the world and I'm not gonna bankroll them with the dollars I scrape together slavin away at a hamburger stand."

"So if you hit hard times and ended up sleeping on the street, you would want me to let you die?"

"If I can justify my continued existence in some kinda way, then I deserve to continue livin. Maybe that's through bein charmin enough to still have friends that would take care of me. Maybe that's by bein a convincin enough beggar that I could even get somebody like *me* to cough up some money. But that guy was an obvious drunk. If he had any friends, they didn't care enough about him to take him off the street. And I wadn't convinced to part with my cash. Like I said, I wouldn't lift a finger to hurt him, but I think he's probably worthless and I stand by that."

"That is one of the more fucked-up things I've heard you say, and you're pretty creative in that department. Look, I'm gonna hang up now and I hope when I see you tonight you've grown a heart."

"Crystalline?"

Dinner was homemade beef pot pie, with plenty of sweet tea. We sat at the table in the same places we had been assigned by chance and affinity a rememberless age ago. Jerm was beside me, Ginger across from us beside Mom. She had, by relentless willfulness, finally been allowed to use as much hairspray as she wanted, and tonight she was elaborately styled. She saw me looking at her hair and obviously divined my distaste.

"Pass the salt," she said. I passed it to her.

"Thank you *slave*." Score. I was concentrating on the coming night at folk-dance and couldn't work up any enthusiasm for repartee. Jerm sensed my weakness and mechanically moved in. He spoke in a lowered voice, as if this rendered sound inaudible to our parents only inches away:

"You use utensils to manipulate food to your mouth-opening." He then continued eating as if nothing was said. Observing me in the style of a schoolroom biology film was his way of reducing me to the level of a protozoan.

"Can y'all talk *normal* please?" Mom aggressively peppered her vegetables. I was losing my touch, if they both scored on me within the same five-minute period. I decided to change the subject.

"Mom, can you give me a ride to folk-dancin?" Joyce had introduced me to the weekly event, held in the cleared-out cafeteria of a grade school. Crystalline was most always there, too, and Travis made occasional appearances. Of course dancing was sinful, but we kids were pushing boundaries as much as we could and English contra-dancing was just chaste enough to scrape below parental radar.

"OK." She didn't sound happy about it. She had intimated opinions by reading the hippie bumper stickers plastered next to faded college parking passes in the lot where she dropped me off, and I guessed they weren't positive. "College leads people away from God."

After dinner I put on a favorite cotton flannel shirt, open over a white T decorated with my latest cartoon. It was an ad for Filboid Studge *(They Cannot Buy It Now!)*, a product mentioned in a favorite short story by H. H. Munro. I wrote the text in phonetic hieroglyphics just to make it look more interesting. "What does that mean?" Mom asked as we got into the car.

"It's a breakfast cereal from the eighteen hundreds."

"Oh!" She tried to sound enthusiastic about my artistic efforts, but rarely delved too deeply.

The dance was held at Stokes Elementary, seven pm every Wednesday. "You can come in if you want to, Momma, it's just folk dancing. I wish you could see how fun it is…" I was a little surprised at the pleading in my voice.

"Honey, no. And you know why." Mom said it gently, like I *should* know and it made her sad that I would even bring it up.

"Thanks for bringin me, anyway." I wished so badly that she would come see me dancing, share the feelings that ran through me like fresh air and light when I heard the music. I knew if she would just come in and see, it would happen. I never expected that she would dance...That was one fantasy image hidden deeper inside another. It would be enough to just see it in her eyes. I kissed her on the cheek and got out, my vague sadness evanescent in the proximity of otherworldly music and laughter.

Joyce's mother sometimes 'called' the dance, announcing steps with serious authority only occasionally broken by a slight smile. Her father was a witty chemist who did something along the lines of cleaning up the environment. She discouraged me from asking him questions when I shared their organic vegetarian dinners, to avoid a scientific lecture. Her house was old but well kept in that way that never lost the possibility that ghosts crept beneath its floorboards. I always peeped into her refrigerator to gape at the esoteric foods: containers with Japanese writing, vegetarian leftovers and foreign seasonings in little hand-labeled jars. Mom kept our delicious rendered lard in a coffee can on the stove. Antiques and African art were spread around Joyce's house, available for touching, but it looked like it had been a decade or more since anyone living there had found them interesting.

Tonight Joyce was wearing a swirly skirt that flared out dramatically when she spun, and a loose cotton blouse. Her hair moved in typical Medusan clusters of tight, soft curls the color of dark honey. When I drew her in cartoons, five identical looping squiggles radiated out from her face like an iconic dandelion. Or like whirling Egyptian atens, the rays of the sun that denoted God status. At school we passed back and forth ragged books by noted authority Sir E. A. Wallace Budge and cartoon insults using ancient Egyptian principles of pictography. It was deliciously arcane and geeky. She never wore makeup that I could see, instead defiantly radiating wholesome barefaced health, down to her perfect white smile. She poked me in the chest with her finger the moment she noticed me.

"Why weren't you at Madrigals yesterday?"

"I couldn't get a ride. I'm wearin Mom out as it is."

"Is your car still down?"

"Yeah, after the *Witches of Bucksnort* incident I haven't been able to start it again." Bucksnort was a rural city we passed through near Hohenwald, where I had chauffeured a carload of wanna-be Wiccans from school who promised to show me its legendary thrift stores. We waded through clothes released from bundles as big as refrigerators that collapsed into vintage paradise when the bindings were snapped. We took all we could stuff into a paper grocery bag for just five dollars. Our happy mood was cut short when my car died somewhere in the country hills of Bucksnort on the way back. After several failed attempts at ignition and some discussion, the girls laid hands on the hood. To everyone's surprise, the engine started when I turned the key. We managed to get back to Nashville, but it hadn't run since.

"Well, the songbooks came in. I have yours in the car." They cost three hours work at Expressway Hand-burgers, but was worth it to me. Aside from folk dancing, singing in the Madrigal group was just about my only social activity.

The beginner's instruction was ending, so we went inside and stuck on our nametags. The familiar double-length lunchroom tables were folded against the wall into giant standing panels of white Formica with the little round seats lining each side. Normal school chairs lined the left wall and people sat and stood talking as the band retuned their fiddles and guitars. There was no retuning the piano, which had presumably been hammered into senility through countless children's recitals. Joyce and I took our place in the contra line as one of our favorite dances, "Petronella," began. The fiddle skipped brightly down a sectioned scale and then tripped off the end before returning to the beginning. It had a lot of swinging, a move in which the partners clung together against the centrifugal force of their turning and stared into each others' eyes. I rarely made eye contact in real life. The overall sensation was exhilarated resistance of inertia, pulling together against the spinning. When it was done, we were breathing deeply and a pleasant flush colored our faces. I made my way toward the water fountain in the hall and Crystalline was just coming in the school's front door still wearing her school backpack.

"Hey!" I hugged her. She felt cool against my dance-warmed body.

"Hi, Scotts. God, I thought I was never going to get here. I had to finish a paper for Mrs. Stewart." That was the difference between us: She did her homework. When I left school, I left all thoughts of work behind. I felt a twinge of depression whenever I saw my friends exhibiting responsibility. One of the many skills I hadn't mastered. "Come outside. I've got something for you."

"What?"

She pulled me down the hall and we slipped out into the back yard of the school. Notes of guitar music like raindrops on water followed us through the door, muting as it closed slowly on its pneumatic hinge. We walked over to the swings and sat next to each other. Her hair was pinned up in anticipation of sweating, but I knew it would be down before the night was done, pulled loose in the dancing. Rhinestones in antique-looking earrings caught the streetlights, showcased by the exposure of her white neck. She pumped her legs a little to set the swing in motion, but had to stop when her skirt proved unmanageable.

"What did you want to show me?"

"I got you a birthday present. I stole it."

My stomach turned over, but I was excited. My birthday was a week ago, and as usual we did nothing special beyond a nice homemade cake and ice cream after supper. Our family had never had any tradition of exchanging presents or having birthday parties. I couldn't believe she had actually stolen anything. She opened her backpack, decorated with needle-pointed designs around sewn on patches, and pulled out a small package. It was wrapped in silver Christmas paper with a fine red design of pine boughs. I took it and immediately knew it was a book. There was something written on the wrapping paper, in powdery-looking burgundy.

"What's this?"

"That's mine and Travis's name written in our blood." The flyaway hairs stood out from her head and made a halo in the streetlights.

"Wow...Can I open it?"

"Yes, just be careful, there's two things in there."

I separated the strips of clear tape from their holds and slid out a book and a cardboard container in the shape of a book. The container was a set of ceramic rune-stones and their accompanying manual. The book was *The Necronomicon*.

"Uh, thanks..." *The Necronomicon*. Despite its origins at the Rivergate Mall chain bookstore, it tingled with forbidden evilness. The only thing worse would have been *The Satanic Bible*, and she couldn't have paid me to touch that. But the thought of connecting with vast forces beyond Christianity was desperately fascinating. It made my flesh prickle and conjured spirits of menace in the dark corners of the sky above us. Jesus had had his chance and I was none the better for it. I wondered if the Bible weren't just a piece of masterful propaganda, Devil and all, and perhaps an entirely different system was actually in place outside that entire mythology.

"What if angels were actually something horrible like vultures," she said, cutting her shoe with a pocketknife. "Showing up when people die to catch and eat the energy of their newly homeless soul."

"What, and we just built up the legends about 'em being holy emissaries because they seemed magical?"

"Yeah exactly. We don't know what all that shit is." She wore no makeup and her unpainted eyes and lips were lush and colorful. I wondered if she knew how beautiful she was. "If they want us to believe there are angels, I mean *really believe* it, then that means there are spirits and ghosts and all that stuff out there. Real. What makes them think we know what any of it actually is?"

"My parents have never seen an angel. Or a demon. You can bet they're totally sure about all that stuff though. How could somebody believe all that, without ever havin any proof?" I already knew, though.

'Faith is the substance of things hoped for, the evidence of things not seen.' I had heard this quoted a million times.

"I'll tell you how. They *have* to believe it, or else their whole lives have zero meaning, and they have no excuse for not playing the hard games out there that real people play every day."

"Like wishin people liked 'em. Because in their little belief system it 'shouldn't matter' since God likes 'em and that's the important thing."

"Yeah, and not having sex."

"How come things got so messed up?" I stopped for a second, debating whether or not to say what had been on my mind so much. "I'll be honest, Crystalline. If I could make it so I was never born, I would. I promise if somebody gave me a button right this second and said, 'Push this, and you will never have been born,' I would. I wouldn't know the difference once it was pushed, so why not."

She seemed to snap out of a reverie and looked back at me. "Don't start that shit. You're not going to kill yourself."

I suppressed a sudden surge of embarrassed hurt before any damage could be done. Don't take me so lightly, I thought. "I'm not talkin about that. I just mean, I feel so messed up sometimes. Like I wish I had been born perfect, is all. I guess I wish that more than anything, that I had been born perfect and beautiful and normal." I waited for the required counterculture response of 'but what is normal?' Instead she was silent, moving a little in her swing. With both hands clutching the chains she looked like a little girl. Long electric shadows ran from the streetlights into the dark playground, wearing our shapes.

"Yeah. I wish that too."

That night at home I opened The Necronomicon and began to read. It seemed to be talking about something like the big, open sky I had always seen in my dreams, the thickness of worlds upon worlds that crowded dark space outside the circle of waking life's firelight. But the places I saw were never so ugly as the ones described on its pages. My dreams felt primordial, empty of intelligent menace. Only gray skies and cold water, or infinite womb-like forests of spongy moss under a glowing green cathedral ceiling of leaves. I drifted into sleep that night threatened by vague entities carrying names long and curved as scorpion tails.

"When me and Karen were little we used to sit in her front yard—"

"Where the creek is?" Jerm and I were walking to the Tenneco to get some candy, something to do on a warmer than average February day.

"Yeah, and we'd look across the road at that big cow field when it started to get dark and try to imagine somethin comin at us from over the hills."

"Why?"

"It was just fun, scarin ourselves."

"Remember those hamburgers y'all made on that little grill you dug outta the trash at her gramma's *trailer*?" We were well aware of Southern stereotypes and thought it hilarious when they actually happened. Karen's grandma lived in a small, neat trailer on her family's property, rolling Bugler tobacco into cigarettes and smoking them in the shade of her giant string-bean tree. She used a little device that magically popped them out in her expert hands. I tried rolling one once, but couldn't make the machine snap correctly. I wouldn't have ever smoked it, nor would she have allowed me to, but the process was interesting to me.

"Yeah, those were good, cooked over burnin newspaper and twigs, ha ha."

"Did y'all ever really see anything comin over that hill?"

"Not really…it seemed like it sometimes, though. No matter what we always ran in the house screamin before it got too dark anyway."

"Did you finish *Interview with a Vampire* yet?" Crystalline and I didn't have any classes together, which was probably a good thing since I would have gotten no work done if we had. The lunchroom ceiling was sloped and disrupted the echoes that might have otherwise been overpowering in such a small area.

"Yes, I read it all just about the first day you brought it. Have you read the next one?"

"Yeah, Travis has my copy, but you can borrow it next, *IF* you give it back before the end of the semester this time." I was a bad borrower. "It talks mostly more about Lestat."

"Well I guess so, since it's called *The Vampire Lestat*"

"You're brilliant, Scotts. Anyway I drew some cartoons while I was waiting for Mom at the doctor's office, they're of when we went to the Scottish Fest." Crystalline played the violin, gigging out with her pianist Dad at weddings for cash occasionally. She was pretty serious about it, but I didn't get to take much part in that side of her music. Her idol was Suzy Perry, the fiddler in a Celtic band some students had started that actually got on NPR's *Thistle and Shamrock* with Fiona Ritchie and everything, and we followed them at local events like the Scottish Fest. Crystalline produced a clear three-holed sleeve like we used to protect the title page of an essay, but inside were three spiral-bound notepad sheets with delicate pictures drawn in colored pencil. They were a triptych of our adventures in the botanical gardens at Cheekwood where the fest was held. Crystalline drew us with huge almond eyes and pointy ears, me wearing a vampire cape and her body voluptuously curved. In the first she was playing her fiddle beside a detailed tree and I produced little eighth notes from a flute or recorder. Next we were running across native brushy hills beyond the imported bamboo garden, drawn without color because we had been invisible then. Finally Crystalline was laying in a bath of milk, with just her blissful elfin face and toes visible against the white paper. Each picture was cut across with the faint blue guidelines for writing, but we never saw those.

"Scott-ty, tell-a-phone!" We had used the same sing-song forever, except when we were little it was for bedtime tattling: "Mom-ma, Jer-mee's up!" I scrambled to grab the receiver and it was Crystalline.

"Scott, what are you doing?"

"Nothing."

"Come over." Click.

Dad had finally found time to look under my hood the day before and, after summoning me to his side, showed me where my starter was and how easy it came off. For some reason the open hood of a car repelled me. I immediately recognized Dad's rare attempts at old-fash-ioned male bonding and they made me feel physically ill. Such things embarrassed me terribly, because I knew I lacked whatever catalyst made these interactions easy between other fathers and sons. I felt bad I wasn't giving Dad what any other boy would or could. Certainly he never seemed anything but a little tired from work and dreading more greasy labor in his scarce free time, but the stress I felt kept me from behaving normally. In any case, after a quick trip to the Napa car-parts place and some pained ratcheting, I was mobile again.

Crystalline lived in the city of White House, almost exactly a thirty-minute drive North on I-65. Once past Nashville's most modern mall, Rivergate, it was a ride through hills and hills full of trees. Her neigh-borhood was typical small-town residential, and although the front side of her house faced a house-lined street like my own, her back yard contained a small pond the size of another lot. Beyond that were miles of trees.

Her room was patchouli-scented and full of candles. Tins of rocks were scattered about that had looked magical when encountered in the creeks and moss beds of her forest. A collage of Faery pictures domi-nated one wall, across from a smaller constellation composed of Linda Hamilton, star of television's *Beauty and the Beast*. The live action gothic drama, not the cartoon. I knew that hidden in her drawers, under stacks of elaborate letters from friends and gypsy clothes, were books on "good" witchcraft. Safer books were stacked in every corner, spilling out from under her bed, by Tolkien and Anne Rice, fiction and fantasy and horror. Crystalline had thick binders of drawings she had made of everyone she cared about, with the upturned eyes and pointed ears of elves, dancing and reclining in mystical locations. She wanted so much to be something magical and free.

"I'd never want to be a vampire, though."

"Why not? I'd rather be one than an elf."

"Scotts, Lestat is cool, but can you imagine if you had to survive by killing someone different *every single night?* Of your *life?* At least as an elf I'd be immortal and beautiful without hurting anyone."

"What if you only killed and drank the blood of people who deserved to die?" I casually flipped through her picture book.

"Who's to say who deserves to die? Look, this one is David and me singing madrigals." She indicated a delicate, spare rendering in lines of colored pencil.

"Some are just obvious. Like I could move to New York and kill all the drug dealers."

"I don't know, that's all so complicated. What if they were selling drugs to support their families?" She got up and selected a record, placing it on the turntable. It was Kate Bush, singing about Wuthering Heights. Only Kate could make a top-ten song about a piece of literature on our required reading list at school.

"Drugs kill people and ruin other families. It's the greater good to kill them first. I'd rather be anything that just a guy. Being human is disgusting anyway. Look at all the possibilities for things to go wrong."

"Most of the time stuff goes wrong because people don't make an effort."

"I mean genetically wrong, like freaks and Down's Syndrome and stuff."

"So obviously you have some kind of theory here."

I had been thinking about this for ages, trying to figure myself out. It was a relief to try and express it to someone. "Well, in terms of genetics, our body is a mathematic idea expressed organically. The DNA is code, which is math, but it has to make itself happen with cells and flesh and blood. That's where the horrible mistakes can happen, because flesh and blood is totally wild and susceptible to its environment." I was excited, and the words came easily like practiced movements of dance or music. "Error is even built in, on top of that. It's innate to physical reproduction in biology. It's a survival mechanism."

"I know. Evolution."

"But for every error that luckily results in a more successful organism, there are the heaps and heaps of freaks left struggling by the wayside. It's like the Fibonacci sequence…this perfect series of numbers that comes out all kinds of ways in nature. Pine-cones, sunflowers, rabbits…"

"Scott, what the Hell are you talking about?"

"I don't know. Never mind."

"Let's go downstairs and watch TV. I rented *Legend* again."

"Did you ever find out that guy's name in it?"

"Tom Cruise or something."

"Works for me." We went back downstairs. I felt as if something dangerous had been avoided and was glad to move on to more familiar diversions.

6

Camping

I wondered if I could ever change the way I was, looking up into the darkest blue remnants of the October night. It was screened through the naked whips of a weeping willow tree, faraway and ancient. I waited for Travis in the cool semi-dark, the wood railing of her deck swollen with mist risen from the depths of the Cumberland river running a short drop below. She had been playing her harp, as she called the skeleton of some piano that lay against the outer wall of her snug log home. It was curved like a strange bone whose function was only understood when viewed in the context of a living body. Its rusting strings were intact across the frame, and Travis would come to lull herself into a thoughtless contemplation by pulling her fingers over them in light strokes.

"I'm ready." She appeared at the door dressed warmly in a vintage sweater and knit cap. Straight, shining hair draped her shoulders in a henna-red veil. She was so beautiful. Travis was elfin, tiny, delicate; the differences between us made her magnetic to me. I felt like an oaf moving alongside her ballerina steps. If I could ever be...My thought stopped, like a record needle lifted and placed somewhere else entirely: "So graceful," I finished. I had never *wanted* a girl. There was no self-deceived lust. But at moments like this some hopeless sensation engulfed me like thick, boiling water when I looked at the women I surrounded myself with. It was a longing, sad and melting like snowflake dreams on feverish skin before I could ever discern its pattern.

Leaving for a camping trip before the dawn kept these ventures separate from the waking world. The ritual of allowing sunrise to set the pace was broken, and we moved freely through the back hallways of the day. She and I crept through her sleeping house, past her drowsy mother cradling sweet coffee on the couch, and accepted that goodbye as our last contact with the mundane world. Through her door we went out in the darkness.

My car was blue, and big and old. I honestly could not quote the make and model without reading it off the trunk, a subconscious rejection of dad's love of such things. Travis slid her pack next to mine in the back seat, and when I turned the ignition, Kate Bush's liquid voice poured from a mix tape already in progress.

We met Crystalline and David at the school building downtown. The stars were fading out, and the sky had clarified from indigo to pale. It was still cold enough that our breaths were visible, and I was glad of the extra flannel I put on at home.

Crystalline's hair hung loose and wavy as always. She had exchanged the usual skirts for a pair of battered jeans with a bit of her simple embroidery just below the front pocket: a red rose. Her t-shirt was topped with a man's flannel left open across her full chest. Two unopened Cracker-Jack prizes dangled from wire loops in her ears, another set of her countless homemade earrings.

"Every girl is in love with David Heiser." Crystalline had once said. At our bohemian school his facility with a guitar and famous braying laugh were cherished points discussed in whispers at slumber parties. I was always the only boy at these events, but the mothers never seemed threatened. David wore a long-sleeved thermal shirt beneath a loose short-sleeved Tee with the wheel of arrows that represented recycling. His hair was long and brown, always in a ponytail. David had terrible acne in high school, but his face was so animated with the most genuine, elemental smiles that no one seemed to notice. He was vigorous with emotion, infectious joy made sweeter by occasional flickers of what looked to my adolescent eyes like the passing of deeper clouds.

"*Hey!*" He was illuminated with his familiar grin, and before I could react he crossed the distance between us and lifted me up in his arms.

He spun in a quick circle and set me down, unbalanced and thrilled. "I'm so glad you made it! Cool!" My composure was completely blown, as I was not lifted into the air very often. It was up in the air whether or not I would be going on this trip at all because my parents worried over the influence of my new friends, but apparently David was happy to see me.

"Yeah, me too." I looked away and felt a flush color my shy smile. I was totally in love with David Heiser.

Travis and I put our packs into David's trunk and we settled in for the drive of a few hours to Frozen Head State Park. We would be meeting some other members of the Ecology Club there, along with its faculty sponsor, Mr. Brown. For me, the drive to the site was one of the best parts of the whole trip.

Throughout high school, the relief of finding a group of people to feel a part of was always commingled with the poisoning fear of their rejection. The more I loved them, the more it burned when I was not invited to any little impromptu hike or jam-session or get-together. I drank in every detail of their cool eccentricities, the way the girls dressed and each inside joke. I had to feel 'on the inside,' and at Hume-Fogg, with these people I got heady injections of this feeling often enough that my undernourished ego finally began to grow and develop. Memories of that time are colored in the earth tones of fall, brown and gold and gray. Clothing was thrift and Goodwill, on purpose now instead of being all I was morally allowed. And the wind always carried a soft odor of moss and vegetation. In dark-hour moments at the muted house on McAlpine, I told myself if I ever lost this new world I had been admitted to, I would die. I counted the ways like a secret hoard of electric coins. "Leap of faith, razor, pill, the only ways myself to kill."

Our camping trips were a time to showcase wit and skill in front of the only people that mattered. Crystalline was my confidant, her position in the hierarchy a bit more secure than mine, but to my great comfort she also had her doubts about whether 'everyone' liked her. We worried for hours on the phone, ears aching from the pressure of the hard plastic receiver.

"I just don't feel like I fit in anywhere..." She said before the trip, some weird earring scratching against the receiver. "Let's break it down: I love nature, but I'm only an 'honorary granola' because I never really get to go camping. Oh, and every one of them has read stuff like *The Hobbit*, and just *swears* by it. You know what? I thought *The Hobbit* was *boring*..."

"I know! I mean, I like a lot of the stuff everybody talks about, but they all seem to know every little detail about it and I'm just now hearing of it..."

"Scotts, I can't name *one song* by Pink Floyd! Not one! Joyce was playing the whole record at her thing last week and I thought it was cool, but..."

"You are so magical and cool, anyway." Magical: this was a high compliment in our circle, where the most envied rooms were decorated with things forbidden to me: candles, stolen occult guides and posters of faeries. "It doesn't matter...everybody likes you. I wasn't even invited last time Travis and Joyce went camping. I wouldn't have known about it if I hadn't seen the reminder on Joyce's refrigerator."

"And at Madrigals I haven't memorized any of the words. Everybody thinks we are completely counter-culture and out-there..."

"And we just saw *Brazil* for the first time..."

"God, we are such total *frauds*!" A nervous, guilty laugh buzzed from the receiver. "And by the way, bring my *Vampire Lestat* tomorrow. You borrowed that two weeks ago, at least."

On the drive I produced a copy of *The Weekly World News*, the unbelievably phony black and white tabloid with headlines that challenged the most credulous reader.

"Amorous Anemones Attack U.S. Government Divers!" I attempted an announcer's flourish. Joyce and David were talking in the front seat, a detailed description of some foible her mother had demonstrated, eliciting more laughter. Joyce's sentences were broken by her gasping and choked exclamations. Crystalline opened a bag of dried apples and passed it around. One of a clattering stack of mix-tapes was playing...We usually decorated the labels with various tiny designs and pictures. David had put in one of Crosby, Stills and Nash and the music felt light, amplifying our rising good spirits in the breaking dawn.

The trailhead was a simple parking area next to the beginning of a partially clear path into the half-snowy woods. We pulled in next to the van that was already there, side door open and kids lounging in the seats and on the running board. Layered flannel and jeans was the cold-weather uniform of choice, variety found in color and the wryly chosen thrift t-shirts with obscure advertising. Mr. Brown and Miss Harmon began shouldering their packs, and our arrival set everyone else looking for their gear. I couldn't wait to jump out and join them. With little said other than greetings and organizational strategy, we entered one by one the forest.

My layered shirts were stiff with the cold when I pulled up a corner to blot the clammy sweat from my face after hiking for an hour. With the heavy pack off and leaning against a tree, I felt like I was walking on the moon. Crystalline and I took giant steps around each other as our muscles reacquainted themselves to carrying normal weight. Crisp fallen leaves rustled beneath the searching feet of tent-setters looking for stones, and Crystalline stayed close by me, watching the activity. This was actually her first camping trip, which we had made a pact not to reveal, and I could see she was somewhat nervous that she wouldn't know what to do at this stage.

"I'll set up the tent this time, since you did it last time." I un-bungeed my compact tent from the pack and looked around for a good spot. Travis and Joyce were in one tent, and David had a narrow ultra-hip one-man next to them.

"Let me help." She took a side after I had unrolled it and shaken out a few of last year's crumbs and leaves. We spread it out and Crystalline immediately understood how the fiberglass rods connected together and crossed to support the dome-shaped roof. Amidst easy, joking conversation the camp was set up in a short time and firewood gathered inside a circle of stones to one side. I noticed at the end of our work that the sky had already begun to deepen and lose its pale light.

"Hey, you want to go see the ranger's tower?" David was asking me. Someone had packed a tiny guitar and several people sat near the fire talking over its music. Mr. Brown had set off after a wild turkey sighted by one of his poetry students and everyone seemed to be settling into doing their own thing. Joyce appeared behind David, looking effortlessly snug and cool in a sweater she had knit herself, thick curly hair struggling to expand out the bottom of her knit cap. In our freshman year her hair had been a short, wooly cap, but it had grown out into bucketfuls of spirals. Once someone had asked a short-haired Joyce if she was a boy or a girl. When she related this incident back to us, I was stunned at the response she gave to the malicious questioner: "Guess!" With her knitting and natural hair and sharp wit she always seemed dryly wholesome, an earth-mother with claws. We rescued Travis from the attentions of some foolish boy, and David led the way out of the camp and up the mountain.

The space between and beneath each tree seemed a continuous chamber divided by the irregular columns of wood. Snow lay in a shallow blue-white crust on the ground and absorbed the sounds of our movement. I felt drugged as I watched the sun fall early below the tree line and refract into arctic colors, cold blue broken by the jagged black cracks of silhouetted branches. The land was uneven, spreading out around me in miniature valleys and peaks. One moment the horizon was very close and then, cresting a hill, it had receded far away across a frozen field of matted golden grass poking up from the snow.

When the rain began to fall I looked up into it and felt the heavy drops sting my face. The trees were tall and thin, and it seemed the clouds had begun to descend in great sections of gray-black mist to better part branches and soak the ground. They moved in layers, the closest opening in gaps to reveal a far off landscape as big as the mountain we stood on, surreally inverted miles above our heads. Lightning illuminated from within the complex patterns of soft hills and valleys, its flash defining great distances in an instant between us. Thunder followed immediately, thickly resonant. I had the sensation of observing something immense and ancient, like the movement of whales, drawing me up into that cold largeness and whispering lonely freedom. We continued up the mountain, playing at urgency in the excitement of a quickening storm. Slick dead leaves were revealed under the melting snow and fallen apples, half-rotted, shifted dangerously beneath our feet. At the top, deliciously sinister against the Chthonic structures moving in the sky, stood the ranger's tower. It was a wood shack reached by climbing squares of stairs coiling up inside the brown metal lattice of the structure. The wind was crazy, sliced to bits as it rushed through the trees. The struggle of it on my skin, pulling at my clothes and hair, called up an eldritch excitement, the same that broke civilized people throughout time into scrambles and shouts at a downpour. Raindrops filled every space, seeming to pop and tremble in place without falling. The wetness bound everything together, so that clothing seemed only another layer of skin. Bark and metal ran down, slick, to shiny earth. Strange light came diffused from every direction, melted in the rain and hung in dying tatters from the branches.

I cannot say what possessed us to ascend a metal structure in a storm, other than fatalistic pursuance of adventure, but without dissent we began to climb. I would have died before I left this band of people in this moment. A strike of lightning would have electrified the entire tower; we would have crackled like insects on the grid. But we made it to the top, pushed up into the cabin, and were inside.

There is a feeling, of being warm in the cold. Of being dry in the wetness. It is the sensation, for me, of complete inviolability. Comfort. Inside this wooden cube, thrust up into the turbulent atmosphere, I felt immeasurably excited and safe. David went to one of the large windows and stood against the shifting glow of its gray and black. I joined him, and he placed an arm across my shoulder, hypnotized by the visions roiling outside. Wet fabric and skin, heat translated from his body to mine through the water. Beyond the window the sight of the entire valley, writhing in the turbulence of the storm, made me reel for an instant as my soul lurched and stretched to a bigger size encompassing this vision. I had never felt this way before. Far below I saw the movement of air trace molten footprints across the vegetation. I saw the secret activities of rain, billowing in exploding swarms before it reached the ground. And then the warm bodies of Crystalline and Joyce, pressing against David and me to see out the window, as we silently observed it all.

7

The Fall

One day in my sophomore year I brought home a report card that was less than stellar, one of several, and after a moment's thoughtful consideration my mother said I was not to continue at Hume-Fogg. The room receded suddenly, unexpectedly. There was a moment of disorientation and I heard a whistling in my ears, perhaps the sound of air rushing past the torn edges of my soul as it fell, disappearing, into fathomless blackness.

"Momma I'll…I can do better…" I had trouble forming the words. I hadn't expected to be onstage, pleading for my life. I felt like one of those blinking, freshly guillotined heads that didn't quite realize it was dead yet.

"Honey, this isn't the first bunch of bad grades you've had. We told you last time if you didn't keep up we would have to do something. You're gonna ruin yourself and not graduate, and we can't have that."

I started to cry. Crystalline. Travis. Music. Dancing. A door was closing, with me on the outside, and I sensed that in some way I would never be allowed back inside. I shouldn't have been allowed in anyway, and now it was discovered. I was being cast out of heaven, never to return. "Momma please…I'll do anything…" Hysterical.

"Your Daddy and I have already talked about this, Scotty. You can't keep on at that school. It's not good for you."

"Can I call Daddy at work and ask him? I'll buckle down next six weeks…I promise…"

"That's what you said before, honey. No. And those kids there have been nothin but trouble for you, anyway. Dancin. Those books you read, all that Dungeons and Dragons trash. That's nothin but the Devil leading you away from God—I know you don't want to hear that, but it is. This is what's best, we have already talked about it."

"Momma, if I don't have my friends, I won't be able to do anything, I need them. I never had any good friends before, I never did, not at church or school or anywhere…"

Mom wanted to say something. She sighed and went ahead. "Scotty, that Crystalline is a witch, I know it and you know it. That other girl has a boy's name and those kids are every one into diabolism and Satanism and who knows what else. Maybe they're just playin at it for now, but the Devil starts some out on milk before the meat and that's where they're headed. Hume-Fogg is out. We're callin Stratford today."

Stratford High was an old school. Not as old as Hume-Fogg, but it had its traditions and trophies. They endured, 'cohered' as Tolkien said, imprisoned in their glass cases. The ridicule of children is an indignity reserved for the utterly powerless, and these symbols of past achievement got their full measure whenever anyone even deigned to take notice of them. It was the late Eighties and at Stratford there were no hippies. No folk music or subversive R. Crumb comic-book artists. No magic or dancing in deserted halls.

Smooth, natural hair was laziness, and girls and boys energetically shook their cans of mousse every morning to pile up frothy stacks in hives and tidal waves and mullets. I sat behind stupid, gray kids in dirty classrooms full of nobodies on the edge and wished I was dead almost every day of that last year and a half. I sat behind Darryl Simmons in Algebra and watched droplets of aromatic oil fall from one tight curl to the next in his dark hair. The teacher was talking about something, but I couldn't rouse myself to care. My grandmother had a lamp of a naked woman in a garden surrounded by a lattice of what looked like fishing line, and drops of oil traveled down these wires to simulate rain when it was turned on. I thought of that lamp as I watched his hair-oil gather and roll down a curl, growing until its weight dislodged the fluid and sent it onwards. Eventually they all reached the creeping stain on the back of his puffy vest-jacket.

Stratford was two stories, and had some classes in portables outside. They looked like mini-trailers and I wondered if the teachers who taught in them were lower on some list than the ones who taught inside. I shuffled from class to class clutching my notebook to my chest, looking down at the ground. One day someone shot off a bottle rocket in the parking lot, and when I glanced at the puff of smoke in the sky where it had exploded, I realized I had never seen the roof of the school before. I had never looked up. I made no friends and the ones at Hume-Fogg continued their campouts and jam sessions without me after a few awkward attempts to keep in touch. *I'll call you,* is what they always said. Less and less. Intentions faded into regrets, regrets to guilt, guilt to resentment until all was wiped away and attention focused on hopes of something new and fresh and clean. I watched them go, towards college and onward. I died and died and died, like a monster in a movie that always came back to be killed again in some new and horrible way. Those were black days. I barely survived them.

8

"Graduation"

When I was very young, Shelby Park was a nice place to go and feed the ducks. On certain summer days something about the temperature or the slant of light struck Mom just right, and she would surprise us by announcing a trip to the park. If we didn't have the tail end of a loaf of bread left over, she would send me into a market on the way with a dollar in hand to pick one out. Even though it was just going to the ducks, I carefully pressed on the tops with my open palm to find the softest, freshest one. Mom had taught me that trick, and I felt like we were getting one over on the devious stores trying to sell stale baked goods. After the ducks there was a giant fort with a spiral slide and iron shapes on swivels meant to represent cannons or machine guns at the turrets. Plenty of fun.

Once, after a bucket of frogs I had collected began to fester, Mom took us there to let them go. My cousin Karen and I had scraped handfuls of the tiny animals from the inside of a big culvert in her creek, and I just had to take some home. I can't imagine why Mom let me. I guess she knew I liked to look at little things like that under my microscope. They were so tiny, but fully formed...I have never seen frogs that small since. The size of chocolate chips, I said then. Probably more like Hershey's Kisses, but a lot jumpier. We got to the park in the late afternoon, hurrying to finish this joyless errand before Dad got home from work. It was still hot, and I remember Mom looking awkward in a nice dress and her hair done, brushing back a stray bit stuck in some perspiration on her forehead. She had the bucket in one hand and squinted across the park's manmade lake looking for somewhere marshy to dump them. The shore was uniformly clear and free of anything looking like a froggy environment. We knew it had to happen but we weren't helping her because we were sad to see the babies go. We just stood by the car and watched. Finally Mom just said, "Well..." to no one in particular and scooped up a handful of them. She hesitated a second, as if someone might be watching, and cast them into the water like seeds into a field. I was surprised at the large ripples each one made as it hit. Mom took another handful and gently flung them into the sunset's reflection on the water's surface. Again huge black ripples on the gold. The last ones were sticking to the inside of the bucket, and she went right to the edge to upend it and tap them out. It was then that we saw the ripples were caused by swarms of scaly, muscular fish sucking them in the instant they hit the water. Mom made a startled noise at the unexpected churning of the fish and dropped the whole bucket into the water. When she got back into the car she tried to laugh at herself, but none of us said much on the way home.

Now Shelby Park was beginning to run down. Our visits had trailed off as we got older and inexpert graffiti spread like mold on its sandy concrete structures. It was too far away from the city and too deep at the tail end of a declining neighborhood to attract the usual seekers of places for dirty deeds. Instead it just sort of faded, like a crazy relative left to rot in a nursing home. Other than the occasional visits of neighborhood ball teams in need of its diamonds, it waited. Empty. And exactly because of its obscurity, its emptiness, this was where I drove my old car to wait out the hours I was supposed to be in school but could not bear to go.

Some days when my face was broken out just a little too much for me to take, and I looked in despair at the way my fashionless clothes hung on my thin body, my heart just couldn't take another noticeless passage through my school day and I went to agonize alone in the park. Sometimes I ducked out between classes after a particular incident, and sometimes I just never went to class at all. Any little comment or insult could crush me on the weaker days. I received the occasional cuts blankly, or worse: with a smile, as if we were both in on the joke. In my Senior year at the joyless Stratford, this happened more frequently. I had been established as a passive recipient of scorn and used accordingly. Each morning I woke up and took a shower, selected my favorite comfortable jeans and blanket-like flannel shirt, and then would come the mirror. My dull, elongated face spattered with red spots. Thin lips. Big teeth. Shapeless brown hair. Nobody ever said to me, "You are UGLY." Certainly my parents thought I was a handsome enough boy. But nothing in the mirror was the way it should be. Sometimes looking at my face I felt everything inside my head drop away, displaced by a rising, boiling pressure, a hot anger without direction. Why couldn't I look good? Why couldn't I look right? Why didn't I see *beauty* when I looked there? Beauty was the word, the most important thing in the whole universe for a person to have, I thought, running over and over the benefits it conferred. The love, the desire like a drug that made people overlook your faults, or want to heal them. I never wished I was handsome. It was always beauty, although I didn't see long hair and painted lips when I thought of it. I couldn't see, couldn't allow myself to see what this beautiful ideal was. I just knew I didn't have it. On the worst days I could not imagine walking down the halls of school, everyone looking at me and thinking, 'Did you see *that?* What's wrong with that *freak?*' When I could endure it I walked the halls with a blank face, shouting in my head 'I KNOW! YES, YOU CAN STOP *THINKING* IT, I ALREADY KNOW!' But all I really knew was that I was so ugly. Unendurably ugly.

The hours in the park were long. Time passed divided carefully into each second, pausing an instant before ticking off into oblivion. I lay down. I tried to sleep. I played my mix tapes, biting back tears because I was not with *them* anymore. Right that second Crystalline was in class at Hume-Fogg. Travis. Joyce. Working their way towards college and real lives. In-jokes and poetry, bonfires and cartoons I showed them how to draw. The more I thought about it, the more the sweet music coalesced ghosts of people I would never really reconnect with again. Drowning fathoms of hopelessness poured in on top of me. *'But you're still alive, aren't you?'* I thought hatefully at myself. Thin bitter tears oozed out and onto the plastic seat where I had pressed my face. *'God wants you to stay right here and suffer.* Let me—entertain you—'I sang in a tiny, choked voice. Then I laughed, a wry, defeated sound that released gasping spasms of sobs and tears. High above the derelict fort with a spiral slide a train crossed the broad stretch of visible horizon. Hours later I awoke in a sticky patch of saliva, eyes crusted from dried tears. It was late, darkening, and the park had been a sinister watcher of my unconscious form. My face showed a pattern of lines from the seat when I looked into the rearview mirror. I looked away and swatted at my nose with a snuffle. I started the car and went home.

"So you're not going to graduate. Your school called today." I had never stopped loving my mother. Never stopped respecting her. The flat tone, the pulling back of gentleness to allow something akin to dislike still hurt. But I knew I deserved it.

As she talked I tried to imagine the snow. Lightly at first, soft and blue-white it began to fall inside my head. Hot juices surging through the veins in my brain slowed as the ice came like sleep across my inner landscape. I thought of the forests of Narnia, the books I had read, and their cold seemed like the most wonderful safety I could ever imagine. Through a magic wardrobe and out into somewhere else.

"What is *wrong* with you!? What were you thinking?" Her voice told me this had been building for a long while. Mothers always know things. Sometimes they are just afraid to ask. "Scotty...I don't know what to say...You're not going to *graduate?*"

I had just walked in. I was still unbalanced from waking up and I felt itches crawling across my face like electric mosquitoes. I wanted to swat, scratch, tear my stupid ugly face off and just bleed to death in front of her so that she would understand how much I hated myself. I *knew* I was stupid. I couldn't believe I had let myself get so far down and desperately wished for the calm of my little frozen world.

"Look at me! Do you even *care?*"

Silence. What could I say? I knew. I knew. Over and over I said in my head, "I *know,* I *know.*" I know I'm an idiot. My fingers spelled it in nervous, slurring signs at my side. I know. I know what you're thinking, Mom. I already know what everyone is thinking, but they don't understand that I can't control how things happen. I already know, you don't have to say it. *Stop saying it.*

"I know, Mom." I mumbled.

"You *don't* know. If you *knew* you would have told me you were having a problem in school and we would have helped you." She was mad because I hadn't let her in, but I didn't know how. My whole life had been covering things up from her. "*Well Mom,*" I thought, "*I didn't go to school because I'm too ugly to live, and I want to fuck every boy I see, and everyone that ever made me feel worth anything is out of my life now.*" How did I open up when I already knew it would make her hate me? It was crushing, to know at seventeen every single thing in the world except how to fix my life.

"You've taken this whole thing on yourself and won't ever ask anybody for help, and now look at you." I couldn't bear to look at me, that was the problem. I knew I would see a big stupid unbeautiful face, raw and red with nothing to offer but an embodiment of my misery. Mom kept standing there, right where she stopped me when I walked in the door. I moved past her and sat on the couch. Silence. Where was Crystalline right now? A bowling alley, a skating rink, a swimming pool? I silently recited forbidden pastimes like clicking abacus beads, always adding them up into resentment and a feeling of loss that left me hopeless. I could never get back the years of being different. What they had built in me was all I had to work with now, to cover over or augment however I might manage, but I would never move comfortably through the world as my peers did. Some things would always be a second language on my tongue, heavily accented, awkward. I bitterly remembered the answer I received the few times I tried to explain this feeling of being a freak to Mom and Dad. *Deuteronomy 14:2, For thou art an holy people unto the Lord thy God, and the Lord hath chosen thee to be a peculiar people unto himself, above all the nations that are upon the earth.*

"We are a peculiar people!" Mom would say with a bright dismissing laugh. Yeah.

In bed that night I felt the absence of light on my skin like a lifting of heavy atmosphere. Burning thread had been looped throughout every part of me and drawn in tight. Now alone, it broke and I watched from a distance as everything uncoiled against the sheets. Fingers fell into loose curves, stale breath rushed out as my chest collapsed, and my mouth opened to hang unbeautifully slack. "Fish-mouth..." Jerm whispered in my memory, but I did not care. The time after her confrontation had passed silently when Mom tired of speaking. The remainder of the day was spent sitting uncomfortable in the living room waiting for Dad to get home, waiting for it to be told. I wouldn't graduate. Intelligence was the only quality that I had ever been proud of, and that was completely discounted now. I waited to see how Dad's face would change as the words came. I imagined them piling in, sorted and stripped and ground up for fuel in the angry place behind his eyes. I had almost become lost watching this unfold, watching the fire build in minutes from nothing to shouting as Mom poured on the information like gasoline. I was told in anger that I couldn't stay there forever. I wasn't going to be a nobody. A good-for-nothing. When it was all done I was broken and came stiffly to my room, closed the door. I undressed in the dark and went to bed. I know you didn't mean it, Daddy. I'm sorry.

Hell is a very personal place to me. I dreamt of it often, in many different ways. Creative minds have explored themes of degradation and torture set in its mythos, but I still favored the versions I built for myself. Right from the source, stories lifted from translucent Bible pages and embellished with good intention by suburbanized country women. From this rich material I evolved a familiar vision of hell.

Over years the details became clearer. Dark honeycombed passages of razor obsidian and measureless caverns made of rock so red it was almost black. A great curtain snatched away to reveal, all in an instant, absolute helplessness on a cosmic scale. The realization that this was the first moment of my eternal, ineluctable punishment materializing deep in my gut as a sick dread. The moment of sitting alone in front of a roller coaster as high as the clouds, just as it begins to fall.

Sometimes when my brain swelled up and broke through its confining shell, I closed my eyes and drew my legs and arms in tight like a wounded spider. I crushed my face into the pillow and screamed inside harder than I could ever do out loud. All I heard then was the air moving across a limitless empty plane of glittering darkness. Hell could be mine, familiar, defused. Even a cage becomes home if it is the only open destination.

I imagined laying on the floor of a vaulted cavern whose ceiling receded upwards into Damoclean shadows. Sprawled in fine sand that glowed like numberless embers, illuminating my face from below in yellow and orange and crimson. Thick white worms "that dieth not" writhed and the grains, jewels, churned in a scintillating illusion of molten fire. The horror could become beautiful, the heat a welcome quickening after the dead world outside.

The barque was always unattended, and I left yellow burning footprints as I crossed heated air to its mooring. Curls of steam rose from the water's black surface. My hair stuck to my skin in thick spirals of black. All was quiet but the knocking of the pole against the boat in its gentle propulsion across miles of glass.

My skin was as white as the worms, as white as snow, and smooth in timeless grace. A gentle finger could trace the curves of its condensation-beaded surface and never find a sharp angle. My face was sheened with feverish beauty, lips swollen in the heat and I tasted salt of my own human essence in sweat and vapor. Across an ageless dark sea I skimmed, ever smaller and further from the world I knew. I slept. I dreamed.

9

Leaving Home

When it was finally time to leave home, my overriding feeling was guilt. My high-school career had sputtered out, all fire lost in the effort to simply get through. Despite spending several years in a school designed to prep its students for college, I had no understanding of the process, thanks to the discouragement of my family and a depressed lack of ambition on my part. "Don't worry about college. I make more than every guy I know with a degree, and besides we don't have the money to send you." Dad was actually right about the money part, on both counts. So at age eighteen I was given vague suggestions to look for a trade school or apprenticeship somewhere while I worked an unskilled job, and I turned this prospect over and over in my mind. I just couldn't imagine it. When a recruiter for the Navy discovered my nearly perfect score on the Armed Services Vocational Aptitude Battery, I was offered a good deal and I took it. I didn't see any other option.

I managed to escape, but Jerm was still at home and now would be alone. Ginger had been lost to me for many years, and that familiar pain was only highlighted, the abandonment of a grave. Jerm still needed me. I felt there would never be anyone else who would understood me as he once did. I had thought up the rules of our secret worlds, and he fell into them unquestioning. He was smarter than I, and funnier. I was ahead in age and so always had an edge, but I knew he would make an incredible rival if we had not loved each other so much. I knew if there was anyone in the world I could trust completely, it was him. All I could think of as I packed was the time when I had first been allowed to ride my bike to the library. He was still forbidden to take his out of the yard. That day Jerm pedaled with me to the edge, looking small. Hopeful. Then the understanding that I was leaving him behind twisted his face into a terribly raw and visible misery. As I heartlessly kept going past the grass and out onto the road, his bike fell away, he stumbled to drop it while his squinting eyes were fixed on me, and he ran after a little ways, crying. My name was drawn out in a long wail of dissolving syllables, *"Scah—aah—aah— ahtt—eee!,"* each punctuated with heavy footfalls that collapsed into a weeping crouch as I receded beyond his sight. If there was ever a moment I could go back to, I would go back there and pick up that little boy and take him with me. But you don't know these things when you are a child. And when you become an adult it is too late.

10

Boot Camp

I have always known that I could do whatever was necessary to survive. There seemed to be an unseen force dragging me, a relentless internal drive that kept me moving constantly forward through and beyond each draining, obstacle-ridden landscape. Not self-confidence so much as an inability to stop, no matter how tired or hopeless, even if I wanted to. I never felt empowered by this ability. I never felt particularly tough or strong, but as I traveled to Boot Camp there was no question in my mind that I would make it through.

The long bus ride from the airport was finally about to end, and I could see the Illinois landscape silhouetted by the coming day outside my window. I was too tired to care. My fears and wonderings about what this next part of my life held were exhausted. I could only lean my head against the hard black seat and float in a familiar sense of surrealism. What was I doing? I wasn't ashamed to be afraid. This emergence into the real world was just another uncomfortable passage to be endured, I told myself. You only have to get through it, let the days pass over you and do your part. Patience was a skill well developed from tolerating endless hours spent in church. Years of isolation.

We had completed our physicals in Nashville at the Military Entrance Processing Station, and stayed overnight in a nearby government-contracted motel. The next day I was pulled from sleep beneath the stiff blankets by a buzzing phone.

"Wakeup call."

We boarded another government shuttle and when we arrived at the airport the Navy escort divided us into groups. "Stick together and good luck." He appointed a skinny wisecracking guy named Kytle leader of my group. I analyzed them, distantly, hardly aware I was doing it anymore. Greenman was thick in a high-school football way and had a sense of humor and style rooted in years of general acceptance by other guys. The other two boys in the group were nonentities, the kind of people who existed to amplify Kytle and Greenman.

"Hey man, let's get some pizza." Man, man, man. I hated it when guys said that. It sounded so stupid. Kytle was talking to Greenman, similar gym bags hanging from their shoulders. I assumed I was to tag along. My blue plastic suitcase was the same one I had carried to Church Camp every year since I was nine. Its handle had broken off long ago, so I held it awkwardly under one arm and walked at the rear of our little group. I was eager to sit down somewhere before our flight so I could begin reading the book I had brought along. We stopped at one of the food counters and ordered huge greasy slices of overpriced pizza, pulling extra chairs up to the tiny café table in the dining area to sit and eat. In that short time our group dynamic was defined and I tried to withdraw into my own comfortable silence.

"So, you bring a picture of your girlfriend?" Greenman patted the bulge of a wallet in his hip pocket. "I got mine."

"Shit yeah, man. That's the closest we get to pussy for eight weeks." Kytle laughed, tapping one of the non-entities on the shoulder with his fist. "Show Greenman yours, man. That's a fine lookin woman."

In the midst of a mental eye-roll I realized I might be expected to participate. I desperately hoped I would not be asked to produce a photo. I snapped open my suitcase just wide enough to retrieve my paperback and hunched forward on the hard airport café chair to see the pages better.

"What, you're gonna read? Damn, Lawson. You ain't got a girlfriend?" Non-entity boy met the gaze of the others in a wordless communication of my obvious geek status. Must it really be like this? I thought. Do I have to play these games? I put my book aside, embarrassed despite myself, and reflexively touched my glasses. I felt exposed when I wore them. They could be crushed into my face in the event of a fight. Lighthearted sex talk was so easy for them, a verbalization of their primal urges. I was unarmed in this arena. I had no similar urges to verbalize. In one of its few occasions of usefulness, my religious upbringing had allowed me sanctuary from this demoralizing ritual. When I explained the church I was raised in to people, they assumed I was uptight and straining to hold back my lust and masculine urges. They didn't really expect me to join in sexual conversations. Of course the feelings actually just weren't there. Not the ones they wanted me to have. Nothing about their aggression and easy masculinity came naturally to me, and I felt cheated by God. Why did I have to fight unarmed?

This was supposed to be my fresh start. This time I was going to change and blend in. But events unfolded the same as they always had, awkward and unnatural and despairing. I couldn't work up the nerve to attempt a face-saving emulation of their banter, so instead I smiled where called for and picked at my food. I would wish very soon that I had gorged on that pizza, because it was the last good meal I was to have for two long months.

I was eighteen, my birthday coming up in exactly two weeks on February twentieth. A week before my hair had been almost to my shoulders, a quiet bit of rebellion permitted because of my impending enlistment. "He's gonna cut all that off when he leaves for the Navy," my parents said to anyone who would listen, mortified. When I was little I used to cry during haircuts because I had to take off my shirt. Any kind of nudity was mortifying to me. They had never known what to make of my bookish shyness, and were glad I joined the Navy. Long hair was just a sign of the burgeoning rebel that the military would nip right in the bud. I kept the truth to myself: the Navy was my escape from their ideals, haircut or not. When I look back at my old bus pass and ID cards now I *do* think the long hair was hideous, though. On a boy.

In preparation for my trip I got a short six-dollar hair cut, feeling good about myself because I was planning ahead. I knew non-conformity would be singled out. I wore old blue jeans, a cotton shirt, and white running shoes. I liked the way the short hair felt against my fingers when I rubbed my head and I began to realize that my life was finally changing. I had been lacking something, indefinable but magnetic. Making this drastic commitment of joining the Navy sent prickles of excitement through my paralyzing hopelessness. I was taking action. Maybe this was what I needed. Maybe I could warm to this assigned role and be a man. If nothing else I was getting away to be by myself and do what I wanted.

When our bus rolled through the broad, tall chain-link gates crested with barbed-wire coils and past a sentry, my dread and excitement began to stir. It was early morning, a time when things have an edge of dreamlike significance to me, and when a man stepped into the bus and began speaking loudly, I sat up ready to listen. The smell of daybreak and wet pavement floated in behind him and bright street lamps illuminated blinking and sleep-swollen faces. A mist had begun to fall from the clouding sky, and companies of serious men our age marched up and down the blacktop. They radiated masculine superiority and their glances said, "I know what you're in for and I've already done it." I would see this attitude in the smirks and faces of upperclassmen in every training school, exercise, and new job I undertook in the Navy. It was universal.

We were instructed to line up on one side of the central square of asphalt they referred to as the 'grinder,' surrounded by utilitarian three-story structures on all sides. I climbed out and stood among the guys, hands tucked under my arms for warmth. Everyone was quiet and serious, street clothes rumpled, a few preemptive military cuts showing pale scalp contrasted with the other boys' heads of sleep-mussed hair.

We were soon grouped together and loosely marched to our first building. Everything was gray: sky, buildings, faces. The chilly, moist air was actually invigorating to me, inspiring an optimism I was careful not to reveal surrounded by the stoic boys. Once inside we were told to line up and wait. I stood uncomfortably in my now two-day-old clothes, struggling with fear at what I'd gotten myself into. I noticed how handsome some of the boys were, short haircuts making their features appear more defined and heroic. Not being discovered was a top priority, but thankfully fear made it easy to put away sexual thoughts. After a short wait we were admitted into a large lead-painted brick-o-block room lined with rows of wooden laboratory tables covered in scarred black Formica. The entire wall to the right was a serving counter in front of bins containing underwear and clothing. No one dared speak except the hard-looking men in charge. Their voices sounded wet and broken from shouting as they instructed us to empty our travel bags and pockets on the table in front of us. Apparently the various recruiting stations across the country had yet to entirely synchronize in advising us what to bring to Boot Camp, and this combined with the usual human penchant to try to get away with anything possible made it necessary that they go through our belongings and standardize everyone. I produced various hygiene supplies, including a razor, some soap, a toothbrush and paste. I also brought out the baggie half full of Hershey's Kisses my grandmother had pressed into my hand as she kissed me goodbye. I hadn't eaten them all, there being so much food available in the airports. I guess I had naively thought that I could save them in Boot Camp. A uniformed man was making rounds of the tables while shouting instructions, admonishing us to keep quiet and not try to hide anything. Whatever was taken from us would be returned after basic training. He had three red chevrons on his left sleeve that looked like wide V's, and a tiny pair of white crossed anchors with an eagle above them. Hardly looking at me, he took the bag of chocolate as he passed. "No food." he said, and moved on. I felt so stupid. I could have eaten all of them right then.

After our belongings had been sorted through to their satisfaction, we were marched single file into another drably functional room cut across by rows of black tables. Each of us received a cardboard box and a magic marker. We piled the things we wouldn't need or couldn't keep into them, taped them shut, addressed them, and they were taken away to be mailed back to our families. For me, that was a coat, change of clothes, and some writing paper. My suitcase had to be boxed separately, an added step that made me feel foolish. Everything was so quiet during all of this, just the harsh bark of the Navy people giving rehearsed instructions and the rustle of clothing being stuffed into paper boxes. I hardly looked at anyone, and when I did peek I saw that most guys were focused on their bundles, learning to give up their clothes and identities. Months later I flew back home for a week of leave a stronger person and found this box waiting for me. When I opened it the smell of that first day rose up like the faded scent from a pressed flower. It seemed like a present sent from a child and I wondered how I had ever made it here from there.

We returned to the first room and were issued some items of clothing and supplies. We received a ridiculous boxed jock strap, which I hid away under the other things in my hands, a bundle of underwear (I was given size 34, I wore 28), and packets of t-shirts. They gave us chit-booklets—the money would come out of our first paycheck—and we had the option of buying plain blue Nike running shoes. I said I was already wearing Nike running shoes, and was told I didn't have to buy a pair. Fool! I turned out to be the only person in my company with white shoes.

The day progressed quickly, clouds opening to reveal a diffuse sunlight pierced by sudden gusts of wind. From one duplicate structure to the next we were split and divided, assigned company commanders and shown our barracks. After some paperwork and bunk assignments we went to the infamous boot-camp barbershop to have our heads shaved.

Aside from one humiliating attempt at 80's styling with some mousse, I had never troubled with my hair. If my parents saw it getting too long Mom sat me down on the floor and cut it. I was shy about my body even with my Mom. I kept my shirt on despite the prickles from bits of hair that fell down my collar, running to shower after she was done. Once I had my own job I drove my junk car to Supercuts whenever I felt the need, purchasing a side-parted style some kids unkindly likened to that of our local TV weatherman in Nashville. Now as I waited for my turn in one of the barber chairs I found I was not dreading the buzzing clippers. I was kind of excited to see what I would look like with no hair, if I would look handsome and tough like a man. Gay rumors had been whispered about me since grade school because I was gentle and quiet. I had never had the courage to do anything so manly as shaving my head. Now the choice was made for me, and I was glad.

Some of the guys had already found the first stages of friendship in the motel and on the bus, and were now sharing subdued smiles and glances as each buddy had his turn in the chair. Wide bald stripes were left in the wake of the clippers, back to front, then up the sides. After some edge work around the ears the recruit was clapped on the back and hopped up to make room for the next guy. When it was my turn I looked around to see if anyone was watching, if there was anyone to commiserate the nervousness and newness of the situation, but there was not.

The barbers were old men. From their tattoos and manner of speech I assumed they were retired Navy themselves, and as they cut they talked back and forth about lawn mowers, trucks and medical problems. My skull was vibrating from the clippers and as the last of my hair fell away I hoped passionately that I would never become like them: rough, leathery geezers whose lives centered on lawn care and bad health reaped from excessive living.

A rough slap on the back of my neck shattered my thoughts. Looking in the mirror at the results of my disinterested barber's work simply showed a balder version of me. So that's what my skull looks like…"Move along. *NEXT!*"

Late that night the men of newly formed Company 080 fell exhausted into their bunks, and I remember the remarkable scent of eighty-two newly shaved heads pressing the air from pillows redolent with industrial laundry detergent. The smell of scalps was so strangely powerful and recognizable. It was the same scent I remembered on my fingers whenever I scratched my head deep beneath the hair I used to have. Feeling every pillow crease on my sensitive newly exposed skull, I fell asleep in a top bunk, one of forty-one in double rows down our long rectangular room.

Boot Camp passed quickly for me. Each moment was filled with intensity, my actions vital. Phenomenally high scores on the military entrance exam prompted my CC's to make me company yeoman, an administrative role held in addition to my other responsibilities. I carried a canvas over-the-shoulder bag stenciled with our company number, 080, and filled with sick-call chits, the barracks check out sheet and writing supplies. I still had to participate in all our physical activities, but being yeoman allowed me some time alone in the tiny office of our company preparing the routine paperwork of the unit, letting me recover briefly from the cumulative stresses of training.

I often had to deliver papers to various offices in the enormous bureaucracy of the camp. This gave me a unique freedom to move independently around the base during times when the other recruits were struggling to stay awake in droning classroom lessons packed between exercise. To improve our constitution, constant "double-time" was in effect, meaning we could not walk when outside and had to run everywhere we went. With my Dixie-cup hat securely molded to the contours of my cranium and denim bell-bottom dungarees flapping I ran in the vast silence of the desolate wintertime compound. My footfalls echoed against the boxlike structures, streets empty and all people inside working in steam-heated concrete rooms. Cold always made me feel clean, the drop in temperature calming my overactive mind and bringing me peace. Icy air found its way inside my blue cotton shirt and through the scratchy wool sweater worn underneath, making me feel smooth and light and tingly. A heavy silver emblem pinned to my collar showed my temporary rank as a yeoman and it bounced against my shoulder with each jogging step. I loved these times alone with the immeasurable gray sky. When I looked up, squinting into the snow, I was hypnotized by the swirling flakes and could imagine falling up into the great ocean of atmosphere. I knew I was not meant to go to heaven, but when I looked into the cold silver clouds I felt I at least understood what it would be like to walk there.

Despite my intentions of slipping through Boot Camp unnoticed, a strange thing happened. There among boys who would never have given me a second look in real life, athletes and paragons of easy, traditional masculinity, I became popular. The passive silence I had meant to hide behind soon crumbled against my deeper need to connect and I began cracking jokes and insults with the guys in the dark before sleep.

I put all my effort into doing my best. It had taken my entire spiritual reserve to commit to joining the Navy despite being a wildly improbable candidate, and I was determined it wouldn't be wasted. I was going to be a man. I never committed the sin of falling out of runs or dropping from exhaustion first when being 'mashed,' punishment by exercise. A huge portion of our time was spent in this kind of 'physical therapy,' known as 'PT' in military abbreviation-speak. You didn't stop until someone vomited or the CC grew bored of counting. To my great surprise, my company mates were fascinated by the fact that I had never seen a movie, never tasted alcohol, and treated me like a foreign visitor from a third world country. They were eager to initiate me into their modern ways. In spite of myself, I was having fun.

One evening after classes and our daily exercise, I was sorting sick-call slips and making notation onto each recruits Hard Card, a sort of 'permanent record' of our testing and behavior in training. Our Company Commander, Chief Adams, was telling someone on the phone that he had found an accordion at a yard sale. It was amusing to think of my strict CC scouring yard sales for musical instruments.

"I can play the accordion." I blurted, instantly regretting attracting Chief Adams' attention.

He looked at me for a second before speaking. Although the other recruits regarded me as disadvantaged and delighted in my naïve observations, Chief Adams was less enchanted with my lack of common experience. "I'm sure you can, rick." The CC's called all of us "rick," short for "recruit." He finished his phone call and looked at his desk for a moment, thinking. I gave an embarrassed close-mouthed smile and resumed typing.

Chief Adams stood up, hands splayed on his desk. "You know what, Lawson? I'm gonna bring that accordion in, and you better be able to play it or I'm gonna mash the whole fucking company until I get tired." My stomach clenched and I immediately regretted breaking my vow of silence.

True to his word, Chief Adams brought in a serviceable-looking accordion the next morning. It was an excellent specimen: bright red bake-lite casing swirled with glitter. For an instant I wondered why our manly Chief had been yard-saling anyway, and even more mysterious to me, why had he purchased *this*? It sat in our little office on his desk, gaudy and out of place, waiting for the evening when we had down time before lights-out.

When the day was done we settled into the barracks to sort laundry and to iron. I wondered nervously what would happen with the accordion. Just when I decided Chief Adams had forgotten, the recruit on watch shouted "ATTENTION ON DECK!" heralding the arrival of our company commander. We had barely scrambled up to attention before he strolled in and said "At ease."

"Listen up. As a special treat for you, *Lawson* here is going to play us a song on this accordion. You guys up for that?"

Silence.

"Now I know I'm not talking to my fucking self, here. Are you guys ready to hear Lawson play us a song?!"

"Yes SIR!" Everyone shouted in practiced unison.

"Go get the damn thing, rick. Go on." I hurried past Chief Adams and into the office, lifted the heavy instrument and slipped my arms into the shoulder straps. It wheezed loudly as I emerged, eliciting a few snickers from the boys. Whatever bonds we had developed, I was still somewhat of an enigma to them and this was yet another strange facet of a strange person.

"Um, it's been awhile since I've played so I don't know how good this will be…" I had always been aware of the accordion's high built-in nerd factor and felt ridiculed by this command performance.

"I don't want to hear a fucking sound in this room while he's playing, and I personally think Lawson is bullshitting me, so if he can't get a song out of this thing I'm gonna make sure you're sorry he lied to me."

Perhaps one more cuss word, and then your vocabulary would be complete, I thought. I knew Chief Adams didn't hate me, but he had never seemed to respect me either, favoring the rougher guys over my bag-toting yeomanry. Oh well, I could do this. The guys looked at me expectantly; anyone who had never seen a movie *must* be able to play the accordion. I felt carefully for the "C" chord button with my left fingers, locating the raised diamond shape on its surface. I launched into my least shaky accordion tune, "Behold the Lord."

The giant sound immediately filled the room and I tapped my foot in time with the jaunty yet sad Jewish song I had learned a lifetime ago playing music with Crystalline. The guys looked shocked by the loudness and layers of sound pumped from the reeds ever-so-slightly out of tune with each other as they always are in old accordions. On the rousing beer-hall style chorus of this religious song my fingers danced over the buttons down the spine of the instrument to the classic finish, a hard squeeze bringing out the last chord with sharp finality. Everyone cheered and hooted like I had scored a touchdown, talking to each other in a rush of amused surprise. Grinning through my stage fright, I had cemented my position as fabulous freak with the guys and even Chief Adams smiled, disarmed by the spectacle of a skinny bald boy proudly displaying this geekiest of skills.

"Well, fuckin A, Lawson. You did good. That was outstanding." Chief Adams directed me to replace the instrument on his desk and he put on his hat and coat. Ready to leave us for the night, he said as he exited: "Out-fucking-standing."

Because most every pool in existence was mixed-sex, I had never learned to swim. Public pools were hotbeds of lust and immorality, and no one I knew had their own at home where such things could be regulated. The day before our swim test I confided this to Raynor, a tall blonde farm boy with a crooked smile whom I talked to a lot before lights-out. We were both from the country. The Chiefs had gone home for the night, and I was in the little office at the end of our floor annotating hard cards. Raynor was only wearing his stenciled white underwear, a kind of public display many of the guys had adopted one by one with a bit of defiant nervousness at first but which was now the norm. Most all of us had been briefly unclothed in front of other men in school locker rooms, but an extended run of socializing in nothing but tiny briefs was a bit of a new thing for many. I remained modestly covered in green shorts and a shirt.

"You joined the Navy and you can't swim? What the fuck's wrong with you, Lawson?"

"Thanks for the compassion. I don't know, I guess I thought I'd get around to learnin before I came here, but I never did." His body was lean and natural looking, shaped by high-school sports and hard work. Sitting across from him, it was all I could do not to look at the bleached whiteness of his crotch. Being alone with him like this, mostly naked, made my skin tingle. My fingers felt almost numb and I stopped writing. I could smell his skin.

"We'll see tomorrow, I guess. Don't drown on us, man."

"I'm not the one who fell out on a three mile run. I got my end of things, you worry about yourself, Rick."

He stood up and shifted from one bare foot to the other. I couldn't look at him and studied my paper covered in numbers. Something felt different. The air seemed thinner and hard to breathe. He stepped forward and I felt his hand on the back of my head, pulling me forward.

"Fuck you, Lawson. Suck my dick." He said it playfully, and I played it like a game although I knew this was not like the taunts the boys made in groups. They never touched each other. I slipped my head away to the side and out of his hand. He moved to stand more directly in front of me and caught it again. He pulled me forward and I was inches from the soft bulge in cotton. His name, Raynor, seemed enormous spelled across the front. I pulled away again. Terror coursed through me, burning my insides. My ears were buzzing and the concrete walls seemed to recede. I looked at his face. There was no smile. I pulled back again and pushed his stomach lightly away. The touch, that warm skin moist with the slightest misting of sweat. That memory would carry me through some private moments the rest of training.

Raynor laughed and gave me a little slap on the side of my head as he turned to walk out. "Ok dude. See you in the mornin." I watched the pneumatic door hiss closed, obscuring his perfect ass and broad shoulders walking away from me down rows and rows of iron bunk beds. I lay my head on the desk and could do nothing but breathe with my eyes closed until I was sure every one of them had fallen asleep.

The pool was Olympic-sized, and as my experience with swimming in general was extremely limited, this was the hugest indoor body of water I had ever seen. It was housed in what looked like an airplane hangar, unfinished walls with visible struts and supports shrunk into tinker-toy proportion on the distant ceiling. Our entire company had to strip naked and pass through what was perhaps the most humiliating moment in Boot Camp, a close first against the duck-walk during our physical. All eighty-two of us had to walk through a passageway fitted with showerheads along the walls and a knee-high pipe running down the middle of the floor that squirted water up between our legs. Naked. There was little conversation during this experience. Once past this we put on loose fitting white swim trunks and were shouted into a long line of ghastly pale bodies only broken in four places by darker-skinned boys. I noted with horror that the line led up a ladder to a div-ing board at least twelve feet above the water.

"I thought we were just going to get in and swim…" I mumbled to Raynor, standing next to me.

"Shut up, you're gonna get us in trouble."

The line moved fairly rapidly, each recruit pausing at the top for the shirtless NCO standing there to hit him on the shoulder and shout, "GO!" Some boys paused too long, unnerved by the height, and were yelled at until they jumped. Several had admitted up front that they couldn't swim and they were taken off to the side and dumped into the shallow end, where several NCOs leaned down from the edge of the pool and screamed at them to "Kick! Kick! Come on, you piece of shit, kick your fuckin feet and swim!"

"You better go get in the kiddie pool with them, Lawson," Raynor whispered, not looking back at me.

"Shut up, you're gonna get us in trouble." The line diminished, and I moved closer and closer, chilled and barefoot on the tile. The smell of chlorine was overpowering, and the echo-distorted sounds of scream-ing and splashing. Light reflected up off the water made everyone appear slightly blue and paler than I would have thought possible. I reached the ladder and watched Raynor climb up over me. I hesitated and a voice exploded from somewhere behind me, "Get up that ladder, Rick! Move Move Move!" Our Company Commanders were pretty relaxed so this hard-core attitude was doubly intimidating. I pushed up the ladder, Raynor's feet in my face. We continued up, one by one, and I felt a bit of vertigo as the floor got farther away. It seemed harder, the tile, the more distant it became, and the rail seemed to shrink in my hand until it was a small cold thread of metal I clung to desperately, slippery from so many hands. At the top I was terrified to let go, climb up and stand without support on the minuscule stage. The man taking up half of my space there grabbed my hand, at which point I almost panicked and let go entirely. He pulled and I crawled up. I was on my knees. He leaned to my ear and I could not look up from the fiberglass surface and meet his eyes.

"You got cum in your ears, Rick?" He was shouting, hoarse from doing it all morning. "I said stand up. Stand up, boy. Stand up!"

I stood up, a robot. My perception of the floor fell away and I was balanced on the head of a pin over a bottomless chasm.

"Take a hold of that rail. Go on." I think he figured out how terrified I was then. I have always been told my face cannot hide anything, even when I try my hardest. He must have seen it there. "Son, you do this right now or you go through the rest of this two months a broke-dick dog in these men's eyes. I'm not gonna sit here and talk you through it. Suck it up and go. Right this second. Now!"

I took hold of the rail and walked to the end of the diving board. I will never forget the sensation of so much empty space spreading out before me, the translucent blue water so far below filled with splashing boys in white trunks and the endlessly cantilevered ceiling far above. "But I can't swim..." I thought, and took a deep breath. I was leaping to my death. It was exactly the same feeling. I stepped off.

There was a moment of weightlessness, my eyes closed, and everything inside me expanded like a supernova exploding in the blackness of space. 'I'm going to...'

And I hit the water. '...Die.' It smacked the soles of my feet and then opened up to take me, drowning the chaotic sounds and echoes in a world of muted quiet. I opened my eyes and kicked, clawed at the water with open fingers before remembering to cup my hands. I struggled up to the surface and a man was shouting, "This way, over here..." I swam towards him, to the side of the pool and climbed out, joining the other boys who were done. Nobody knew. I had faked it. Nobody but Raynor knew that I was a fraud and I walked among them back to the showers glad to pass unnoticed.

In April the graduation ceremony Mom and Dad had been waiting for finally came to pass, more than a year late. It wasn't high school, but anything was better than nothing. I earned meritorious advancement to the second pay grade, E-2, as the top academic of my company and spent the night before sewing a little two-stripe emblem onto my dress blues. Dad borrowed a home-made camper of plywood and two-by-fours from someone, secured it into the bed of his blue truck, and the whole family drove up to watch me march past and receive my certificate. Mom and Dad hugged me so much, and we all cried a little. I had finally done it. We were all so proud, me of my accomplishment and they of their son and brother. Relief, a release of fear and self loathing, is what I remember most from that day. It was worth it.

11

Desert Storm

When I stepped off the plane it was raining. A light mist, really, but coherent enough to call rain, and I laughed aloud. Here was the desert, I thought. I was stiff from numberless hours in the transport aircraft, sitting on cargo nets with hundreds of others, all of us wearing pale desert camouflage and black boots. There had been a shortage of the suede camel-colored ones, and only a few people with rank or connections had them. Likewise the soft desert hats were scarce, and I only managed to grab one after the whole war was over, just before we got on the plane back home. So there I was, bareheaded and black-booted, gas mask clipped to my belt and a little pack of medical supplies slung over one shoulder. My sea bag was on my back and in its center, padded by all my uniforms, was the hard-shell case containing my old fiddle.

We staged on planks of plywood over pallets on the sand beside the runway, separating into our little companies in preparation for loading up and driving to various duty stations. Overall I knew remarkably little about this war or much of anything that was going on. People were loading and unloading crates and pallets of supplies, organizing groups of people with subdued commands in the new dawn's sleepy light. I didn't know exactly what any of the things were for. I didn't know what kind of plane we had just stepped off of or even really why we were here. Something about Saddam Hussein. He was forcing his will on Iraq or something, which threatened U.S. oil interests. I didn't know. Everyone was talking about it every day with their own little opinions, but I just wanted to get through my classes, read my books and try not to think about sex with men too much. The officers had the knowing, superior looks of low-level insiders, and the NCOs had their gritty, in-the-trenches ideas that were oh-so-much more in touch with reality. It all bored me. I looked out across the sand on the other side from the airport and thought about Aladdin and Indiana Jones.

I was assigned to Charlie Company, 1st Medical Battalion, 1st Field Service Support group. This resulted in a long ride through residential-looking neighborhoods of Al-Jubail to a barricaded hospital that we were to rehabilitate from its current abandoned state into a functioning medical facility. I wondered briefly if it had been abandoned all along or just conveniently when the war started. But ultimately it was nothing to me. It was so easy to coast in the military...As long as I completed my assigned tasks and stayed quiet, everything else was taken care of. Food. Housing. My life in general. The Navy was my dad and I was safely asleep in his arms.

We were admitted past sentries into a courtyard delineated by huge blocks of concrete rubble and sandbags, a place which I would come to know well as the war progressed. We walked up a decorative looking sidewalk to the front door of the hospital and got into formation for our first briefing.

The air was crisp and had an entirely different smell than I was used to, expectably. It was similar to that of California, but very clean and surprisingly damp that morning. I supposed it was the dew burning off and the last of that unusual rain. Tropical looking plants and trees grew in the same places that hedges and oaks held residential court in my own neighborhood back home. There were no other cars on the streets and no people. The neighborhood was quiet. Watching. Some officer checked names off a list, assigning people to various duty sections and then excused us to go find beds among the unused hospital rooms inside. Finally released, I clopped in my boots past a stripped grand entry and down the echoing halls where normally patients recovered under the practiced care of nurses. Now bored sentries sat at the nurse's stations, reading or making log entries as repetitive as write-offs:

1100 Made rounds. No suspicious activity noted.
1200 Made rounds. No Suspicious activity noted.
1300 Made rounds. No Suspicious activity noted.

Everything seemed empty, staged for an event no one had bothered attending. A few televisions had been rigged up to play CNN in darkened hallways, on top of boxes or furniture dragged out of some unused room. I walked through their islands of radiated blue and static to the area set aside for enlisted men in the back of the hospital. I took a room where I saw a free bed and laid my sea bag on its uncovered mattress. A handsome Marine was asleep in the next bunk, his gear set up neatly on the rolling bedside table. They were here to protect us, and the hospital. The bed was an old fashioned kind, with crank handles that lowered and raised it into the various positions, Fowlers, Shock and Trendelenburg. I cranked mine flat and lay down for a moment. It felt surreally homey, to be on a mattress beneath fluorescent lights, and I had to remind myself I was on the other side of the world in a war. 'You might even die,' I thought. Finally.

Standing twelve-hour gun barrel duty was exquisitely dull. Outside each entrance was a metal barrel filled with sand, and before entering the hospital everyone had to aim their weapon into it and pull the trigger. They were supposed to keep the chamber empty of bullets anyway, and the cartridge in their belt, but just to make sure everyone had to perform this test and I was set there to ensure compliance. The USO had sent stacks and stacks of books and magazines in boxes, some of them quite bizarre, and I sat in various duty stations reading Sarum, some magazine about role-playing games done in full costume outdoors, and the collected short stories of H.G. Wells for most of the war.

"Hey y'all, check your weapon in the barrel."

Click!
"Check your weapon."
Click!
"Weaponscheck."
Click!

Eventually I just pointed at the barrel from behind a book. If there had ever been a *Blam!*, someone would have been in big trouble. Luckily this never happened, allowing me to avoid an embarrassing scream and fall from my chair.

When the anticipated casualties of war failed to materialize, we found ourselves looking for things to do. On television we heard about scores of enemies surrendering and being carted off to holding camps. The medical personnel assigned to these came back with generally positive accounts of the prisoners' treatment and seemed to have enjoyed the extra labor...real injuries to work on and everything. Frustrated officers began tentatively loaning us out for duties which walked the fine edge of what was allowed in the Geneva Convention for corpsmen. I was assigned a twelve-hour-on, twelve-off duty rotation standing perimeter watch with a Marine in one of the several sandbag bunkers around our hospital, glad to be issued a double-barrel shotgun in addition to the nine millimeter pistol clipped to my belt at all times. It was heavy and cold, and actually an insult since they only gave it to medical personnel. Anyone could do some damage with the spray of pellets from a shotgun. I didn't care, really. I couldn't imagine having to use it. I just didn't feel it in my gut that the occasion would ever come up, although I knew I could kill if it ever came down to him versus me. I wouldn't enjoy it, but I could.

After several days of sleeping twelve, working twelve, time began to blur into desert scenes of light and dark sand, split by the always-shocking squawk of some faraway mosque's prayer recording drifting down into the neighborhood from lonesome speakers high on a pole. At night our own speakers wailed, testing some warning system I imagined, and it was the loneliest sound I had ever heard. Slow and human, from low up to high and then back down again. I couldn't believe such a living sound could come from a simple siren.

My Marine, Jim, was a big, thick quarterback kind of boy, Midwestern and innocent with his killer's hands and prom-night eyes. We sat for hours on two chairs of exactly the type that we had ridden throughout our high school years, padded with Army blankets, and talked around intent scans of empty streets. It was easy to sneak glances at his body when he was watching the road, where it showed beneath his sweat stained bulletproof vest and BDUs.

"I'm studying theoretical mathematics in school right now. For computer programming." Jim didn't look the type. I was surprised.

"Explain it to me."

"What part? Shit, there's too much to tell."

"Just start at the beginning. All we got's time."

Sometimes I darted out to collect little flowers and plants to press in whatever book I was reading and then mail home to Mom.

"Dude, get back in here. You're gonna get snipered!"

"I need somethin to remember this by," I said, breathing heavy in the heat. We weren't supposed to take anything back, it might bring some horrible pest back to the U.S., but I had seen plenty of officers showing off bottles of sand and other memorabilia to each other when they thought no one was looking. They're not any better than me, I thought, as I secreted away my little keepsakes.

One day back inside the hospital we were issued blister packs of twenty-one pills and instructed to take them, one a day, to protect against nerve gas. Jim and I had just finished our watch and he was already down to the marine green version of tightie-whitie underwear and thick socks, ready for bed. I had put on a more modest soft green undershirt and shorts. Our beds were next to each other and I felt safe with him beside me at night. Protecting me.

"Pyridostigmine Bromide..." Jim read with effort. The tiny print was hard to see on silver foil.

"I think that's just another way to spell 'Agent Orange.' I'm not takin any of that."

"You could spell anything with all those letters. What about Agent Orange? What's that?"

"Good lord, how old are you, Jim? It's that stuff they used to kill plants in Viet Nam, and it turns out later that all the guys who got exposed to it have cancer and deformed babies and stuff."

"Shit. But we're supposed to take it."

I almost said, *If they told you to jump off a cliff, would you do that?* But that was what the Marines were all about. Of course he would. He probably had jumped off a few cliffs already. "Some fat officer in a custom made triple-extra-large uniform sitting in front of an air conditioner in Washington probably said, 'We spent ten million last year on this crap, I'll be darned if we don't use it.'" The pills were tiny. They weren't in my PDR or any of the other drug reference manuals we kept handy.

"I highly doubt he said 'darn' and 'crap,' Lawson. But anyway, that other shit was back in the sixties. Let's just take one and see what it does." He pushed a pill through the foil and it looked even tinier in his thick fingers. "Take it." He shoved it at my face.

"I'm not takin that pill…" *I* was the pill pusher here.

"Dude, your orders are to take this medicine and as your Marine I am going to ensure you fucking well do it." He smiled as he grabbed the back of my head, roughhousing, and pushed it between my lips. We were laughing, wrestling, and fell onto his bed. His hands on my face, his powerful arms subduing my reed-thin body, caused a shock to wash over me like a cool breeze on wet skin. A man was touching me. My mind reeled. The poison pill was in my mouth, along with his salty thumb and finger. Then he was off me.

"Now. I don't want any more insubordination out of you, damn squid." He took his own pill and we settled in to sleep.

"I spit it out…" I said quietly. I lay in bed facing towards his back and wished.

"No you didn't. I saw you swallow it." He was grumbling, half asleep. I liked being here alone with him. It felt so right. As I fell asleep I wished I was his girlfriend and we were making love and getting married after the war and everything else was just a horrible dream. I could still taste the pill and his skin. Outside the occasional distant sound of bombs came from somewhere beyond the horizon, and I slept until the next watch.

The war ended suddenly, when it had no more political purpose, and the entire experience was wadded up like a piece of paper and tossed into my past without a backward glance. I flew back to California first on a commercial airliner, and at each airport we went through on our way back to wherever we had come from, there were throngs of people cheering and applauding with signs and banners that said 'Thank You' in some way or other. I was tired and glad it was over. It was exciting, the cheering, and I felt like I had done something. I felt a little like a hero.

I was given a bit of leave before I had to report to my next duty station in Alaska, and I went back to Nashville, to Mom and Dad and Ginger and Jerm. When I stepped off the plane the air was so thick with vegetable smells I felt like I could have chewed it. Everyone came to the airport to meet me and cried and cried…They couldn't keep their hands off me and I loved it. I loved them and it felt great to be back home, finally bearing something we could all be proud of. I was a war hero, a combat veteran. There was a wall dedicated to me in the living room, with shadowboxed desert flowers and certificates and medals and ribbons all surrounding an eight by ten of my Boot Camp photo, the graduation I'd never had in the dark days when I was a rebel and a failure. They could finally be proud of me, and for a moment I could relax. But I knew it was only a matter of time before things would change. I could not deny myself for very much longer. Things were awakening inside me, ideas breaking out that would not be laid back to rest.

12

Adak

I saw my first dead body on Adak Island. A volcanic speck located 1300 miles of deadly-cold water away from Anchorage, Alaska, its primal landscape was carpeted in spongy tundra, crowded by the sleeping volcano of Mount Moffett on one side and a horizon of gray-blue Bering Sea on the other. Flying in from the mainland, fresh from the war and strung tight as a new fiddle string ready to sing, I wondered if Adak was a well-chosen destination. I always thought the water was the color of sweet, unconcerned death, that private moment past the point of no return. Supposedly in winter hypothermia killed within minutes, and I imagined all the brain's missioned sparks like stars slowing and sinking away into the blackness. Our tiny base was the only civilized section of an otherwise raw wilderness spotted by occasional ruins from the war with Japan and dumped military techno-waste.

Our groceries came in on planes and barges every few weeks and MTV was shipped a month behind to our basement TV station in blocks of videocassettes. "Happy Halloween!" VJ's proclaimed, as we secured imported Christmas decorations against the constant powerful winds. The Aleutian Chain of islands veered southward as it trailed off the United States, so our weather was not Arctic, but the hottest summer day was like a Nashville Autumn. Winter was deeply cold, our little isle absorbing the freeze like a lone penny at the bottom of a cold sea. Most of the year averaged out to a general ambience of compensated chill in the daytime, and our Navy-issue parkas kept the nights tolerable. The numbing snow and winds always returned to whisk away any complacency, angrily rolling dumpsters and swinging the eagle-lined phone wires to announce a reappearance from wanderings through our barren sister islands. Adak's sky was eternally spread with a blanket of gray clouds, and random gusts threatened to unbalance naive walkers. On this raw stone, sterilized by the flaying breath of the North, my soul opened like a long-clenched fist. My sleep was untroubled, scoured clean by the exaltation of my childhood companion, omnipotent here. The wind.

Not everyone found the island or its conditions so comforting. Depression led to alcoholism for some, and then on to all manner of bad decisions. In my first months a resident named Petty Officer Franks apparently had a liaison with a woman in Anchorage and contracted HIV. Or so island gossip went. Unable to face the consequences of this or tell his wife and child, he decided to drive his truck off the pier and into the void of our bottomless bay.

Sweeper's Cove dropped away to untold depths of thick, cold ocean full of unimaginable things. Members of the Polar-bear club dived off the pier in the summer, requiring our ambulance to wait by the dockside in case of hypothermia. They shivered past us with tales of jellies the size of Volkswagens and clouds of cold-water fish jetting around them with frightened, soulless eyes. I watched them diving singly and in pairs from the warm safety of my cab and imagined one plunging straight down into one of those enormous jellyfish, sticking right in the middle. Stung to death while slowly drowning in the gelatinous guts, feeling a lurch as the wounded creature headed away from a blurred view of the barnacled dock supports and toward open water. Very H.P. Lovecraft, I noted, resolving to recreate the image later in the form of a cartoon.

When someone realized Franks was missing, our Search and Rescue, or SAR, team was activated with little optimism. It was a small island. There was nowhere to go that you could not be found almost immediately, except for the wilderness. People without supplies and shelter did not last long there. A SAR helicopter scoured the island looking for him, and from above a glistening oil slick was noted off Pier 5. They surmised his missing truck must be down there, and I was called out of a warm bed in the E.R. duty lounge to once again wait by the freezing water for someone to emerge who should not have been there in the first place.

There were so many beautiful things on Adak. At any moment my attention could pluck an image or sensation to be savored privately amidst mundane activities. Starting the diesel ambulance was a process of several steps, and I felt like a child play-acting some game as I spoke into the chunky radio mike at the end of its twisty cord. The two other watchstanders, Banks and Lipetzkey, were quiet with sleep still evaporating from their hunched shoulders. Banks rode in the back with his head in his hands, so that below his silky black brush-cut I could see the creamy, flawless skin of his neck disappearing into a blue duty-shirt. He usually walked from room to room in the barracks at night in just his pristine bleached underwear and t-shirt, last name stenciled in faded black on each. Once, in excitement over some assignment, he had grabbed me and danced around his room like this for a brief moment, before realizing the gayness of it all and punching me in the shoulder. I hoarded these moments and images in my most private place. Crumbs.

It was an emergency call, so I flicked on the siren and strobing colored lights. Beyond the windshield swirling snowflakes caught and hung in frozen curtains of red and then blue crystal, backed by dark mountains on a distant treeless horizon. Each rapid flash of the lights captured a different three-dimensional pattern of suspended sparks like stars, and we rode without speaking wrapped in the thick sound of our trucks engine. Then in front of us was the steel-colored water stretching out to veiled, shifted constellations and snow-clouds. The nearest land to me right now is Russia, I thought. Various military people, the same who I saw picking over sales and carting babies in our abbreviated island stores, were now uniformed and moved in and out of the lights. Some dragged on invisible cigarettes, keeping the murderous ember at the tip alive with their inhalations. The SAR team divers had been busy, so I got out to chat in puffs of innocently smoky breath with the other emergency response workers. We were all waiting. This was where dread might have manifested, or fear, but such things were run down by constant overworked appearances and I found it easier to ignore them now. Earlier in the day I had sliced on my wrists again, but I still hadn't been able to go beyond the epidermis. I think I just liked the sting of it, and the sight of blood. Cold air made the band-aids on my wrists stiff. The rubbing of my long sleeves reminded me of their presence with each movement. Sometimes when I was alone in my room I put on Le Mystere Des Voix Bulgares and used scalpel blades stolen from the E.R. to see how deep I could cut. Never very. The precise blades left only the thinnest of stinging red lines. Now I sat on the edge of the ambulance and watched metal cable wind onto a winch bolted to Pier 5. Dull. Its other end disappeared into the mist playing on top of the water, presumably down to where divers had attached it to the truck. Cold wind came out of the darkness, and that slow grinding motor turned, drawing up from the depths. Minutes passed.

Then just before it broke the surface there was the sudden apparition of a pale leviathan rising up from below. I felt terror, as if it were a shark or whale about to explode from the water. Anything could be down there. The edge of the hood broke the surface, crazy at that angle, in that circumstance, and the feeling dispelled as quickly as it had manifested. It was replaced by the usual reigned-in empathy I felt at the sight of injured bodies. The stronger I felt their damage, the calmer I became as walls went up and connections were severed, so that in the worst situations I almost felt completely blank of real emotion and proffered honestly manufactured smiles and comfort as necessary tools along with bandages and Betadine. Up came the truck, hanging longways like a trophy fish. Everyone instinctively played their flash-lights onto the glass. Trapped water refracted the beams into an ethereal luminescence, revealing a dark form drifting inside. I could make out that the cab was filled with milky colored seawater, like a horrible aquarium, and as it rushed out from the edges of the doors, its currents caused the blue white body inside to turn and swirl ever so slightly. We would later see that his hands were clumsily bound together and his movement in the escaping fluid looked like a slow motion reenactment of what must have been his last moments, panicked and beating against the door.

His waxy form had tried to curl into a fetal position against the steering column and now rested against the windshield, in the sideways hanging truck above the icy bay on that tiny island a thousand miles from nowhere. The truck was arduously cantilevered into a better position over the dock and guided back down onto its sagging tires. The rubbery concessions to gravity made by the body inside mesmerized me with each change in orientation. That was a person in there, I thought. *Dead.* The sight of the body, now wasted, now unable to run the infinite functions of self preservation and upkeep, now vulnerable…I imagined my own hands and face unprotected against insects, bacteria, even the soulless fish. I knew my soul wouldn't be inside anymore to care, but the thought was revolting. I felt embarrassed for Franks as we pulled his form from the truck. There was no angelic transcendence visible to me there. Only a supreme indignity.

My friend Chris and I went hiking whenever we could. He was the skinniest guy I had ever seen. He had short thick curls the color of wheat and his thin skin was stretched taut over a delicately structured, elfin face. His eyes were dreamy and rarely met my own, not that I would have known since I avoided the discomfort of looking people in the eye as much as I could anyway. It seemed an unpleasantly revealing connection. I imagined him a lean spirit of nature, a sober and thoughtful Pan, hiking the tundra and spending his earnings on Gore-Tex and boots from catalogs. His barracks locker archived trays and boxes of sea-sponges, shells and dried plants, and when he spoke his words were arranged with the same thoughtful care. Failing weather cut short a day's venture into the wilderness, so I left him playing basketball at the Kuluk Rec Center and took the yellow bus back to our barracks. I had spent the day with him and Laurie, a Mormon girl who was a TV makeup artist before the Navy and looked like Snow White. In the area of the base our roads were paved, but beyond that small grid they were loud, crunchy gravel. We had just followed a narrow offshoot into the tundra and reached the top of a hill when the snow began to fall. Standing on the rim of a valley cut through by a ribbon of glassy water, I watched the flakes rush away from my outstretched hands and into the rapidly whitening gulf of air before us. From that height we saw it fill slowly with roiling snow, and the sight of so much raw space overtaken was like witnessing a solemn predator subdue its prey.

Chris and Laurie were Aviation Aerographer's Mates, one of the more obscure Navy Ratings that people usually fell into through a recruiter's quota-filling encouragement. Basically their job was to man the small but powerful weather forecasting and data collection station on the island. It provided information to Adak's pilots and important warnings of impending natural Armageddon to inhabitants. One of the duties Chris rotated was the launching of a small weather balloon into the pewter sky, and I liked to follow him out whenever I could. This evening he came to get me before making the short walk to his weather station. It took almost an hour for the balloon to fill, and we talked about life, the universe and everything while we waited.

"So Clinton's gonna let gays in the military." I didn't know why I decided to chance this topic today.

The balloon expanded. The sound of hissing gas echoed inside the aluminum shelter that kept the winds from snatching it away before it was ready. Chris was intent on setting up the instrument box that was to be attached and released.

"I think they're already here, don't you? I don't care. Doesn't hurt me, you know. Let's get this thing up in the air." He unfastened the balloon, secured it and secured the box to a long cord. Carrying the whole thing outside was awkward on the tricky, spongy tundra.

"Maybe they're here, but they're not free. I mean, I would guess."

"You're as free as you wanna be, man. Stand back..." He waited for me to move and then jumped back himself. The rubbery sphere leapt up into the air and we stood, watching it race up toward the layer of shifting clouds. It quickly became too small to see, but I imagined what it must be like to dip into the wet darkness and then out the other side. Silver sunlight and an ocean of softness below. So beautiful.

"I've got some spice tea, if you want some." Chris always had the simple comforts.

"Let's go." Far above us the box and balloon sent back messages of open space and platinum-tinged clouds and the cleanest cool air imaginable. I could hear it, somehow, and was reassured.

Two years passed quickly on my chilly paradise. I made friends, started a weekly coffee house and community theater group and generally came to understand myself free of the outside world's pressures. Near the end of my enlistment I was discovered and adopted by a tribe of lesbians, who took me camping when they weren't fixing airplanes and decoding top-secret submarine messages. We talked about love in the smoke of tundra campfires and I began to believe. I left the island with my head full of their stories of how free and normal it could be in the outside world, and was determined to discover it for myself. When I finally came home to stay with my parents and get back on my feet, they met a very happy and excited person.

13

Confrontation

"Scott, come on in here. We need to talk to you about somethin."
I had been asleep, something I was doing a lot of since returning home
from the Navy. It was dark outside, disorienting since I had laid down
for a nap around noon. My father's tone was serious-sad, one usually
reserved for talking to me about Jesus. I sensed ambush and struggled
to snap out of lingering confusion enough to defend myself.

In the living room I saw Mom sitting in her spot and the always
unwelcome figure of Brother Jerry, pacing like a nervous pinch hitter.
So they had brought in some champion to slay me in Christ and return
me to the fold. Anger bled through my torpor like the hot, wet stain
around a bullet hole.

Mom spoke first. "Scotty, we know that you're...ah, living in the
gay lifestyle." Her voice was flat and empty. I'm sure the love was
there, inside her, but none of it came out into the air. A lifetime of
training had rendered her eyes as impossible to meet as the full glare of
the sun. The edges of my vision disintegrated inward until only an
indirectly viewed model of the scene surrounded by blackness existed
in my brain, with all human figures torn out. I felt full of wet sand and
could only sit down on the couch. Brother Jerry continued to pace.

My anger remained, through static and darkness that threatened to
expand into unconsciousness. I took hold of it and pulled back up into
the light. I focused. I looked at them, first Dad, then Mom, then
Brother Jerry. My lungs released a sigh, a breath of years and years of
lies they had begged me to tell them, out and away and into nothingness.

"Good. Good. I'm glad you know." At this point, were my life a movie, the ass-kicking techno music would begin.

Dad jumped in. "You've got your brother talking about gay rights and gay parades on TV and I saw that…in your drawer yesterday." I remembered the wig in my top drawer. Oops.

Brother Jerry stopped across the living room and began to speak. He told the tale I had heard many times in our mostly working class church, of a man who had learned his spiritual lessons after a youth spent in sin and debauchery. I never got to have a youth spent in sin and debauchery. "And I used to know a gay fella, and son, I'll tell you…he took me to one a them *gay* clubs," and here he paused, perhaps dredging up some long repressed memory. "And I'll tell you, it was a lotta things goin on there with a lotta very, very sad people, and ev'ry one a them is bound for a lot more sufferin in their life and afterwards, boy, and they know it." I wanted to ask him why his own son had spent every night of our missionary trip in Germany looking through the bathroom keyhole at our other male bunkmate getting naked. My mind was racing with rebellious thoughts unleashed and I felt at that moment, with everything out on the table, more free than I ever had. Brother Jerry suddenly seemed like a sacrificial target representing everything in the church I hated so much, served up to me for destruction.

I stood up and a new tone of voice came to me, like the day I learned just how far to slide up my violin's neck to play in second position. An entire range there all along but never explored. "I don't know what roller-coaster ride into the underbelly of gay life he took you on, but not every gay person dresses up in leather straps and wigs and has sex in back alleys. They're all different, just like you. And what do you expect anyway, after you beat down every one of 'em till they don't have anybody, and nowhere to go, and nothin to do!"

I saw the recognition in his eyes, of my complete loss to the Devil, and with that his gesture at reasoning with me dissolved into sour, calculating silence. He looked towards my father for support, prompting Dad to speak.

"Boy, I know they's a lotta things in this world set out there to trip you up, and deceive you, and they're the ones that seem the most right sometimes, but that's just the Devil's way of leadin you against God."

"Daddy I ain't doin anything that feels wrong. What feels awful is what people do to *me*...the judgin and names and excludin me. Everybody knows I'm gay, Daddy. In school and at church. I'm not makin any of this up, or learnin it off of people. It's been in me from the start, and y'all have known it, too. I know you knew I wasn't right ever since I was little. Y'all knew it and you just hoped it wasn't what you thought it was. You hoped it would just go away, and it didn't, and now here we all are."

"The Bible is very clear. Whether you like it or not." Brother Jerry was getting angry.

"That Bible just sits there two thousand years old, and most of it doesn't make any sense unless you say it stands for somethin else anyway. Unicorns. Fig trees. Pillars of fire and smoke. Come *on*." I dismissed him and turned to Mom and Dad. "But you saw me grow up every day of my life right in front of your eyes. You know what I am, and it came natural."

Mom, long silent, broke in with her point of reason: "Scotty, livin your life this way is a *choice*. If you would try..." But I was laughing, a wretched sound dreadfully close to tears.

"Momma, you don't even know. You have no idea. See, everybody says that. It's a choice. It ain't no more a choice that you likin Daddy is. It's *in* me. The only thing I can choose is whether or not to lie about it." My hands trembled and sweat gathered beneath my shirt. I felt like every word slashed a thread tethering me to the safe world I had known. I was ready to go up into the sky, away from the hiding. I felt terribly alive.

Brother Jerry was ready for this to end. "I can see that we're not gonna accomplish anything here tonight. I'll be prayin for you, son. We all will."

Something had broken inside Dad, something important that I had missed while staring down Brother Jerry. He stood up, tears brimming in his weary, work-worn eyes. "It ain't your choice to be this way, son. I know it. But I don't want you to suffer…there has to be a way. You can pray with me about it." He was pleading. My own father. Yet another jagged piece broke from my heart and fell into the blackness. I loved him so much right then, because I finally understood that he truly believed what he was saying. In his mind he was watching his firstborn fall backwards into the pit of a real hell, and he was begging me to come away with him instead. In some way almost every day for as long as I could remember I had wished for death, and finally seeing my father admit he cared was all I really needed. I crossed the few feet of an impassable gulf and hugged him. I fit inside his arms so perfectly. In his ear, through hot slow tears I whispered, "I cain't, Daddy. I'm sorry. I cain't."

After that day I rarely spoke to or saw my parents again, or any of my family really. A few phone calls or uncomfortable visits a year, maybe. Old chapters closed with quiet finality and new ones went unwritten. I missed them, more the people I wished they had been than the real ones a fifteen minute drive away. I'm sure a similar could-have-been son received their longing thoughts and similarly made no appearances to quiet the pain. It's funny how things turn out. I'm sorry, and I love you, Mom and Dad.

14

Showgirl

I almost immediately enrolled in Middle Tennessee State University to major in Biology. My military medical training had come easily to me, and I liked the hospital's environment of educated and intellectual people. Medical school seemed like a good goal to work towards, one that no one could criticize. I lived between couches in Nashville and my dorm on the Murfreesboro campus thirty minutes away with some Navy money I had saved up, carried by my trusty red Chevy truck and a feeling of liberation. I was finally an adult and could do anything I wanted. So there! My first priority was to discover more about the gay community in Nashville and jump in with both feet. It was only a matter of time before I found the biggest gay club in the city, a few streets off Broadway. It was called the Link.

After several agonized drive-bys followed by defeated trips home to bed, I managed to work up the courage to go inside. I spent that first night sitting at a table alone in the lounge, sipping a three dollar Sprite and trying to stop my legs from trembling. My next visits led me to the enormous dance floor where gorgeous masses danced and made out in the wild music, and one night I ventured past this bacchanalia, towards two glass doors through which I could see another huge room. It was filled to capacity with people standing and seated at café tables, and beyond them was some bright focus of colored lights and music. I pushed in and through the crowd I saw a recessed, elevated stage on which three figures of amazing beauty danced in unison to a bounding theatrical show-stopper. It ended with all of them striking poses in silhouette to its final flourish. I had never seen such stunning creatures outside of a movie screen.

People who have not seen drag in the South probably have no idea what I'm talking about. Most everywhere has some kind of female-impersonator show, but Nashville is an entertainment town, land of big hair, heavy makeup and cut-throat pageantry. We take it quite seriously, and looking as real as possible was priority one. I could not take my eyes away from the show, and as weekends passed I came so often that eventually I was watching from up in the lighting booth, talking to the employees by name and getting in free. In those first few months I picked up how to run the lights and sound and eventually started filling in as a technician. It was the easiest way I could study the girls and slip into their community, goals which became strangely urgent the more I watched them. For the first time I began to feel like I had found the friends I had been looking for since high school.

Most people's only visual encounters with drag queens are on talk shows, which almost universally select the most hideous and primitive girls they can find, or in movies, where they give them the same distanced psuedo-glamorization they use on prostitutes. In my later travels I had expected to find girls of unsurpassed beauty in bigger cities North and West, and while I certainly did encounter a few goddesses, by and large I was shocked by how primitive the general understanding of female illusion was. For example, in the South girls wear hip-pads. Most amateur queens expend all their effort on breasts and face and hair, because that's what they see in their waist-high makeup mirrors, but when they step onstage the unmistakable V-shaped torso slams the viewer's subconscious 'MAN ALERT' button with an iron fist. Girls in the know cut out foam pads roughly in the shape of Africa and placed them on their hips, held in place and smoothed by many layers of flesh toned tights. On stage, if done correctly, it was a nearly flawless illusion of a round, hourglass figure and in my mind made all the difference in the world in creating a convincing overall illusion.

I had not worked at the Link very long before I began to realize I was living a mostly straight-free life. I had never felt a part of any group I had lived among before, in church or school or the military. Now the pressure was off in a setting where everyone shared a common thread of experiences and feelings. I worked at night, in a club with up to two thousand gay people of every kind. My bosses were gay, my coworkers. I slept all day, missing most of the time when straights are active, and then gathered with my gay friends to discuss our gay loves and enemies. We read gay magazines and gay books. If I ever saw straight people, it was on television or when I went out shopping. I didn't talk to them. They didn't talk to me. My friends and I lived among them almost completely apart.

We worked in a gay bar and went to other gay bars on our nights off. They were pretty much the universal common ground for an otherwise diverse group of people who all shared one similar experience: being loathed by most of the entire world. Despite a few popular TV shows and movie appearances where sexless homos were trotted out for non-threatening *aren't they funny!* roles, people generally didn't like to include gays too deeply in their lives. There were the few sympathizers that most gay people know, the beloved 'fag-hags' and PFLAG fantasy moms that really only lived inside televisions. It was easy to forget that they were the exceptions, until the soon-to-be familiar snickers or cruel comments in the mall, the restaurant, or the dinner table.

The more I saw of it, the more drag fascinated me. Clubs never carded queens, so underage gender outlaws sailed into worlds of sex and glamour with ease. Skinny sissy-boys and chubby train wrecks who would never get a second glance beyond the initial one of scorn in real life could put on some makeup and spandex and suddenly unlock the door to hoarded years of bitterness or ambition. Talents hidden by a lack of traditional beauty could finally be explored. A 'fat boy' dancing might be seen as comical, but put him in some gorgeous makeup and a fringed outfit first and the kids would line up to scream and tip. The ugliest boy could, if he found the right mentor, be painted up and costumed and coiffed into a glittering entity of ritualized beauty to float through the dark spaces of gay nightlife and for a time know what it was to be Marilyn or Janet or even, for the first time, simply herself. There was no similar outlet in the straight world for such people, and I often felt it was one of the luckiest things about being gay. An ugly heterosexual man was pretty much stuck with himself, but I had seen many ugly gay boys grow into Olympian figures of power and popularity in their own community.

The failures were cannibalized, forced to sell off to more established girls the expensive gowns purchased during rent-sacrificing shopping sprees. I avoided the cruel ones. When successful, they blossomed into full diva-hood with a vengeance against every kind of person who had ever wronged them. They sexually intimidated pretty boys and lorded over weaker queens. Their fingernails were ornamented scimitars, their wigs enormous lions manes. They became exactly the kind of woman a man would: exaggerated, bosomy, loud and aggressive. Never a nice comment from these girls, nor a genuine smile unless it was at some tragedy. I imagined the dissolution of the spell at night when they washed off their face at some cracked sink in a run-down space paid for by daytime hours bedrudged in menial labor. My first impulse was to look for the human element. How lonely they must be inside. Why had they become that way. But eventually I learned to let go and just say, "Fuck 'em." Or "Fudge 'em," as my mind unconsciously edited it.

The nicer ones became benevolent social figures, quickly learning that although they were not cut out for performing as a profession, they could sustain their personalities through attaching themselves to social causes and benefit shows. This gave them enough of a defensible justification for appearing out in their more popular drag personas that they could eventually shed the drab male image entirely. Some of these girls were completely unknown out of drag and would never consider allowing anyone from the club to see them without makeup.

Then there were the entertainers. These were driven girls with some beauty and some talent, be it acting or dancing or costume making, or a deadly combination of all three. They usually won a few low level pageants, expanding their wardrobes through the purchase of competition level gowns and talent costumes. Pageants got their faces known to bar owners and put them in front of large crowds for which they would not normally get to perform. I watched these girls with great interest, especially the cast members at the Link. They had already won their share of competitions, a requirement before getting a position on cast. They were stunning, incredible celebrities in our secret world, but touchable like no one in a movie could ever be to me. I wanted to be one of them, and this became my secret, impossible ambition.

Drag is a complex thing. It was a way to experience a tantalizing approximation of a what it is to be a woman socially, even if only in the useless context of a gay bar, but ultimately to me it was unsatisfying. It was like a drug, the golden hours of being called 'she' and 'her,' feeling beautiful and famous. It was never enough. I hated to take everything off and shrink back down to the colorless nobody I had been all my life and every night I wished I could be this person outside the magical borders of our clubs. The better I could learn to perform the illusion, the sooner I could chance the risky forays into straight bars some of the girls related with excitement and screams of laughter. The other queens and gay boys listened jealously to what it felt like to kiss a straight man, and to feel one's ass in public, with his consent. We said *straight man* like some hetero porn aficionados might say *Asian schoolgirl* or *lesbian twin*. But kissing them or groping them was only counting coup and then dashing back into the dark underworld to tell the tale. None of the girls expected anything more. To me, successfully achieving the illusion of womanhood was being allowed access to a man's sexuality first, and then his heart. I was desperate for this, even if only to start with the 'drag-chasers' who came to the club beginning their own journeys, tentative first steps into homosexuality with girls whose breasts came off in the dark. I wanted to be straight, as a woman, but fate had not been cooperative. They wanted to be gay, but society had not been permissive. Two people moving in opposite directions along the sexual continuum, touching as they passed.

I sat hidden from the audience in a cramped space with our anti-quated spotlight, which was held together by bent coat hanger wire and mismatched screws. I tapped the bumper buttons on a tiny fader board with my toes in time to the beat and ran the spotlight with one hand. I used the other to hold whatever book I was reading, a needed distraction from the unendurable repeats of Whitney Houston and Celine Dion that polluted every show. My own musical tastes were rarely represented onstage. "Learning to love yourself—It is the greatest love of all?" Rather egotistical, Whitney, I thought. Aside from rigidly ignoring these loathed songs, I watched, learned, and began to deal with the idea that it didn't look that difficult, really. In fact, *I* could probably do it as well as anyone. The more I watched, the more I saw how the transformation was done. I studied. I took notes. Whenever I could I slipped upstairs to watch the girls get ready, to learn and make connections. I was going to be one of them someday. I knew it.

The upstairs dressing rooms displayed the recent decay of a modern-day ruin. The space had obviously been intended for some other purpose, but the imposition of our needs created an interesting clash of old and new. The internal walls were exposed sheets of gypsum and particle board, with parts of the external structure visible in slabs of dark, scorched brick. The ceiling was little more than the underside of the roof, lost in gloom, silently absorbing the scintillations and bright conversation from below.

There was a dressing room in the back left empty by the recent vanishing of another cast member. Girls came and went, each new bloom eventually desiccated into legends and memories. This one had gone to model in New York. Or was in prison. Who knew? Who cared? The back of the room was a still life of chaos. Moldering drywall sagged against the bricks below broken panes of a low-set window. Someone had hung a few rags by forcing the points of wire hangers into the crumbly stuff, and now lines of rust trailed down and expanded into sad shades of black and brown. It looked as if the deserted show-clothes had been crying, or bleeding. A crude table remained in the middle of the room. It was made of an unhinged door laid across two stacks of bricks, probably gathered from the unused recesses beyond our converted area. It stood like an altar and I wished it were mine to sit behind, to work a transformation upon myself like the vanished girl who built it. I approached, stepping over debris carefully in the semi dark, inhaling the cloistered attic musk. The window must have been above the level of the streetlights, by the angle of blue-white that made a place for the dust to drift in languorous undersea patterns. I passed the table and saw for the first time that the window was set on hinges and could be swung in like a small door. I brought the dressing table's chair back against the wall and climbed up, opened the window, and saw beyond it a level of the black-tarred roof. I went through and stepped out into vertiginous space, all of Nashville immediate and laid out around me. I felt as if I were suddenly on the deck of a moving ship, and grasped for reassurance from the wall behind me. The tall buildings clustered together a distance away, and where I stood the sky seemed closer than I had ever noticed in the parking lot below. This was a secret place, the other side, and I felt the club throb under my feet with contained energy. The night was exceptionally clear, and cold air passed unconcerned around my powerless figure. I looked up towards the bright moon and its presence unlocked a moment's understanding of perspective. The cosmic arena was rich with stars strung like beads on curtains, behind which the mysteries sat so grim that I could not have found a question on my tongue to ask them. However I stared at the moon, its detail was not exhausted, and the abstract knowledge of it I carried became energized by belief: the glowing speck was a real place, a dusty world, and I could see its craters and mountains. There above my head was a luminous landscape as real as the ground below me, floating in the sky. Mountains in the sky. It seemed touchable, an impossible miracle below which the city lay drab and tired.

Why did I yearn to see a woman's face when I looked into the mirror? There were people below me who cared about how I lived enough to kill me, yet they were directed by the same sourceless passions that moved me. Lust. Need. Desire. Why was I magnetized by the strong bodies of men? Did any of the boys in ball caps and SUVs wonder at the origins of the heat that came when they ogled a straining tube-top? That I even had to question myself defined my place in the world, where their own lusts went unchallenged. Celebrated. They were so misguidedly righteous in the secure position of overwhelming majority. When I watched a straight couple kiss, I immediately imagined how revolted and scandalized they would be if I were to do the same with a man. Even though my need came from the same deep place inside. The empathic understanding of their smug confidence in satiating a physical need, their snobbish nausea toward my own hunger, stirred bitter anger. They were feasting at a table set by millennia of human tradition and, mouths full, disgustedly denied me even a crumb. I didn't deserve this. I didn't even want to be here, considering piecing myself together from the cast off trash of 'normal' society like some post apocalyptic scavenger. Black market hormones. Thick makeup designed for burn-victims to cover a face ravaged by the electrolysis needle. Implants. Wigs. Lasers. It sounded ridiculous. Frightening. None of these technologies were created for making a male body over into that of a woman. If I had been a girl from the start, I could have had the love I wanted, and the carnal passion. I could live the life that came so naturally to my heart yet was denied to my physical self. I needed to be one, and I felt it pure and acknowledged for the first time, unclouded by hopeless shame. However horrifying the process, it was possible. The streets ran with people and cars below me, below the cold moon, and I rained down jealous hatred on them all. I pulled at the stars to fall and burn away this stupid life, so full of impossible contradictions, but they remained fixed in place and offered nothing but a blurred image to my wet eyes. I made no sound other than a sigh, and blinked the moisture away. The window was still open behind me. The city was before me, beyond the edge of the roof. I could step off and never have to worry about making the choice. Fall broken at the feet of those who would crush me anyway in horrified scorn.

But there was really no question, only the slow acceptance of the harder path. I turned around and went back into the window, into the dark room, knowing what I had to do. It was not the best solution. It would never be a complete one. But other than death, it was the only one.

The Link moved into a bigger space down by the river, displaced by Nashville's new sports arena, and I moved with it. Employees came and went, but I stayed constant behind the spotlight, illuminating each passing face. I watched up to eighty-four individual numbers a weekend. I learned every step, every word, of every song repeated again and again and then again. I noted what poses looked cool, which color shoes went with what color outfits. I saw how some girls handled drunks, how some enticed tips from cemetery crowds. Months passed and somehow I lived on one hundred and five dollars a week, plus occasional day jobs that I never took seriously and usually ended up walking out of just before being fired. Wednesday nights the B-cast performed on the dance floor, and joining them was the first step in my mind to making the weekend cast. It did not occur to me that a girl could transition outside the framework of the shows, and besides I desperately wanted the validation that came from hundreds of screaming fans. If I could make everyone think I was beautiful, then that was almost as good as being it really.

My first attempts at drag were probably painful to watch. I was determined to hold onto a "Morticia" look (or "Man-ticia," as my 'friends' so kindly remarked), and thus my foundation was Dermablend Chroma 0—the palest ivory. My wig was color 0—jet black. I liked the matching zeros that meant two opposite things.

"Mmm, You'd do well as a comedy queen..." One of the more experienced girls offered, sizing me up.

"Comedy is just a way for ugly people to become famous. Obviously it doesn't work for all of you..."

"Your plate is full, honey. Don't worry about me."

Red lipstick and black eyeliner, a stuffed bra under my Halloween dress, and I was done. I was seriously convinced this look could carry any song, and I wobbled onto the dance floor for Tuesday talent-night determined to catch the eye of the Wednesday show director. I'm quite certain I managed that.

Chyna was a beautiful black queen famous, in my mind, for three things: a microscopic waist, full hips and the ability to spin like an Olympic ice-skater in heels. She put Whitney to shame with an impassioned delivery of lip-synced lyrics and the lightning snap of her dancing. On the climactic, drawn-out crescendo of a song she would twirl until she blurred and her earrings shot off across the stage. The note carried and she spun faster, more jewelry unfastening through centripetal force and flying away. Everyone screamed, shouting, "SPIN BITCH! SPIN!" until it became unbelievable that she could keep it up another second, and then the note finished and Chyna stopped as easily as she started, rounding out into a grapevine step.

One of her odious duties as second-string cast member was running the Tuesday talent night. She performed a few numbers and hosted a motley lineup of amateurs who came in thrift store drag and out-of-date ensembles 'borrowed' from their mothers closets. After the show the audience awarded fifty dollars by applause to whomever they liked the most. There was rarely much of an audience. Mostly bored fags looking for laughs and predatory closeted grandfathers seeking an insecure young queen to flatter into bed.

I had inexplicably chosen "Red Football" by Sinead O'Connor as my debut song. This was by no means a popular tune, nor a popular album. Sinead had topped out among queens with "Nothing Compares 2 U" (still a moneymaker for me, by the way), but "Red Football" was a sullen, timorous reclaiming of identity by an abused woman, ending without warning in a shocking beer-hall chorus of shouted LA LA LA's. Absolute stage death. I couldn't be paid to do it now. My entire plan for the number was to break into a spin during the final exultation. Perhaps I felt like I could communicate some complex sentiment about my own tragic disenfranchisement. More likely, I was just trying to buck the system. It was only after years of experimenting that I perfected a balance that allowed both positive cash flow and individuality.

The music started, and Sinead's pure voice was different enough from the prevailing pop of the night to attract everyone's attention. I made my tentative way out onto the performance space while lip-synching, pale and weird looking. Towards the end someone gave me a single mercy tip, and then as I sensed the finish coming near I drew back away from the audience. When the LA!'s screamed out, completely startling everyone, I did my best to spin, managing a few circles before dizziness overcame me and I tottered off the stage. The song ended abruptly. Crickets must have been lined up for weeks to audition for that moment. After a bit of silence I heard a few laughs, then someone clapped, weak and conciliatory. I didn't win that night. But maybe it was my spin, or perhaps just simple pity. As I was preparing to leave, gathering my things together in the dressing area, Chyna came up behind me.

"Lemme see what you've got in your makeup box."

I felt stupid next to her beauty. I lifted the lid. "I was kinda goin for a Morticia look, I know it's pale…"

"Girl, what the *hell*…" She spoke in quick, clipped tones of authority, holding up my pot of Dermablend. "Chroma *Zero?!* What are you usin for powder?" She scrabbled among my meager supplies and took out my round paper box of Coty airspun. "Natu-*Relle!* Bitch, that's as white as damn paper." She looked me over. "And you don't have on no lip liner, no lashes…Girl, you look a hot *shitty* mess." She was sitting down next to me as she said this and reaching for my makeup brushes. Somehow it didn't seem hurtful the way she said it. More maternal. She sighed when she found my contour: a package of CoverGirl with three stripes of blush in it. She looked me right in the eye and said:

"Rule number one: Cover-G*irl* does NOT Cover *Boy.*"

Much like the kid everyone knew who could burp the entire Pledge of Allegiance, Chyna had the ability to speak whole sentences in a genuine, Janet Leigh *Psycho* scream. We would be getting ready side by side, some old school drag music from the 80's playing in the background, and without any change in her demeanor Chyna would lean delicately into my ear. There was a minuscule pause. I felt the damp warmth of her breath and then before I could react my eardrums were pierced with: "AIN'T YER HAIR A HOT SHITTY *MESSSSSS!*" The last word would always rip away into an even higher screech, completely beyond the bounds of human sanity, and then she was back at her mirror painting with a tiny suppressed smile. I always took that time to clean up the spilled powder and hairpins.

Within weeks I was a regular at talent night, fully adopted into Chyna's eclectic family. Big girls, skinny girls, pretty ones and plain. Black and white, transie and drag. There were no rules, only acceptance. Chyna did not use drugs, and if she taught us anything, it was the rewards of simple hard work. We informally referred to ourselves as the *House of the Orient*, although it was not a clan identifier in the way that Houses exist in New York and elsewhere. It was just our name, like the Smiths or Joneses. Most of us had been shut out by our genetic relatives, or else tacitly compelled to keep our non-hetero lives completely out of the picture, so we made our own relations. A typical country family, supportive, accepting and completely loyal. Oh, and heavily made up.

"Girl, I would never have believed it, but you look good." Chyna was behind me, picking and spraying my red wig and looking at our reflection in the mirror. It had only been a year and a half, and tonight was my first audition for a full time cast position at the Link. I had finally won my first pageant and wrangled enough special guest spots for them to get a sense of my freaky glam take on performing. The audience liked me, if they didn't always understand the sometimes obscure music I performed, and I had concentrated all of my energy in making the transition from behind the spotlight to in front of it.

"Calpernia, you're next." The backstage manager was gone before I turned around to look.

"Now girl, the owner is out there watchin, so don't do any of that freaky shit tonight. Do it like we practiced it and make me proud." Chyna had choreographed an entire routine to Crystal Waters' "What I Need," and we spent most of last night hot-gluing dangling strings of silver beads onto a bra and panty set for me to wear. The beads sounded like rain falling and shifting against one another as I moved. I looked in the mirror and saw the results of Chyna's expert hands in my makeup and hair. I really was beautiful. It filled me with excitement, an electric charge of confidence. I really was beautiful. Amazing. It never got old, that feeling.

"Well get up, bitch. You're next."

"I don't think I can do this…"

"I know you can do it."

One year later.

"I know I can do it, whore. I'm sorry you missed rehearsal, but I know the steps and you don't so there's no other way." Brigitte was in my dressing room for the third time in twenty minutes, hovering behind me. All I saw of her were two enormous naked breasts in my makeup mirror.

"Girl, You're already the lead in two other productions. You can't have everything."

I scooted back from the mirror and began peeling off strips of duct tape to form my personal favorite Y-shaped pattern. I looked her in the eye. "What do you wanna do, go out there not knowin the routine and fake it? You can have it next weekend after you've learned everything. I don't care. I'm not really a Fosse girl anyway."

"What's Fosse?"

"Brigitte. The production we're doing? The song's from *All That Jazz?*" I struck a pose. "Never mind. Whatever. Go ask Robyn." Our show director.

"Okay then, next weekend. Don't forget, you hateful beast." Brigitte always breezed into rehearsals late in sunglasses with her cellphone attached to one ear, living that whole image. I went through steps in my schlubby t-shirt and jeans, scanning her trendy skirt and top and heels. We were completely different creatures.

Finally alone, I put on my short, dark wig and slicked it into place then searched for my flapper-girl dress somewhere in a pile of clothes on the floor. The overture was about to end. I stopped a moment to look at myself—quick approximation of a Marcel wave, ruby lips glistening against ivory skin. I usually only wore stage foundation, red lipstick and a dramatic curve of liquid eyeliner behind huge false lashes. Simple. Like a movie star, the real black and white kind.

"Calpernia, you have…thirty seconds. Twenty-nine. Twenty-eight…" The backstage manager, Devin, was looking up at the ceiling, the place where I imagined he saw the voices that whispered information into his little earpiece.

"How is it out there?"

"Standing room only. Twenty-five…" I ran down the hall and steps in four-inch stilettos and took my place in the dark between Judy and Rebecca. The show began.

My dressing room was the size of a very tiny studio apartment, and I could have lived there without much complaint. I pretty much did for seven years. As time passed and I developed a sense of the show's rhythm I realized there were large chunks of time with nothing to do. Other girls had their dressers to talk to, and their entourage, but I could not stand to have anyone over my shoulder and kept my room free of intrusion. I carted in two boxes of turn-of-the-century school-room encyclopedias Sissy had given me, full of hilarious horse and buggy photos captioned "London Today" and children's science exper-iments. I stuffed the empty cracks around the larger books with some of my yellowing Mad Magazine paperbacks. I bought a pawn store television and VCR and set them up next to my makeup mirror. One entire wall was covered in wigs of every description hanging from nails, and a rack of shoes. My makeup station was a collage of mirrors, lean-ing against the middle wall behind my smaller lighted mirror. The right side of the room was a long pipe hung on wire from one end to the other, packed with hanging costumes. Magazine photos of Ange-lina Jolie and Bebe ads covered whatever spaces were left on walls painted two different shades of mental institution green.

The house was packed with tables and tables of drunk, loud men and women and queens, gay and straight. Hundreds of them. Similar throngs filled the balcony, screaming and sometimes tossing wadded up bills at the stage. First time visitors to the Link were always over-whelmed at how many people came there to dance and see our show. I was dressed for my first solo number, a remix I had made of Patsy Cline's 'Crazy' going into the psychotic death-metal version by Kidney Thieves. My hair was a huge cloud of curls that I had spritzed with water just before going on to make it stick to my face when I began to fling it around. I didn't change my makeup at all except to smudge my lipstick a little. The performance was all in the face. Underneath an absolutely enormous burgundy Mongolian lambswool coat I wore a sequined patch in the shape of a red and orange flame between my legs and two smaller versions covering my breasts. A pair of thigh high boots in red patent leather finished the look. Robyn had just enough time as I hustled past to say, "Girl, when Wal-Mart says, 'Dollar-a-yard fabric table,' you can buy more than one yard."

My music began, an echoing Patsy playing at uneven speed with the hisses and pops of a Victrola in the background. I walked out, smooth and surreal, like an image of her projected onto the wall of an abandoned building at midnight. My fans began to scream, knowing what was in store, and they were backed up by some country aficionados who probably thought I was just performing to a bad recording. I felt so beautiful, in exactly the way I wanted to be: erotic, powerful, and a little scary. My gestures were slow, expressions of internal struggle. I was damaged. I wanted to fuck someone. Kill someone.

"Crazy...I'm crazy for feelin so lonely."

They were already lining up on the sides of the runway, people pressing their way through the capacity crowd to tip me and say hello and give me kisses.

"I'm crazy...crazy for feelin so blue."

"I knew...you'd love me as long as you wanted."

"And someday...you'd leave me for somebody new."

The song melted, slowed as if a finger had been laid on the record to stop it. My head dropped, hair obscuring my face. The stage went dark and two red can lights slammed on just as the other version started, eerie and darker. My head snapped back in an explosion of curls. I felt myself begin to expand, filled with some kind of fire and venom and power fueled by the music and people. Everyone was yelling now, louder than before. I raised my face to the audience and I was looking at them, making eye contact. Now I was really present. As I ripped off my coat the music detonated into distorted guitars and an agonized, diabolical wail. Some newcomers were looking away, disapproving, frightened. I stood virtually naked, back arched, posed in a rictus of betrayed desperation and begging to be loved, leaning back and looking up towards the ceiling with clawed hands hanging uselessly at my sides:

"Worry? Why do I let myself worry?" The guitars pounded out an agonized march and I moved stiffly down the runway, looking desperately at the thousand faces of my unfaithful lover.

"Wonderin…what in the world should I do?" I sank fluidly to my knees and cupped their faces in my hands, searching for some sign of humanity. I took their dollars.

"Crazy…for thinkin that my love could hold you." I tossed my head and arched my body, crawling on hands and knees. The guitars screeched. My hair was wild and unkempt and as planned stuck to my face and dragged through my lipstick to leave red slashes across my skin.

"Crazy…for thinkin that my love could hold you." I had fistfuls of bills and stood back up to finish the song. I looked defiantly into the spotlight, a Vallejo heroine staring down the specter of death, broken by self-realization.

"I'm crazy for tryin, crazy for cryin, and I'm crazy for lovin you." I walked to the back of the stage and turned back to peer at the crowd from the tiny window of a pinpoint spotlight on my face. The last line was whispered over the sound of night insects and the wind.

"I'm crazy for tryin, crazy for cryin, and I'm crazy for lovin you." The spot winked out and I picked up my coat and left the stage. Robyn was next up, smiling at me in the dark. She had the microphone and as she looked me in the eye her inimitable ghetto grandmother voice filled the theater.

"That bitch is fucking *CRAZY*. Damn. Let's hear it for Calpernia Addams, everybody!"

I could imagine Robyn Dupree seated behind a desk in some forgotten bureaucracy, an endless line of supplicants filling the un-airconditioned hall awaiting her bored consideration. She seemed born to utter the classically biting "*Next!*" Each word she spoke fell heavy and theatrical, intended to amuse and devastate simultaneously, carried by a rich throaty voice resonant with a lifetime of demanding respect. She enunciated deliberately, speaking from deep within her large body. She was a big woman, heavy but compact, her face defined by sculpted cheekbones and wide, unbelievably full lips. Mixed Black and Puerto-Rican ancestry gave her the smooth caramel skin that inspired her stage billing, 'The Bronze Beauty,' and her relaxed hair glistened with burgundy dye. She slicked it against her skull with quivering handfuls of brown gel scooped up in jungle-red nails so long and straight she had to have them specially made every time she had a manicure. It was all secured with elastic to form a classic Mother Hubbard bun. Robyn was in her fifties and had been performing since the days when record players provided the sound for cabaret shows. Before that she had been an MP in the Marines, which developed her commanding presence and ability to make people around her do almost anything she wanted. Her movements had the dignity possessed by the very large and she sat regally in front of her makeup mirror, massive breasts hanging free as she finished her old-school makeup and readied herself to announce the next entertainer, her ex-lover Rebecca Lynne Blackwell.

"Ladies and Gentlemen," she began wearily, wireless mike clutched in her large taloned hand backstage. "Please welcome to the stage our very own," voice heavy with sarcasm, painted eyes rolling theatrically to rest on me, "She's already *here*, we *may* as well bring her out…"

Her cruelty was so blatant, unrepentant and funny that I could only watch in stupefied amazement. Rebecca preened herself nervously at the bottom of the stairs beside the stage, sublimating annoyance. Robyn's body collapsed in her chair, mouth slack. Her eyes bulged from behind half-closed lids: the face of an annoyed corpse fished out of the river. Every syllable was accomplished with supreme, apparent effort. "Ladies and gentlemen, I give you…*Rebecca…Lynn…Black-well.*" Terrifying silence filled the theater for a second, then Rebecca's music started. Robyn's voice, impossibly false and bright, rang out over the intro: "Come on! Let's hear it for Rebecca Lynn Blackwell!" A few cheers blended in with Dolly Parton's energetic singing and a broad smile framed Robyn's sinister chuckle. She leaned into her mirror to apply more black to her eyes.

"Robyn how can you *do* that to her?" I said around a smile. I was always in awe after one of her personal performances.

"Mother has her ways, baby. If you stick around long enough you'll learn."

"I've been here for a year."

"Awww, the Baby." She reached back and fondled my breast with her claws. "Aw yeah, Mommy. Now that's what I'm talkin about…"

I recoiled and laughed and accepted that as her way of ending the conversation. I had a complicated evening gown to get into and left her to her painting. Below us Rebecca's Dolly Parton chirped through an upbeat number for the shell-shocked masses I had left behind.

15

Brigitte Carmichael

Her eyes were swollen behind drooping lids, a dreamy look that made it difficult to guess which person, which drug, I was talking to at the moment. So many drugs here. "This club would close if it weren't for the coke and X and G. Nobody would come..." the management had told me when I complained. Brigitte's words ran together and dribbled out like heavy smoke, tired from traveling the million miles between her brain and where we were standing, in the dark, backstage.

"You've got fucking *cute* shoes, you've got face and you've got *body*. Fuck those *bitches*." She took my arm and we catwalked through the maze of passages that led to the stage entrance, down the steps and stopped in front of the mirror in the glittering dark swell of the production's beginning. Dust and hair and scraps of the bright costumes that moved through here were swept back into corners, against baseboards, hopeful, discarded. Brigitte leaned against the unpainted wall and her unfocused gaze placed her somewhere on the remotest, loneliest island I could imagine. Only the hot boiling surf exploding against sharp coral and her languid contemplation of bleached out sand through those lidded eyes. I wondered what she ever thought about anymore. Her part began and she dropped my hand, sailed out past me and onto the stage, into the pounding applause and lighted darkness. I followed when my turn came, stomach in, back up, to feed the glare that was my sun. The spotlight fringed with shadowy figures, nodding heads and smoke, waiting to see us perform.

The music. It took up every bit of space and I moved in it like a figure through liquid fire. Beats suggested clicks and explosions of cameras, goddess-like attitude and confidence, and Brigitte and I walked through it down the runway like supermodels. To our audience, three feet below us, we *were* supermodels. As I well knew, in the blaze of lights and amphetamine sound my familiar showgirl friends could fascinate, hypnotize even me. Acquaintances for whom I would not answer the phone in daily life drew interest on stage with the lines of their movement and projected emotion. Whether to gain ammunition for criticism or store up points of worship, the crowd watched, shifting at our feet, loud, cheering, commenting, encouraging, taking the energy focused in and channeled out of we two girls walking, walking down the runway. Brigitte clasped my hand, this secret touch a realness in the tempest of light and sound. We reached the end and paused, knowing we were beautiful, resonantly fulfilling the ravenous desire to be wanted and loved that everyone felt, us included. We turned in place, dropped hands and rejoined opposite ones, ponytails swinging, jewels flashing, and made our way back to the main stage to allow room for the next two girls to walk out. There is nothing like that evanescent feeling. In those moments, I knew what it is to be completely beautiful and perfect, filled to the top with a homogenous confidence unblemished by any doubt.

Then it's over and I go back to my dressing room walled in mirrors, to start over again at zero. Like Tinkerbell I needed everyone to clap to keep me from dying.

My room used to be someone's office, as did everyone else's. My life seemed to be made up of cast off things. Cast off rooms, cast off clothes from thrift and resale stores. Wigs and heels purchased at black-girl stores, makeup with enclosed illustrations showing how well it covered over burns and birthmarks. Hormones for menopausal matrons. Nothing I had was meant to be used the way I used it. A sudden dive of spirits carried my thoughts into a familiar hopeless place where nothing looked right and I lost grip on the feeling that someday I would make everything work outOk. My next number was to be 'Somewhere Over the Rainbow' and I gathered together all the things I would need. Long

habit blocked out the unpleasant clash of whatever song the girl
onstage was performing with the heavy pounding of music from the
dance floor. I slipped on the blue country dress and white apron, the
white socks and red-glittered mary-janes. My hair was already long and
brown, so I shook it out upside down and then braided it into two
loose pigtails, tied with red ribbon. It was a good approximation and I
felt pleasantly amused at the old-school campiness of the image I presented in the mirror. 'You look more real than campy, of course.' I
reassured myself. I had gotten ready rather quickly and still had several
numbers to go before I was on, so I sat at my dressing table and took
out a book to read. I started my favorite Enya CD as the latest Des-
tiny's Child single boomed up from below, faintly excoriating yet
another in a legion of poorly chosen lovers. I laughed to myself, thinking about the part in the video where the girls lip-synched a line about
their Christianity while wearing stripper outfits and then went back to
chastising their out-of-wedlock ex-sexual partner.

I was snatched from this reverie by a knock on my door as it was
pushed open. It was a bar manager, Amy, looking serious.

"Callie, there's a phone call for you in the office. It's your Mom."

My first thought was that Jerm was dead. Only the most dire of circumstances could drive her to call this hellhole of depravity. I felt
immediately and deeply ill. I followed Amy back into the dark warren
of hallways that led to his office, feeling incredibly foolish dressed as I
was, ruby slippers and all. The plastic receiver lay on his desk like a
fallen power line, off the hook, and I knew she was there breathing on
the other end, listening for me to pick up. I didn't want to talk to her.
I panicked for an instant and my stomach, already sour, clotted into
bile and acid. I did not want to pick up that phone.

"Well Mary, pick up the phone." Amy, so called because of an abandoned drag persona many years past, was one of the few people left
who still said Mary. I knew she had probably heard him say this and I
snatched it up before she could hear any other time-warped homosex-
ual patois.

"Mom what's the matter?" All in a rush I felt angry at her for calling me here, for stirring me into jitters and poison right before I had to go on stage.

"Scott! Where've you been, honey? I was worried about you…" She was talking quickly, breathless. Nervous and relieved. My own mother, nervous to talk to me. I hated myself. "I just…I didn't know if you we'reOk. You don't ever answer the phone." She had been calling. Every time my phone rang it was in my bones, the ringing. I hated the phone so much. It was never anything good.

"I'm sorry Momma, I've just been busy…you know, working and stuff." Did she really know what I did? Did she know I was standing here dressed like Dorothy right this second? I wished she could see me, see how good I was. I'm good, Momma. People like me, what I do, and it makes them happy. It makes it not so bad when people laugh at them all day, and call them names, if they can come somewhere and watch a show and have a few drinks.

"Honey, I miss you. I love you…you know that, don't you?" That voice. It was flowers and biscuits and gravy and Christmas trees. It was hugs and kisses and laughter and snowflakes.

"I'm sorry. I'm…" I knew I had failed her on some cosmic level, and that she still loved me, and all I could do was cry. My throat closed up and the tears burned and spilled down my face. I patted them carefully so as not to smudge my makeup and twisted the mouthpiece away so that she would not hear. I took a deep breath and swallowed everything down, in my special secret way, and spoke again. "I'll come visit you. Sunday, when you're back from Church, Ok?"

"Ok…I just want to see you, you know…I don't never get to see you no more. You're my son and I love you." My son. Love and poison mixed so well, you could hardly taste where one stopped and the other began. She didn't mean to hurt me. I know it.

"I love you Mom. I'll call you."

"I love you too. Bye honey. I'll see you tomorrow."

"Bye Mom."

Amy had been there the entire time, watching. He patted my hand, a little hesitant. "Parents are a bitch, aren't they?"

"They're somethin."

"Here, Take this tissue and clean up your face. You better get to followin the yellow brick road, bitch. You got a lot of people waiting out there to see your tired act."

"You're the best, Amy."

"I know I am. Now hit it."

The next morning I slept, deeply, in a quiet and dark apartment. My phone did not ring and when I awoke that night it was just in time to grab a cup of coffee on the way in to the show. I drove with my window down, sipping the bitter cup. The sky was clear and full of stars, and the air felt nice against my face. There was something hard inside me, a regret. She would never accept me as I was. I could not bear it.

16

Murderous Friends

"Look at Calpernia. She's the hottest bitch in here." David was drunk. This was nothing new. It's what bar-people did when they were off work. We all told everyone, "I *work* in a bar, why would I want to *go* to one?" and yet there we were, every other night without fail.

"And she's got a fucking *cock*." Mikey clapped me on the back, truly proud of this accomplishment, and everyone laughed. It was just us friends. He would never have said it where anyone else could hear. I smiled. A barricade in front of the deepest howling pit of despair flapped open for an instant like a shutter in a gale and the ghosting presentiment of acid tears tingled behind my eyes. You're so beautiful...*for a man*. We think of you, ultimately, as a man. Would I ever be able to leave that behind and just be a woman to anyone? I dispatched another demon of hopelessness with weary ease and regained my composure, all in the blink of a burning eye.

It was dark and close inside the club, horrible and comfortable. Comfortably horrible. Every second I spent there I wanted to go home, but possibility floated above our heads in the curling smoke of a thousand cigarettes and I could not kill the faceless image of some perfect lover I might meet if only I could stand the hellish atmosphere for one more moment. Hyper-real music beat along with my heart, faster every year, some new remake of an old song sampled and sliced down into its most exhilarating five percent and looped again and again over the pounding of a ten-ton metronome. My new best friends and I stood in a group near the back wall. Best friends just kept coming, too, it seemed. Wave after wave through the years, each group different but the same. It reminded me of that Twilight Zone where the guy woke up each morning in prison to the same day over and over. All the same people were there, just in slightly different parts. Despite this I loved these friends, and needed them to fill their roles. The disbelieved compliments came just in time, the shallow concern was just enough that I felt cared for. There was no malice, only a group of people holding hands in the dark, and as long as no one grew too heavy or walked too slow, the circle would remain unbroken.

"Wait, wait...watch this!" It was a Monday and we were all off, watching the show at our sister-bar, the Chute. A new queen was on stage, special-guesting.

"Ok, now here it comes. *PICK THE APPLE...*" David reached up, palm towards his face, and did a slow, stylized mime of picking an apple that hung just above his head. At that moment onstage the queen performed the same movement, accenting the longing phrase of her Celine Dion ballad. The few people who didn't think I looked like Drew Barrymore felt compelled to point out an imagined resemblance to Celine, which was even more annoying. We joined in David's game and waited for the next move. She swayed awkwardly in an off-the-rack navy polyester J.C. Penney evening gown and two-inch leather pumps. I looked at her paint-by-numbers makeup and felt sorry for her, remembering my own first dabblings with cosmetics. We all knew every lyric by heart of course, some through genuine worship and some, like me, simply through repetitive exposure. Celine was like gamma rays on our little three mile island of drag: unavoidable. She was about to sing, "NO NO NO NO!"

"*WASH THE WINDOW!*" David shouted over the music, although not loud enough for her to hear. As she swiped her hand back and forth in a gesture of negation we all did the same, and we were laughing, everyone exaggerating even more than was necessary. The smallish room was almost unbearably filled with the cacophony of conversation, drag music and the milling of a capacity crowd, so we were generally unnoticed. It was normal to play along with the entertainers, Rocky

Horror style, on busy nights. Personally, it was difficult to perform at all without the charge of the audience screaming at me in some kind of way.

"OPEN THE CURTAINS!" We pushed open the hugest, plushest floor to ceiling velvet drapes we could imagine as Celine talked about something or other dramatic, but the queen missed the opportunity because she was collecting tips.

"You sure you don't want anything to drink, Callie?" Mike held two beers by their necks between his fingers and passed a glass to David. They knew I didn't drink but bartenders couldn't relax unless everyone had something liquid in their hand.

"Here, take my Coke." Neysha presented it disinterestedly. Her mind was on a certain Mexican ex-girlfriend across the floor. Left her for a white girl, she said a bit too often to anyone who would listen.

"Yeah, if that's not diet you better get rid of it, girl." David slapped her celebrated ghetto booty. Neysha made a gesture as if to claw his face and then looked back to pick out her girl again.

"I'm fine." I was watching Ellen flirt. She was taller than me, and because of it I secretly idolized her. I always tried to envision how I, the freakish Amazon, looked in comparison to people around me, and having a taller female to watch as a reference point killed a lot of my obsessive, distorted images. She looked elegant and modelish, which were exactly the qualities people attributed to my height when I worried about it. It was one of the few instances when a cherished point of personal self-loathing was laid bare and defenseless with no recourse but to die, but such comforts evaporated quickly when I was alone. Then I only stared into the mirror and knew I could never hear enough that I was beautiful, because I would never believe it.

Ellen was bisexual, with a preference for women, and we flirted casually all the time. It made me feel more 'real' to pretend that she found me attractive, although I had made it clear that the only woman I could ever get naked with was Angelina Jolie. The early show ended and she came to dance a little in place with me as she drank her beer. People surged around us in hot groups of dancers and talkers, lookers and walkers, everyone a story I had heard or lived in some way. Mikey came up to dance on my other side and our distracted time-keeping movements progressed into the standard bump-and-grind between friends that happens in clubs. Mikey's rough jeans slid along my bare leg and I felt the hard curve of pectoral against my breasts through his cotton shirt. They loved my breasts, always touching them, pushing their faces into them, and I enjoyed the attention. It was sexuality without fire, playing the game of being straight. Behind me the scent of fabric softener somehow penetrated the smoke and Ellen's yielding body pressed into my back. I pushed back against her and pulled her hands up to my breasts. The lightest touch like the fluttering of moth's wings was her hair against my neck as she leaned close to whisper laughter and alcohol into my ear:

"Don't get it cut off…you could please me in so many ways…" She was drunk. Joking. Still, I couldn't think of any witty response just then. What did it mean, that she would say that? It meant I was, on some level, a man to her. The thought was a stone that plopped into the surface of my soul and sank to the bottom, one among many. I just smiled and leaned back against her. Not because I was happy or wanted to arouse. I recognized as I did it that I was only trying not to be rude, not to reject her, and I despaired that I would care about that even as I suffered devastation. A tall guy with the short curly hair and perfect body of a Greek statue joined in as the music continued to pulse, pressing behind Ellen. He smiled, and in his face I saw only a simple enjoyment of the moment. His hands reached past her and found my waist. They were large and strong and felt good against my bare skin. The song changed and we split just as easily as we had intertwined. Ellen disappeared, a strange look quickly suppressed in her large brown eyes.

I smiled. "What's up?" My standard conversation opener.

"You want something to drink?" Mikey, too, had wandered away, sensing the possibility of trade. It was just me and the statue. Every time it came to the booze thing I felt like such a freak. Was I the only person in the world who didn't drink? I took a deep mental breath and said my lines:

"Nah, I don't drink…I'm a cheap date, ha ha…" Self-deprecation, a.k.a. Old Reliable.

"Water? Something?" He was trying. Whenever I said I wasn't thirsty, they always asked at least two more times. It was maddening because it was so predictable, but this time I didn't really care.

"Ok, some soda water would be good. What's your name?"

"Christopher." He had a cute, little-boy face on top of that body. I couldn't stop looking at him. I was being shallow, a voice said without conviction deep inside my head. Whatever. I leaned closer and shook his hand.

"Sarah. Nice to meet you." Mmm, manly.

"So do you come here a lot?" *That's original,* I thought. "I'm here with some friends from work." He looked around as if to point them out, but couldn't find whoever he was looking for. "I think they're outside getting high or something."

"I come here every once in awhile. I'm usually working. The bartender there is my best friend." I indicated Oscar, pouring and smiling diligently behind his bar. I knew I would get a phone call with the full report of his night's amusements once I got home, if not over coffee at Café CoCo after his shift. A sexy Cuban boy behind the bar was a magnetic sight in Nashville, and he had a legion of slavering fans.

"Its cool to talk to a girl here. All night I've just been gettin gay guys on me."

Did that mean he didn't know my deal? "Well, take the attention where you can get it, ha ha…" I playfully punched his arm. It was like a rock. I pretended injury and blew on my fingers. "Ow!" I could play corny too.

"Aww, let me see that." he took my hand in his and kissed it.

I performed a fake swoon, quickly recovered, and said, "Hey where's that soda water you were talkin about?"

"Oh yeah…" He was smiling. I watched him walk away and wondered why he was talking to me. Did he know I was TS? Somehow I got the feeling he didn't, and noticed the familiar nervous excitement that always came when an unknowing straight man flirted with me. *This is what it feels like to be a woman,* I thought. Ellen came back through the crowd and leaned in to talk over the music. There was a spark in her eyes.

"That's Christopher…I kinda know him. He is *so* straight, I can't even believe they got him to come here. I bet he would *totally* freak out if he knew."

"So you don't think he knows?"

"I don't know. I don't think so. You know David wants him *so bad.* Wait, here he comes. *Bye!*"

He gave me a bottled water and we went to lean against the wall and talk. It is standard for some people to deny that they are a 'club person,' to loudly proclaim interest in literature and art as if it made up for standing desperately in the middle of a meat market like everyone else. I was one of these people, but this time it felt more like I was telling the truth. My intellectual side was something I was actually proud of and wanted to show off despite its smallness and rarity of use. If someone had said, "Show me your intellectualism, *one two three—GO!*" I would have just stood there stupefied, but nonetheless the idea was something I valued. So we talked about what writers we liked to read, and what trash. We talked about music, and he told me he played guitar. I imagined us playing music together like Jerm and I used to do. Moments passed and there was no stalling of the flow. We connected, in a real way that was nonetheless simple enough to quicken our physical attractions. I knew this was an uncommon chance, to meet someone I actually found cool here in this soul-dimming place, and I had already begun to anticipate the additional hurt that would come from his more weighted rejection.

"What are you thinkin about? Your face just got all screwed up." He had such a cute smile.

"Nothin...Um, hey Christopher, I think I better get goin. This smoke and noise is wearin me out."

"You know what, I'm gonna go too. This really isn't my scene anyway, you know what I mean?"

What, the gay scene? Surely he knew? But the drag queens here were caked with theatrical makeup and outlandish outfits, capped by elaborate wigs. I was wearing a cute skirt and a baby-doll cropped T, with little to no makeup, my hair loose and curly. I glanced over his shoulder into my old friend the mirror and was relieved to see I looked great. Skin was clear, shiny in the right kinda way. Lipstick holding up, not too garish. And I saw myself next to him, noting that he was almost a head taller than me. Damn, he looked good. And he was not clocking me. I knew it, and it was terrifying and exhilarating all at once. This gorgeous straight stud was all about me, me who God had never intended to be anything beautiful or beloved. In the mirror was a beautiful woman and he wanted her, wanted me, and I was going to give it to him. I never lied to anyone unless they asked me to.

"I live really close, if you want to come over and hang out for a little while. I'd love to hear you play your guitar." He had come right from a rehearsal and had it checked in the coatroom.

"Yeah, sure. That would be cool." He was excited, which excited me. I hoped he knew. I hoped he knew and still wanted to go home with me. If he didn't I was in for an unpleasant evening.

We got our coats and I waved a hasty goodbye to my friends. He followed me out, and it was obvious to them what was happening. It was impossible that some queen hadn't run up and said something to out me, but I supposed Christopher was too new for them to realize he didn't know. David saw us leaving, too, and knowing he wanted this straight man but could never have him made me feel wickedly powerful. Sometimes I cashed in all the trouble and pain, purchasing vile moments like these, and despite the sick loneliness that came later it seemed all worth it. But if I died today, it was worth it at least to know the desire of a man. To make peace with the mirror and not be destroyed by the burning images that lived there. It was worth it.

"You know who you look like?" We were in my apartment, sitting on my bed. I had slipped in a CD of Sade's greatest hits and lit the one candle in my bedroom.
"Who." I waited. Here it comes.
"Drew Barrymore."
"Do you think she's pretty?"
"Its your lips. And eyes. Sure, she's cool."
"Well, thanks. I thank you, and Drew Barrymore thanks you." I smiled instead of sighed. We were sitting close together, and in the improved light of my bedroom his body looked even more incredible. Not an ounce of fat, and that curly brown hair looked so soft, like silky lamb's wool. Plus he played the guitar!

We talked some more, and I persuaded him to get out his instrument. His voice was nice, woodsy and mellow, and the songs were not unbearable. I got my fiddle to improvise along, mildly shocked that this was happening. I had met a cool, super-sexy acoustic guitar-playing guy who appreciates literature in a club? We talked about poetry and he said we would have to write each other one to read the next time. Next time. He kissed me. While we kissed I play-acted in my head how it would be to have a boyfriend like Christopher. I hungrily recorded sensations: the hard smoothness of muscle felt through t-shirt. The smell of cologne and sweat. The taste of salt on his skin. He became a prop in my hands, to aid my imagining. This is my husband, and we're kissing on our anniversary. He's my hometown sweetheart the night of the prom. Anything real and normal, because this couldn't be. He peeled off his shirt and my fingers flew to record the shapes that moved in his skin. So soft, his skin, and the firm muscles underneath. The weight of him on top of me, and the smell. His big, soft lips on mine and the breath that I inhaled as if it were mine. My legs wrapped around his narrow waist and he instinctively forced them apart, exciting me further. We were gorging on each other, thirsting in passion and lust. My fingers traced his delicate eyelids and refined brows. He reached down and I bucked away thinking he meant to touch between my legs, but he only fumbled to roll my shirt up, our lips separating just long enough to pull it past and throw it away. Did he know? He slid down to ravish my breasts and I watched the workings and ripplings of his back, cradled his head at my chest and was mesmerized by the sight and sensation of his greedy suckling. He wanted me. I had given him a straining erection and his whole body was overcome in the ancient need to possess me.

"So *then*—," and this was Mikey's favorite part of the story, "*then* she says, 'Honey, you *DO* know I'm a transsexual?" the last word dissolving into laughter. It was the next evening at the club, a slow Tuesday show-night. This was at least the second telling for everyone and they still died at that part, amazed by yet another miracle I had wrought. Our Calpernia. She can go out and have a straight man and bring back with the most fuckinhilarious stories. It was a kind of worship, but that only made it harder to reject or defend against. I laughed. It *was* kind of funny. How silly that I had tried such a thing. They died laughing.

At home I stripped down and washed the stink and makeup of the club from my body in a hot bath. I leaned forward in the water, my forehead nearly touching its warm surface, and saw like a revelation the small, desperate force inside me that worked like a heart to keep me alive. Keep me from snuffing out my unkind, confusing existence. This revelation was numb, devoid of my usual cynical melancholy. It shone like a small light in a silent room and I realized then that the more clearly I could see it, the easier it would be to someday remove it. But this thought was distant, from outside the moment. I left that quiet room inside. I got up and dried myself. The just-washed towel smelled sweet as a baby's blanket. And there was my penis. I looked at it in the mirror, my beautiful woman's body with its soft curves marred by its jarring presence. If not for that, Christopher would have stayed, I thought. I could have gotten to know him, date him. Fuck him. But I didn't blame him at all…If he had had a vagina in those tight jeans I couldn't have done it. There was no solution, only the hurting.

17

Learning

Bad days were the swollen ones, tired from talking of horses and cancer to help pass hours beneath Amanda's searing electrolysis needle. The hurting ones when too many people looked and laughed. The empty ones when nobody saw my little victories and pinned them in place with a congratulation.

Tension lived behind the locked door of Robyn's dressing room and in her long fingernails clacking against the syringe's chamber to drive out any air. Everyone knew and then learned to let pass my tears unlocked by estrogen and the shut-away days covered in healing scabs. A new face emerged, slow, like a landscape forgotten in winter now revealed through melting snow.

Too tall. Too masculine. Too late. The words flickered and buzzed like a sign in film-noir neon just outside the window in every scene. But still I found that I could not give up. Even when I wanted nothing but to surrender, exhausted by the constant pressure of people's stares and laughter. The only way to give up was to stop living, and I was not ready for that. But the scabs healed. My hair grew. My body began to change. The days began to come when I was more often called "Ma'am" than not, and I collected them, the "Ma'ams," to count at night as I relaxed into sleep. One at the Burger King. One at the mall.

I wore light makeup, earrings, and long peasant skirts. Driving alone in my Chevy pickup I repeated, "Hello! Hello! Hi! My name is Sarah! My name is Sarah! Hi!" in a bright conversational voice, practicing tone and inflection. The simple experience of being treated as a woman by strangers became the focus of my life, and in some way I worked towards it almost every moment I was awake.

One late summer day I felt pretty for no reason and decided to fill out my thin wardrobe. I took fifty dollars and drove to the outlet mall near my apartment, windows down so that I could enjoy the warmth and sunlight.

I had an airy sensation of freedom as I walked through the racks of clothing, past full-length mirrors into which I did not even bother to look. I was enjoying myself and determined not to obsess over my appearance. When I left the store with my bag of purchases I was relaxed and thinking of nothing in particular. Just as I made it to the door, a somewhat short older man tried to pass me.

He said, "Excuse me, *Sir*."

My mood evaporated instantly. I felt prickles of embarrassment dance over my skin and a sudden vulnerability tightened in my chest. These feelings transpired in a second as the man hesitated, waiting for me to move.

And then I felt very angry.

Something was woken from fevered sleep, vicious when wounded, and as ready to cry as claw. I looked at this man, dragging my eyes up from where they had fallen on the floor to fix him in place and take measure of the space he occupied before me. He was one of thousands, a foot-soldier in an army dedicated to the destruction of my soul. I had met too many. Too many. Fury expanded and filled my body, snapping my arms and legs straight, and it seemed that I would reach out and rip this paper figure into shreds without any conscious volition. The height I had always hated gave me a sense of power and I whirled, skirt flaring, pony-tail swinging, and I actually, on purpose, *loomed* over this man. Danger roiled up from my flesh like smoke. I leaned over him, furious, and could barely hiss out my words. "*WHAT DID YOU CALL ME?*" My hands trembled to reach his skin, his face. I stared at him, ready for anything.

The man had not anticipated a throw-down in the dull family clothing store and was ruinously off balance.

"Whoa, let's not make this into somethin'" He tried to laugh it off and looked around for people to meet his nervous smile. He had casually, intentionally stripped away my dignity by calling me 'Sir.' He didn't consider me human, at least not in the way that any human being might deserve the right to walk out a door unmolested. And without dignity or humanity, in that burning moment I felt no obligation to hold anything back.

"Well why don't you pick up your *short, old* little ass and walk it *around* me if you need to get by. I could kill you as soon as look at you, you little bitch." I stood there, trembling. *Eyes,* I thought. *If he attacks, go for his eyes.* People had begun to notice us. He edged around me and pushed out the door. It closed slowly, softly, with a gentle breath of air.

"Well…" I was a bit flustered and losing steam. I turned and walked out, determined not to release the tears burning just behind my eyes. This time I had spoken up. I could have taken him down. I *would* have taken him down, I told myself.

The twentieth of the month had been my twenty-eighth birthday. Unwilling to face my parents' sad eyes, I celebrated alone with a walk at Radnor Lake. The hours of silence touched only by wind in the trees cleared my mind, allowing fragments of thought that had been buried to suddenly present themselves whole. Some of my best thinking had been done as I made my way around the three miles of trails at this mostly-deserted nature preserve. This day, pleasantly toiling my way up the staircase of railroad ties set into the side of a steep hill, I was energized by a new sense of purpose and decided it was time to take my life to the next level. I went home, bagged up all my old male clothing and put it in storage to be given to my brother. Dad's work shirt with tiny burn holes from his sparking blowtorch, the Army jacket Crystalline had bought for me in Hoenwald for 25 cents, all put away. I took some comfort in knowing that Jerm might treasure them as I had, adding his own memories to their history. Giving away these last lifelines to my old self, I was ready to embark on the next phase of my life as a woman.

18

Barry

Sunday nights at the club were quiet. The audience was different, a scattering of die-hard fans, their kidnapped straight friends and people unwilling to endure Saturday's frenetic crowds. The embers of lit cigarettes made constellations of their tiny cliques in the dark sea of empty tables and I mostly performed for myself then, ignoring them. Tips were scarce and applause clattered like a handful of pennies tossed at my dancing feet.

As usual, in the middle of the show I took the microphone and went onstage to emcee. I searched for the faces that needed my attention. The shy first-timers whose only moments of fame would be passed in the spotlit conversation I engaged before moving on, and the desperate seekers. There in the choking smoke I thought of these things while practiced words came out of my mouth as they had so many times before, and would probably for dark nights to come.

"*Alll—RIGHT!*" I began. "How the HELL is everybody!?!" I was on and the inner dialog drowned in a rush of adrenaline. My back arched, my chin went up. I looked away and leaned the microphone toward the audience. A scattering of half-hearted whoops fell dead against the cavernous theater's velvet walls. I laughed at them in exasperation.

"I see. Well, if I cain't make y'all scream as a group, I'll just have to do it one by one, and lap-dances cost money, bitches. I *SAID*, HOW Y'ALL DOIN?" Hand on hip, eyes rolled away from the audience, I pointed the microphone and tapped my patent-leather clad toe.

"WOOO!" They tried harder. They wanted to play the game. I scanned the audience, my eyes fixing on a black girl with ornately styled hair sitting beside her girlfriend.

"Girl, does your Momma still do hair?"

The spotlight picked her out and she smiled, touching the sculptured mass. "Yes!" She looked at her girlfriend. "How did she know my Momma did hair?"

"Well," I turned to the audience, "The next time you see her, tell her to get busy. You look a mess!" The laughter was loud and individual in the nearly empty room. I saw a bit of "No she didn't!" finger wagging melt into impotent darkness as I slipped away and the spotlight followed. They wanted this, I knew. In real life I'd rather gargle broken glass than insult someone. I thought about the girls upstairs rushing to change and looked for more material with which I could stall. The lighting tech panned around the room looking for freaks.

Caught in the edge of the spotlight's circle was a group of four boys who could only be Army. I could always tell by the haircut and demeanor. This group had been particularly vocal during the show, and now that I was on the mike I had every intention of 'getting' them.

"Look, Chelsey," and I directed our tech to their table, "I *knew* I smelled Aqua Velva…Straight people!" Everyone made 'Oooo!' sounds and prepared for their destruction. The boys blinked in the brilliant light, shielding their eyes. Beer bottles glowed as they broke the beam, tipped up to smiling lips. I hopped off the stage, and a few regulars hissed out the vampy count of a brushed snare drum as I moved toward their table in my black spandex mini-dress. When I arrived, the sound stopped and for an instant there was deadly silence. I adjusted my breasts and arranged my hem, then cleared my throat for a shriek.

"No, wait. That sounded fake. Ok, um…," and I shrieked again, this time more shrill, and performed my trademark fake fall into the lap of the nearest boy. My gold dusted breasts almost spilled out and I positioned them right in his face, which I casually pushed into my cleavage by means of the arm thrown around his neck for support.

"Excuse me..." I wiggled into a more secure position, milking his shocked discomfort. "What's your name, baby?"

"Uh, Steve." He looked to his buddies, who were hypnotized and still. As long as it wasn't them.

"I can barely hear you, sugar-dumplin. Lemme put this microphone out of the way so we can get closer." I wedged the cylindrical shaft between my breasts and turned to straddle his lap and face him. "Now, what did you say?" I leaned in and tossed my hair back, looking deeply into his eyes. He sat with hands held stiff out to his sides, eyes darting from my breasts to the floor. He looked like a medical specimen to me, or a child. I tried to focus.

"Steve!" The audience watched, drinking in his embarrassment. He still hadn't moved. Not wanting to overdo it, I smoothly dismounted and went around behind them to lean in between.

"Well you keep those beers comin, Steve. The more you drink, the better we look." The boys at the table broke the spell with relieved laughter and punches as the spotlight swung to follow me back to the stage.

"I'll see *you* later." I feigned clumsiness again climbing back onto the stage, falling forward with a theatrical gasp and rolling in one smooth movement to end up lying on my side with legs crossed, back arched and my head supported on my elbow. "I can't seem to stay on my feet tonight!"

"You mean off your knees!" Chelsey yelled from the lighting booth. The audience howled. I struggled up and made some final announcements before introducing the next girl. Her music started pumping and multicolored lights spilled from the stage into the dark wings, fitfully illuminating the way for me to plod upstairs and get ready for my next number.

After the first set we had a little while before the last show to come downstairs and hobnob with the audience. The other girls had their eighth or ninth cocktails and wandered from table to table, chatting up friends and fans. I remembered the table full of cute military boys and put on a gold lace dress I had just made, completely sheer. I brushed my hair out into lustrous chestnut waves parted in the usual Veronica Lake style and hurried down straight to their table.

"This is the one I told you about," The dark headed guy seemed eager for the other boys to approve. He lifted his beer bottle to his mouth and drained it, placing it among the many empties already on their table.

I smiled. "Y'all know I was just playin with you, right?" Taking the chair next to Steve, I felt powerful and sexy in my show face and clothes.

"Yeah, I've been to drag shows before." Steve seemed more comfortable now, tilting his bottle up to take a swig while talking to me. "So you're really a man?" He looked with disbelief at my figure and chest.

I leaned back in my chair, crossing my legs, and gave my standard response with a half smile. This question almost didn't even hurt tonight. "Well, I was born male but I'm all woman now. Mostly." I moved on. "So, what's everybody's names?"

"I'm Fisher," the dark headed guy said. "That's Winchell down there, and you know Mettinger already."

"Is that what your Mommas call you?"

"What?"

"What's your *first* names?"

"Justin," Fisher said.

"I'm Steve," Mettinger said, "and he's Barry." He indicated the other boy, quiet and lanky, sitting at the far end of the table. I was excited, performing in a more personal way under the attentions of these attractive men. Steve had begun to appear a little bored and excused himself to get another round of beers.

"Hey, you know who she looks like?" Justin was talking to Barry. "That girl from *E.T.*" On closer inspection I didn't find Justin attractive in the least and moved over to sit beside Barry and get a better look, trying to stay confident. The sensuality of my act tended to crumble one on one and I was still the same shy person I had always been when things moved beyond playful flirting.

"So where you from?"

"Kansas city." Barry's voice was gentle, but he looked me in the eye when he spoke.

"Well, you're not in Kansas any more! Ha ha…uh, ha…" I exaggeratedly slapped my knee and my laugh trailed off. Barry generously ignored that one and changed the subject. I realized he had been watching me intently the entire time when he finally looked away.

"You look great. You're the best one up there."

"Oh, I bet you say that to all the girls." I cringed as I said it. I talked in clichés to cover my unease, attempting coquettishness despite my entirely see-through dress and killer pumps. I felt stupid. "But thank you. I love this job…it's like Halloween every night of the year."

"Oh." He didn't seem scared of me like some boys were. Just a little nervous. I couldn't remember a time when a man had cared enough to be nervous around me. He swigged his beer and did not look away this time. Did they always drink like this? I wondered. Who is this guy?

I watched him decide what to say next. "Well, *I* think you're the best one." He set his bottle down with a little thump and leaned back in his chair, satisfied with this statement.

Although I had not even noticed Barry at first, sitting next to blond California boy Steve and extroverted Justin, his fascination and respectful manner intrigued me. As we talked my mind percolated, working out possibilities behind its front of 'Don't even think about it.' Being in the Army, I was sure he had been to occasional strip clubs and the like, and otherwise met plenty of girls, but I could tell I was something new for him. Well, you're something new for most guys who come here the first time, I thought. But for some reason he was a little off balance, and I liked it. I noticed that he allowed me to lead the conversation. I asked what he did in the Army and if he liked his job. He told me about working with weapons, and I could tell he was especially proud of his marksmanship. As a medic I hadn't had much experience in these areas, and it was interesting to hear him talk about them.

Seeing us engrossed in conversation, the other boys passed intermission on the dance floor in the front bar. In the brief span of thirty or forty minutes I began to feel a little bit of something uncomfortable. A little bit of something like dread. Talking to Barry I felt some hope for a connection, but I had felt that so many times before. It had never worked out. Not once. But maybe there was someone. Maybe. So many men had tried me, tried to have the fantasy they sweated for in sick hours alone. For survival's sake I augured their motives, flash-analyzed their sad hearts with probing, gloved fingers and cast them aside before any breach was made. It was almost clinical now, but I realized sitting there that I hadn't even begun to do that this time. The clarity of Barry's personality left me feeling suddenly still, as if a background of whispering voices had unexpectedly stopped. And of course, he was also *very* cute. The nurse inside me smiled and sighed and took off her rubber gloves, happy to have her first night off in a very long time.

His hair was a cap of soft bristles, his face young and smooth with truthful eyes and pouting lower lip. I could tell he was tall despite being folded up in a relaxed slouch, and I asked him to stand so that I could see how big he was. He complied, nervously switching his cigarette to the side of his mouth and looking at the floor. I stood in front of him, eye to eye, brushing my hand across the top of his head ostensibly to gauge his height.

"You're pretty tall yourself." He said around his cigarette, smiling a little. With the cigarette he reminded me of a young Bogart to my attempted Veronica.

"Wait." I *was* tall, but my four-inch heels were partly to blame. I put a hand on his shoulder to steady myself and stepped out of one shoe. He placed his hands on my waist and I pushed the other shoe off against my leg. Now I was looking up into his eyes, still holding on despite being completely stable barefoot. His body was firm under my fingers and the feeling that he was bigger than me was immensely exciting. As easily as I had seen his pride and interest before, I now saw a flicker of surprise and desire. There was a bit of coltish awkwardness in his long limbs, and he was so young, but he was definitely a man. Animalistic sexuality lurking at the edges of control, ready to pounce, easy to tempt and lure but hard to contain once aroused. To me that passion, overpowering and ancient, was integral to manhood and intoxicatingly present in his eyes and the way his hands felt on my body. I had to step back.

And he was definitely taller. "I think you've got me," I said.

He patted me on the head. "I guess I do."

We sat back down and I moved closer. I didn't want to make a scene with my attraction to him, although the mostly cleared out showroom was not paying any attention to us. As we talked the noise receded and I forgot I was painted up like a showgirl. With my shoes off I was vulnerable and relaxed all at once. Our conversation had come to a place where I ceased being a performer. I found myself talking about camping and military life, things I never tried to discuss with my delicate girlfriends. I carefully touched his arm and played with my hair—things *Glamour* had said a girl was supposed to do. I knew all the tricks, I thought. It came as a shock when the backstage manager announced a five-minute warning over the sound system.

"I gotta go, there's a whole 'nother show before I'm off." I stood, feeling sad because I was sure I would not see Barry again. Surprised that I let myself feel anything so quickly and intensely.

"Can I get your number? Maybe we can go out sometime."

He was asking for my number! I strangled my excitement, afraid, thrilled to have the attention of someone I considered attractive. Why does he like me? He won't call. Don't get your hopes up.

Over the years that I had been performing, men had offered me many things for my time. Drab, obese grandfathers trotted out lines about wanting to 'take care of me,' fly me to exotic locations and buy me beautiful clothes, even as photos of neglected families sweated in their leather wallets. To my cynical ear these were empty lures they had used before to score a night or two of passion, but I was no grasping, uneducated novice. I always left them angry or apathetically moving on to the next girl. Some few tried so many times that I dropped pretense and entered into a routine of insult and rejection.

Jimmy always made his way through the throngs of tippers surrounding the catwalk when I was onstage, presenting me with a big bill and locking eyes in a meaningful gaze that said, "See, this is a ten dollar bill, baby. Hot-cha-cha!" Or at least that's what I imagined him saying, in the voice of some 1940's lothario. He held onto the bill for just an instant too long, so that I had to stoop uncomfortably before pulling back. After the show he waited for me at the foot of the stage, usually with one or two pretty call-girls at his table.

After the first set I would prepare myself for intermission and go downstairs. As I stepped off the stage Jimmy sidled up. Years of professionalism stifled a look of dismay before it ever surfaced.

"Have you ever been to Jamaica? What name should I put on the ticket?" he purred, pear shaped and middle-aged in his gray suit and tie-less shirt. He awaited my gushing excitement.

In my flattest tone I said, "Janet Tyler." and tried to move past. He didn't budge, or get the reference.

"It's gorgeous this time of year. The beaches—"

"I hate the sun. I like to be pale."

"You look good pale." If central casting were looking for someone to fill the role of 'salacious octopus,' I could have booked Jimmy out for top wages. His beady eyes rolled over my body and I couldn't help imagining the horror of his sweat-lubricated palms against my flesh. He paid no attention to the working girls waiting a step behind him and I knew anyone accepting his gifts would join them, no longer exciting once under his command.

I excused myself and walked towards the bar. He followed, taking me by the elbow.

"Well, I have my own investment business." As I well knew, since he said so every time we talked. "I can take you anywhere you'd like to go. You like…um, Europe?" He was beginning to sound exasperated, as if he were losing patience with a difficult child.

"Oh, I'd sooner walk seven miles on my tongue over broken glass and lick a lemon than ask you to go to any trouble for *me*." I had begun to feel threatened by his persistence and wild offers, so I resorted to ridiculousness. His face clouded, not amused, temperament shifting like the alcoholic dad's in a movie-of-the-week.

"What's the fucking problem?!? I can give you anything! What do you want?" He said, voice raised in agitation. His brow creased and he seemed so transparent in that moment, like a horrible insect larva whose pulsating organs were visible through the flesh. If I hadn't been so unsettled by his outburst I would have laughed at him. My refusals of his gifts confounded him and his entire demeanor was volatile now.

My self-assurance was far above what it had been in the past, but when a man raised his voice to me my eyes stung where the tears had once come. My playful confidence faltered, but now rather than dissolving I became angry. Polite humor vanished and my face hardened into a disgusted scowl.

"I don't '*want*' anything from you, you stupid freak. I have everything I need. Back off." I pushed past, trembling and trying not to cry.

Tonight I was enthralled. I wanted to get Barry's number before I had to go back to work so I went to the bar, trying not to walk too quickly. I begged a pen and paper from the bartender, Rod. He glanced at Barry and comically arched an eyebrow, giving me a thumbs up.

Steve and Justin were just returning from the front and came up beside me to buy another round of beers. I bumped them, one on each side, with my hips and smiled before going back to the table.

"Here, call me any time night or day, because I'm up all hours." Normally I was emphatic that no one dare wake me before twelve noon. "I would love to take you to this coffeehouse I go to all the time." I was nervous he might be scared to be seen in public with me in case I was clocked, so I threw in "Everybody knows me there, I go all the time and never have any trouble."

"O.K. babe, I'll call you tomorrow and we can see when's a good time." I thought it was cute that he called me 'babe,' a subtle thing that would have caused some of my friends to gag but somehow made me feel more girly.

"Don't go anywhere! Bye!"

The overture was starting as I raced up the few stairs onto the stage, slowing down to an exaggerated strut as I crossed to the break in the curtains. Barry's table hooted and I slipped through with a flourish, blowing him a kiss.

It was difficult for me to finish the show. I felt that in a little window of time Barry had seen past my glittering, sensual stage persona and spoken directly to a person unused to company. The part of me that was left when all the makeup was washed away and the judging eyes shut out behind the walls of my room. I found it sexy when a man looked at me lustfully but treated me with the same respect he would any normal girl. He let me know I was attractive without cheapening it by simultaneously grabbing my ass, a courtesy that made me want to trust my feelings about him. 'You're an idiot.' I said into the mirror. I rushed to repowder my face and fluff my hair. Our backstage manager, Devin, realized I was running behind and zipped me into my big production dress with one hand while making announcements on the mike held in the other. I ran back down the stairs to find Regine and Stephanie clucking like hens in the dark.

"Hmmm! I saw you talking to that man. Cute, girl!" Regine spoke around the hairpins in her mouth, and her slightly accented voice was playful as she twisted her long black hair into a formal knot. "You gonna get you some?"

Stephanie smoothed her dress, lips pursed in mock disapproval. "Pernie's found a little action, I see."

"Y'all, I'm not…"

"And now, ladies and gentlemen, welcome to the stage the *CAST OF LE BOY LA FEMME!*" Devin's eyes bulged as he urged us into place. The curtain parted. We turned on cue and began the routine to "Dream Girls," swaying in our navy-blue gowns.

"WE'RE YOUR DREAM GIRLS...BOY, WE'LL MAKE YOU HAPPY..."

Barry stayed for my first number of the second show, but he must have left immediately after, because when I came out for my second I peered into the dark through the spotlight and saw the table was empty. I tried not to feel let down, and prepared myself for the possibility that there would be no call, no date and no man. 'I didn't have one yesterday, I won't miss one tomorrow.' I told myself.

There is a radio station in Nashville that is only on after dark. WANB 98.7, "*Beautiful Music Through the Night!*," defines its play list as Big Band/Nostalgia. It is solely supported by Music City Sewer and Drain and has one commercial script read by three different voices. Each spot serenely extols the interdependence of plumbing and civilization between a heavy rotation of sultry torch singers, classics from Ellington to Ella, and strange '70's arrangements of preternaturally happy choirs harmonizing entirely in 'Dooo doo de *Doo!*'s. When I drove home in my old Chevy truck after an exhausting show, the music cleared my mind of the soulless pop I'd been bombarded with all night. I liked to imagine I was a tragic heroine in an old movie, hair wavy and carefully arranged, my face a porcelain mask embellished with red lips and arched eyebrows. I didn't know these goddesses intimately the way some fans did, but the women of this era looked so clean to me, so pure and stylish on the screen. They possessed an elegance I feared I would never share. But that night riding home in the dark, my new hope stirred and I allowed it to alight. I turned the radio way up, and was surrounded by bright horns and the fragile glistening of notes like a thousand tiny bubbles floating in air.

The next morning the phone rang. I never got up before noon, but the insistent sound invaded my dreams until I recognized it was real and pulled myself up to look at the caller ID. It was not a local area code, and the previous night came back to me. I snatched up the phone, desperately clearing my throat before answering. My voice was most husky right when I woke up.

"Hello?" I whispered, trying to keep my tone feminine as my just-awoken consciousness fell into place bit by bit.

"Hey, this is Barry...we met last night at the club?" Oh my God, it was him!

"*Hi!* I'm so glad you called!" My hair stuck out in a huge frizz and I rubbed the grit from my eyes. Don't sound too desperate. Remember, *you're* the showgirl. You've probably been called by a man before, I told myself. Don't act like this is all new for you.

But this *was* new to me. It was so exciting to be talking to a normal guy, especially one in the Army. Barry was eager to tell about his day and how he had come to be at the club last night. While speaking, he quickly reacquainted me with the military habit of referring to people only by last name. His crazy roommate Fisher, whom everyone called 'Fish,' was at the show the previous weekend and had come back saying they had to see this one girl who worked there. Me. So out they came the following Sunday. And thus a potential new boyfriend was dropped into my lap, I thought. Or I dropped into his lap...or something. I took a deep mental breath, forcing myself to wake up so that I could go ahead and ask some big questions.

"So, have you ever hung out with a transsexual before? I hate that word...It sounds like an alien or something." Stupid. Let him talk, I thought.

"No, no...I've...I never have," Barry said. "But I've seen a drag show before and I thought the girls were really pretty. I think you're really pretty."

"Well thank you...Um, I know this is stupid to ask..." I paused, compelled to get it over with. "Why are you interested in me? I mean, I'm glad you are, if you are. I'm just wondering..."

Barry didn't say anything and my stomach shrank. He didn't seem quite sure himself, but then he said, "At first, you know, I just thought 'Damn, she's pretty'...but then you came up and talked to me and I thought you were cool, too. I dunno..."

"No, that'sOk, I just have to ask because I get nervous about stuff sometimes. I'm just kinda crazy. In a good way." I laughed, holding on. I hoped that somehow I was coming across as cute and quirky, versus creepy and crazy.

Thankfully, Barry hadn't answered with the dreaded 'I've always wanted to do drag and I was hoping you could teach me,' staple of a performer's dating experience. I knew plenty of queens who had ended up with husbands borrowing their drag to start embarrassing, short-lived careers. *I* didn't even want to be a queen, much less go out with one.

Barry and I made a date to meet around six P.M. at my favorite place downtown, Café CoCo. After I hung up I realized that my face, which had been covered by stage makeup last night, was still irritated from the electrolysis I had on Friday. I knew it would not be very lovely in the light of day. I fell backwards into my pillow, eyes squeezed shut, and groaned.

I dragged myself out of bed and started a cold shower. My plan was to spend all morning babying my face so that it could look its best in the evening. After running frigid water over the inflamed skin and scrubbing myself clean, I pulled my hair into a ponytail and selected a top and jeans to get me through a trip to the grocery store. I knew the only things that might help were aloe vera and Motrin. Going out when my face was messed up was painfully embarrassing for me. Normally I could leave the house fairly confidently without makeup, but I felt my irritated face was too telling and walked with a stiff back against everyone's imagined jeers. It would have required heavy concealer to cover, which was itself a giveaway. In the past my impulse was to choke down my fragile new identity and not even try in order to avoid harassment. This was invariably demoralizing and had become more difficult as my breasts developed, my hips filled out and my hair grew longer and longer.

On this day, in girl's jeans and a T-shirt, hair back and face freshly scrubbed if a little red, I took new confidence in the fact that a straight man wanted to go out with me. He wouldn't have asked if I looked like a man, I reasoned. With this subtle but powerful self-assurance I walked into the supermarket and smiled at the cashier, whatever she thought of me. The fact is, I realized, she probably wasn't thinking anything about me. I was just another face among hundreds.

As the hour of my date approached I looked in the mirror and felt pretty good. Thanks to, or perhaps despite, the ice, the slimy aloe, the pills, and the antibacterial soap, my skin looked nearly normal. I applied a touch more powder and concealer than usual, some cherry Chap Stick for a bit of shine and color, and then mascara. I let my hair fall in its natural curls and wore a full skirt with a simple top the color of ocean storm clouds. One final, critical assessment left me feeling I looked as good as could be expected under the circumstances, and with that grim consolation I was off to the coffeehouse.

The city had expanded and consumed the trees that once shaded the old house that was now Cafe CoCo. Inside, the floors and trim were dark wood. The walls had been finished to look like cracked plaster, and the glass in the windows had settled slightly, so that looking out through the lower edges gave a rippled view of the funky vintage stores and restaurants that made up Nashville's Bohemian district. I felt comfortable in the café's mix of college students, dancers, and eccentrics, but I rarely ventured speaking to anyone. Instead I'd bring a book and sip black coffee, inhaling the nostalgic scent of clove cigarettes and feeling that I was at least making an effort to be near a social group.

This day I was running a little late, as usual, because I had been so busy with my face. My truck had long ago surrendered such amenities as air conditioning and now concentrated solely on the labor of carry-ing me from one place to the next. I hoped I would not entirely sweat off my makeup, and decided to avoid all anxiety by simply not looking into the rear view mirror. In a short time I reached the café and parked, my nervousness and excitement mounting the closer I got to seeing him. I wondered if he would even be here…and what he would think once he saw the way I looked in real life.

I silently repeated my mantra, 'Posture, Voice, Confidence…' as I walked toward the patio, scanning for Barry's shaved head among the dreads and colorful hair of the regulars. No luck. I smiled and mouthed 'hello' to a few stray fans seated on the patio. He was waiting at a table immediately inside.

Barry stood, reaching out to take my hand. I was all curves in my ankle-skimming gray skirt and gauzy top. The black hematite bracelets I never took off sparkled at my wrists.

"Sorry I'm late. I'm so glad you came!" I shook his nervously offered hand and pulled him into a hug.

"Hey, I'm glad you made it. I was getting worried about you." Barry looked down when he smiled, his body draped in a loose shirt and baggy jeans. I gestured him over to the counter, eager hostess in my domain.

"So this is where I come all the time…I practically live here. I love it because you can just have conversation and stuff…" I was talking too much, too fast, not looking at Barry but lightly touching his shoulder as we went toward the register. He slipped his arm loosely around my waist and put both hands on the counter's edge as he leaned in to study the menu, leaving me pleasantly trapped between his body and the counter. This was somewhat forward and lasted only a second, but I thrilled at the contact, at the unspoken acceptance of me that this small public display of affection carried.

My friend Shell, a petite English woman, was tending bar. "Hello, Calpy. Iced Mocha?"

"I'll have black coffee and *this*," I said, popping out from his arms to open the cooler behind us and wrangle a heavy chocolate cheesecake onto the counter. Barry ordered the same and paid both our bills. We went to sit in the deserted smoking room and I looked closely at him in the light for the first time. Sitting across from me was a picture of sprawling boyishness. I sipped black coffee wondering why and how he might really be interested in me. Whether I should be interested in him. I noticed he was looking back at me and smiling.

"You know who you look like…" He began. Dammit.

"Drew Barrymore." I just gave up and didn't even add 'But I don't see it.'

"Yeah…It's your—"

"Mouth." There was a pause.

"What are you thinking?" he asked. I didn't want him to know how insecure I was. What to say…

"Oh, I'm just glad to be out having coffee and conversation. It's been forever since I've had any time with somebody outside the club." There, not bad, not really a lie.

"I would think you'd have tons of guys hitting on you all the time. I couldn't believe you wanted to go out with me."

The poor boy thought I was actually some kind of a rare prize. I hardly ever went on dates because the only men who asked me out were freaks. "Yes, I do get a lot of attention, but it's rarely from anybody I like."

"Ohhh…poor little superstar." He gave my hand a few pats of mock sympathy and then closed his rough fingers over mine. I liked it when someone felt confident enough to poke a little fun at me. I was liking him more every minute.

We talked and I ate, first my cheesecake and then the rest of his. He lit up a cigarette and drank coffee. I drank coffee and ate some more. The pale light coming in through the windows grew darker and hours evaporated unnoticed. The noisy, false life I led at the club was nowhere and nothing, and I allowed myself for a moment to imagine being with someone who accepted me as I was, who didn't think of me as a man in a dress. The club was the only place that had let me in unquestioned, and although I had found success among its drugs and dysfunction, I was not a part of those things. Smoke curled up from his lips, expanding into nothing before half-closed eyes as we sat and talked about everything that came to mind.

Barry drank a lot of coffee. I was pleased, seeing this as confirmation that I had chosen our first meeting spot well.

"Yeah, whenever I go out into the field I hafta have my coffee." Barry leaned in as if telling a favorite story, punctuating his speech with jabs of his cigarette hand. "I fill this thermos with the good stuff and take it with me, not that shit they put in the MRE's. Sarge always says 'Winchell, how 'bout summa that coffee?'" He imitated the gruff voice of his sergeant. I remembered the scientifically engineered 'Meals, Ready to Eat' and their tiny green packets of coffee dust.

"What do you do when you're in the field? Just practice camping and sneaking up on each other and stuff?" My own times in the cold and dirt of field exercises were long ago, and I wanted to hear his story. Besides, it seemed more feminine not to know about such things.

"Yeah, that, and also I get to launch TOW missiles sometimes. That's my main thing."

"Is that what you do? Shoot the missiles?"

"Yeah, whenever we actually get to fire a missile they want me to do it, because they know I can hit the target." He tapped his chest and leaned back with his arms behind his head. "Top Gun here."

I jabbed him in the stomach with my finger and he snapped out of the stretch with a laugh.

"You guys don't get to fire missiles all the time?"

"No, no...They cost about ten thousand dollars each."

"No way!"

"Yeah. After you fire 'em they leave this metal cord behind, it's part of the guidance system, and we have to go pick all that up. Look, I cut the *fuck* outta my hands on it." He held them out for my inspection.

Thin red lacerations were scored across his fingers and palms, partially healed over but still stinging, I imagined. I held one hand in mine and lightly ran my finger over one of the cuts.

"Do they hurt?"

"No, it's just like a paper cut."

I thumped the hand I was holding right on the shallow marks. "Now do they hurt?" I laughed and tried to snatch my hand away but he caught my wrist.

"Ow! You think that's funny?" He was smiling, a little amazed by my twists and turns. If he was like most guys I remembered from the military, this kind of thing was standard play among the boys.

"So you're all famous and everything. What's that like?"

"Oh I'm nobody."

"Half this place jumped up and tried to say hello when we walked in."

"Being famous just gives you a bigger arena to fuck up in. A lotta people know me from the show, is all."

"You just said fuck." Barry did that little salacious smile around his cigarette again.

"Shut up!"

Barry related more small details of his days to me, lovingly quoting statistics for weapons ranges and specifications that I would never have been able to remember. His manuals were normally always close at hand, he said. Except on first dates.

"Mmm, so this is a date then?"

"Well, yeah!"

After way too much coffee and numerous cigarettes, we finally prepared to leave. I realized with a rush of warm excitement deep in my chest that I felt completely normal. I had forgotten that I was anything other than a girl on a date. I almost cried. It was like stepping out of a long confinement into the clean air. As we made our way to the parking lot I tried to commit the sensation to memory, planning to enjoy it later when I was alone.

"I guess I better get back." We were standing beside my truck. I knew he had driven a hour to be here.

"Do you have to, uh, 'work' in the morning?"

"Yeah." The sky was orange and pink behind us, and Baptist Hospital stood two blocks away, outlined in gold.

"That's where I was born." I pointed at it.

"I can come over, if you want." He was looking at me, his eyes meeting mine when I turned back to him.

"Ok."

"Ride with me." We got into his car. He opened my door first. The world rolled past us and we didn't talk much the whole way, except to ask and give directions. I held his hand. I leaned against his shoulder. He kissed my fingers, keeping his eyes on the road. I was so happy. So happy.

19

Visit to Chicago

Maggie Miller was a Nashville girl who had made her transition quietly. Slightly built and petite, it seemed relatively easy for her to blend in and work a normal job, although I'm sure she has her own stories, as all of us in the sisterhood do. While I toiled away on the stage she took classes and built up seniority and eventually moved away to the big city of Chicago, becoming a legend among the struggling girls left behind. A year later a fellow showgirl and friend, Maddie Chamberlain, packed away her gowns and went to live with her. They were beautiful and passable and working corporate jobs in the city, and the first chance I got I took three days off and went to visit, seeking inspiration. Maddie picked me up at the airport looking like a model in huge sunglasses and her thick blond hair.

"Pernie! Honey, you look soft as butter! Look at you!" Soft meant feminine. She hugged me and I smelled her perfume. She was so *real* looking. It always stunned me.

"I cain't believe I'm here! Chicago! Woo hoo!" I had been nervous traveling as a woman, it was my first time, but the moment I saw Maddie I felt energized. Damn them all, there were two of us! We collected my luggage and as we drove toward the suburbs she caught me up on life in the big city.

"Maggie's gonna meet us out later. I know you probably wanna get cleaned up and have a little supper before anything." She almost dropped her cigarette cursing when a cab slammed on its brakes in front of us. "Goddammit, these Chicago fucks are worse drivers than anybody in Nashville ever *thought* about bein. I was in a cab last night

and his breath smelled like he just ate the crotch out of a dead whore."
She had a smoky, sultry voice and whether it was the way it carried her
always-shocking jokes on a thick Southern accent or simply her overall
drop-dead gorgeousness, everyone fell immediately in love with her.

That night we took a cab to Maggie's apartment and decided to
walk to a club called Berlin from there. Maggie wore jeans and a little
top, nothing special. Her hair was black and in shoulder length waves.
Apparently she and Maddie had abandoned their Nashville showgirl
wardrobes for a more casual real-girl look. I felt like a dope in my
stretchy pants and tight top.

"Well, looky here what the cat's drug in!" Maggie's accent was worse
than Maddie's. She held me out at arm's length and looked me over.
"You look mighty nice…for a *praw*-sti-tute!" She then hugged me, the
standard Southern thing to do after an insult. We were laughing so
much.

"She doesn't know any better yet, honey. We'll get her in line."
Maddie patted me on the back.

"Y'all are like the bigger, older sisters I never wanted." I loved the
attention.

"Now sugar, you know all up and down Belmont is where the *workin girls* make their spendin money. You're gonna have to find somewhere else to…"

"This top is not that bad, freaks. It's just tight is all. I cain't help it if
I have a beautiful body."

"Oh lord, let's get it a goin, y'all could do this all night." Maddie
picked up her purse and started for the door.

"So who's this boy you been fuckin?" I had been telling Maddie
about Barry over the phone before I came.

"No, we're actually dating. His name's Barry and he's in the Army."

"Ohhh." Maggie cut her eyes away in an exaggerated pantomime of
poorly concealed embarrassment. "You know them Army boys are
always good news."

"This one is a good guy, Maggie. We've already been on tons of dates and he's nice and calm and actually straight."

Maddie laughed. "Straight onto your cock." Maggie busted out laughing too and they fell on my shoulders from either side.

"Oh we're sorry, honey. Go ahead, you were sayin he was straight..." A car pulled up beside us and honked. "Ignore that. He thinks we're whores." We walked on past, quiet for a second. I was stung by her comment. The car pulled away.

"Barry is straight. He only likes girls. We've already talked about it, he had a girlfriend before me, she was an ice skater."

"Okay, so what then...do you hide it?"

"Well it's not the focus of things, if you know what I mean..."

Maggie patted my shoulder. "So you're gettin yer jibs busted and then he hits the road?" I reeled with a mixture of embarrassment and frustration. A dirty van slowed to match out pace and honked. We ignored it and it went away.

"No! I..."

"So you're the top?" They were teasing me, laughing. I had to laugh too, but they were driving me crazy. It was so exciting to be there, in the city, walking with them in the night. Those bitches.

"No, I'm not the top. No he doesn't just have sex and leave. We go on dates, rent movies, go out to eat and drink coffee. It's really nice. He treats me like a girlfriend." I guess they could hear a little edge in my voice.

"Oh Pernie, you know I'm happy for you. We're just kiddin, you know that." We all took hands and swung out to avoid a bum.

"Wait..." I went back and took a dollar from my purse. "Have fun," I said, dropping it into his cup, and caught back up to the girls.

"Girl, you can't give out money here or they'll be on you like flies on shit..."

"Anyway, back to Barry, so how does he take it that you haven't had your operation yet?"

"He doesn't care if I have it or not, he said. At first I kept myself hidden during sex, you know…"

"You just blew him?"

I halted mid-stride. "God, y'all, stop with the filth for just one minute! Good lord!" They were chastised and silent. "Yeah, we just made out and all that at first, but finally he just said whatever and…you know, while we were kissin…he…stuff…You know. I still kinda don't like him *seein* me, but he said he loves me and it doesn't matter."

The girls put their arms on my shoulders from either side and Maggie kissed me on the cheek. "I'm glad for you, girl. If anybody deserves somethin nice, it's you."

"All them drugged out beasts and bitches up there, I can't believe you've stayed so sweet after all this time. You been drunk yet?"

"Not a drop. To this day I have still never tasted alcohol ever. Well, except when I kiss Barry after he's been drinkin. I guess I can finally say I know what beer tastes like, once removed." A Lexus pulled up beside us at the light just before the club, which I could see ahead with a short, eclectic line of people waiting outside. The driver rolled down his passenger side window and started to speak.

We turned to him in unison and screamed, "*FUCK OFF!*"

"God *bless!* Ain't they hungry for it up here? Why does everybody assume just because we're transies that we're whores?"

"I know, honey. It makes me sick how people always assume the worst."

20

Relationship

"Are you gonna get to come?" It had been a horrible day. I was imagining his firm body against me, and the way his downy short hair felt on my neck when he kissed my collarbone. My piece of crap cordless phone hissed and popped, and I waited for his words to come through sixty miles of overcast trees and limestone hills to my darkened apartment.

"I want to, I really do. I don't know if I can leave tonight or if I have to wait till tomorrow, though. You really want me to come?"

"Yes, Barry!" Softly exasperated. *I like you, get it?*

"Ok. Lemme finish some stuff I have to do and I'll call you later. But it'll be late if I can come tonight at all." He sounded happier, and then I realized he must have been a bit down when I called.

"Well do what you gotta do. The house is ready for you and I have a surprise, too."

"I've already seen it."

"Not that, doofus. Bye, and hurry up." I was smiling.

"Bye."

The patio's sliding glass door was open, along with most of the windows, welcoming a faraway storm that spilled and ran across the clouded afternoon sky from a dark point just beyond the treeline. I knew it was going to be a good night if the rain was coming. The light was stained black and the trees and clouds seemed to glow from within, agitated by gusts of preparation for the coming of a greater wind. I turned off every light and put on the gentlest music, piano like moonlight on water. The stale smell of old carpet was exposed by the fresh air and chased away without resistance. I retrieved a massive green candle from the bathroom and set it on one of the club's café tables I had relocated to my patio, and then swept away the matted leaves and twigs collected there. The wind outside was cool and strong, and I stopped a moment to stand with my eyes closed. Acres of sepia- and tar-colored leaves filled the space behind my eyes, dripping silver. I savored the feel of it on my face, pulling at my hair and swirling the hem of my gypsy skirt. I thought of the shoreline along Kuluk Bay on Adak, and the invisible strength of the living ocean air. I had been so alone there. I had gone there to die. It was a lifetime ago.

I lay on the couch with nothing to do and began to fall in and out of sleep, listening to the movement of leaves outside. The music had played to its end, and now there were only the sounds from outside. In the semi-dark room I could as well have been in some sheltered grotto. Some other place, magical and wild. 'What is the most overused metaphor in bad poetry?' Crystalline asked me, an echo.

'Dancing. The water danced across the rocks. The trees danced in the wind. But I don't know if that's really as much a metaphor as a...'

'Yes. Danced. Don't you ever write me a poem where something dances.'

'I won't.' My consciousness shifted like heavy layers of sand in a Saharan dusk, slow and low to the ground. I saw Barry dancing in the club with me between shows, looking at the floor. I caught his eye and laced my fingers behind his narrow waist. It felt so good to touch someone. To feel that they wanted me to touch them. Sometimes every inch of air between two people was a gauntlet of pain that could not be breached. His free hand rested on my bare shoulder. Played with the thin strap of my top. His fingers were dry and rough.

'Your skin is so soft.' and he slipped his fingers down my back a little, just to feel the place between my shoulder blades where no one else ever touched me. 'Like a baby.' He took a sip of his beer. His lips were deep red, and his eyes smiled back at mine.

'*You* look like a baby. That cute little face...' and I reached up to stroke it. I liked to feel the scratch of his invisible stubble. He looked like a baby but he was a man. He kissed my fingers. The music pounded, meaningless as air, and I was aware in that instant of the people around us, dancing. The sweating, desperate people and the joyous ones. The drugs and drag and secrets open only here, still creased and ready to be folded back up into rotten little packages that no one would mind outside in the daylight. We were one of them, I thought. They were all reflections, distorting whatever we were and making it ugly. I hated them.

But I looked away from this, into his bright face, innocent and happy, and his fingers were still exploring me as we danced.

'Let's go. Back upstairs.'

'Why?'

'I hate this.'

'What? Me?' He was suddenly more present.

'Barry, you're the only thing here I don't hate. These people. These freaks.' I pulled him off the floor and he submitted to my dragging hand. We went into the dark towards one of the secret doors that led backstage. I jammed my key into the lock and turned it without looking, a smoothness of years guiding me in the dark. We slipped out of the noise and I locked the door behind us. Here the walls were exposed lumber and drywall. A string of red Christmas lights had been plugged into an outlet and tossed on the floor in the dust for illumination. Barry stopped, halting my flight, and I did not want to let go of his hand. I sighed. He leaned against the wall, a black shadow in the red lights at his feet, and pulled my body in between his legs. His hands were on my waist and I leaned away, but he drew me back. I pressed my face into his t-shirt, smelling cologne and sweat, and tried not to cry. Barry said something in the dark I couldn't hear and hugged me so tight it squeezed the breath from me.

'That stupid loud stupid *music*. I hate this place so much. I hate it.' His chest was a sanctuary against the blackness outside. I pressed into it and inhaled his scent like oxygen.

'I said I love you.'

'Oh god.' I hadn't been expecting this. You couldn't possibly, I thought. You have no idea. You'll see, you just haven't yet. The flaws. The bad stuff. I'd be waiting every day for you to open your eyes and then you'll go…

'I said I love you. Do you…' He guided me away from his chest and we looked at each other, glistening eyes in black faces in the dark. I couldn't hear the music anymore.

'Barry…I already did. I already did love you. I mean I already do. As much as I can, just having met. I can tell you're special. But you can't take it away, if you say that. At least not for a long time. I was wishing you loved me, and if…I mean you can take it back if you want to. Right now. If you're not sure, take it back right now.'

'Don't tell me to fuckin take it back. If I say something I mean it, and you can take it or leave it, but to be honest I was hoping you would be a little more excited about it than this.'

I found myself laughing. I was so stupid. 'I believe you. I'm sorry…' I could hardly speak. I grabbed at unfinished thoughts not ready for the open air. 'I didn't think you'd ever come. I was just so used to being alone, you know…But…'

'Damn.' He smiled and leaned down to press his lips ever so lightly against mine. I felt the words like satin. 'Shut up.'

I awoke with a sharp gasping inhalation, as if I had been holding my breath for hours. I was still clutching the telephone. It had been raining and the carpet in front of the patio door was wet. "Dern it." The VCR said it was midnight-thirty. Barry wasn't going to come. I got up and walked outside, unwilling to put down the phone yet, and looked out into the trees. The candle was full of water and a suicide from amongst the clouds of chalk and sawdust colored moths gathered around the porch lights of the other apartments. I started to dump it out over the rail and when the phone in my other hand rang I started so violently I dropped the candle into the dark grass a story below.

"Hello? Hello?"

His voice was easy. Tired. "Hey babe. You up for some company?"

"Good lord, Barry. I was afraid you weren't gonna get to come."

"You were? Awww…You know I wouldn't miss seeing you if I could help it."

"Well come on! Get it a goin, it's an hour drive."

"I'm already here. At the 7-Eleven down the street."

"Yay! What did you call from there for, you shoulda…"

"Just wanted to make sure you were there. I'll be right over."

"OK, bye." I rushed to the bathroom to see what I looked like. Not terrible.

I took off my shoes to answer the door, to be as short as possible, but it didn't matter. He was always taller than me. Old habits. At the first knock I pulled him inside and pushed him backwards over the arm of the couch. My hair was loose and curly, wild in the humidity, and my bare face shone free of any makeup. I felt beautiful, like an elemental spirit from out of the earth, and lust coursed in hot, thick rivers across my skin, an ache to be touched.

"Hey…"

I crawled on top, kissing him, starving. My hair fell across our faces and blocked out the room around us and he closed his eyes, tasting my lips. He grabbed hold of my hips with both hands and forced me against him, and I felt his body awaken already, urgent, grinding, desperate to merge. I threw my arm around behind his head and held him tight to kiss him more deeply. Our breathing hissed out from flared nostrils and around probing tongues, and I could not inhale enough of his scent. His fingers scrabbled along my legs to find the bottom of my skirt and then yanked it up, tearing the gauzy cotton. We laughed into each other's mouths at the sound of ripping and I arched myself up to slip it down past my hips enough for him to remove it completely. I loved the feel of my bare skin against his jeans, his dark tanned hands on my pale thighs. He rolled me onto my back, straddling me, and pulled up my shirt to reveal my breasts. I watched him lean back and look at me, exposed and vulnerable beneath his weight. I reached up and he forced my wrist back to the couch, and held it there.

"Take off your shirt." He smiled, released me and took it off. His skin was white and soft and tight across lean muscles. I traced his funny little tattoo of an eye and pulled him down onto me. He was slower now, watching me, gentle. When he kissed my neck I caressed his ear with my lips and whispered, "I love you."

He made a sound, a deep Mmm of contentment into my collarbone and worked his way down. He cupped my breasts and pushed them together, tasting them and exploring the chasm and curves he had created. He kneaded them, devouring and licking and biting until I could not wait another moment and threw him off of me entirely.

"What?"

"To the boudoir. Now."

"Whatever you say."

I led him past the gray glow of the open patio door, two shadows in a sleeping house. In my room a window fan drew in the air and billowed white and burgundy curtains I had hung around the bed. Chiffon. I saw him then, naked and powerful, the figure of a man with his hard, tight frame and long limbs tensed in anticipation of what he was about to enjoy. There was no guile in his eyes, only simple longing and an unwavering gentle kindness that never went out, in all the time he looked at me. We fell inside and his weight was on me.

"Take off your panties."

I didn't want to. I felt embarrassed. I pulled at him to lay on top of me again.

"Sarah. Take them off. It's just me."

"Aw, don't ruin it, Barry. I will, in a minute." He couldn't like that part of me. A deeper part of my mind returned a distorted echo: He shouldn't like that part of me. A girlfriend had once said, 'mostly the only guys who like us, they like us for the one part we wish we didn't have. That's why we hate them.' This time you're wrong, I thought.

He kissed me, inside the pale streaming fabric and it was like we were in the clouds, in that kind of cold heaven I used to imagine that had nothing to do with Jesus and the Bible. Storm clouds and soft light and a beautiful honest man kissing me. Everything else just fell away and did not matter. He slipped a hand between us and I lifted up, allowing them to slide down past and fall to the floor, outside the clouds. Skin to skin now. Warmth in the cold.

"There are so many stories I could tell you…" It was hours and a trip to Café CoCo later. We rode the split from Broadway into Division and West End, following the right side. Barry's car handled smooth, and soft music from the radio was almost carried away in the rush of open windows and into the night. There was Tower Records, where Latarsha had worked as a girl, the amazing first time I had ever seen one of us step into the daylight job world and blend. There was the turn for Dragon Park, where Helen Ziekland from Hume-Fogg had burned an American flag in 1988 and been sprayed in the eyes with mace.

"That's the Parthenon. When I was in junior high, I was still so brainwashed that I called it the 'porn-a-thon' because of the naked statues."

"You don't have much of a problem with being naked now."

"Nope."

"What's this place we're going to?"

"I've never been there—"

"Oh great…" Barry laughed around his cigarette.

"I've never been there, but I know where it is. Pretty much. It's like a 'Lookout Point' kinda thing. You can see the whole city from it."

We rolled on through flashing yellow stoplights, streetlights and past dark cottage stores selling antiques and shampoo. Old houses twinkled on a great uprising in the landscape to our left, among the trees that grew even here at the city's edge, and I directed Barry to turn in. The road zigzagged up the improbably steep hill, past old-people yards free of any toy that cost less than what I made in a year, and after a false turn or two we made the summit. Barry parked in a gravel crescent, and we got out to walk up the last bit to the top of a grassy hill crowned with a single metal spire antenna that reached higher than I could see in the dark. There were two other couples here, college-y teens on a blanket and a middle-aged pair, laughing at something. They paid us no mind.

"Hey, you really can see everything." Barry held my hand and took a drag from his cigarette. He seemed so glad to be with me. It was exciting to be here with him, with other couples, a part of normal life. Where gay couples made out in public they were arrested amidst much disgust at their perversion. Where straight couples made out in public, it was called 'Lovers Lane.' I felt a little guilty here on the other side, towards those I'd left behind. They never let me forget my origins, though. No one told my secret to incredulous straight friends quicker than my dear gay pals. I hugged Barry, and kissed him. He led me over to stand against a fence around the tower and I leaned back into his chest to look at the stars and lights opened up before us. His arms felt nice around me, the one hand holding a little embered cigarette close to my ear. When the breeze carried its scent past my face it seemed like sweet incense, because I wanted him near me, like this, so badly. 'They always leave.' A voice said. 'I know. But there can be a first time for anything...' I replied. Mom had always said that.

"What's your dream?" Barry said.

"Hmm...I don't know. To have somebody I can count on, I guess."

"You're just saying that because I'm here. What else?"

"No, I mean it. But if you mean what else besides that...I want to be an actress. For real. Not like what I do now."

"I like your shows."

I turned in his arms to face him and met his clear eyes with a look that might have been desperate. "Barry, what I do now is a joke. It's as hard as being a real actress, or maybe harder since there's no big payoff outside the gay bars, but when it comes down to it, real people laugh at drag queens. We're a punchline, an episode of Jerry Springer."

"Sarah, straight people aren't 'real people' any more than you are. You're a straight girl to me, anyway, if that matters for anything, but you have to stop putting yourself down like that no matter what. All those people in the club are just like you and me, trying to get some and find somebody they like, and that's not a bad thing. It doesn't make you weird because you're around them. They're normal, and so are you. So am I."

"Barry how do you know all this?"

"If you don't feel the same way, that's cool…"

"No, you're right. I just mean, how can you be so understanding about this stuff? I try, but it makes me sick sometimes…"

"I don't know. It seems right. You can't get all fucked up outta shape just because some drag queens are hitting on people and guys are kissing…"

"Do you know how crazy it is for you to be saying that to me?" I had to laugh, at myself. "God, I am so stupid."

Barry grabbed me tighter, pressed himself into me and tilted his head down to touch noses. "I don't ever want to hear that again. You understand me?" Nose to nose, he shook his head side to side, making me do the same. "Never never never."

I smiled. It felt good to let go. "Ok. I promise."

"You have the most beautiful eyelashes, you know that?"

I pulled back. "Mom told me when I was born the nurse said, 'That baby has the prettiest eyelashes.' That's just about the only compliment on my looks I ever got."

He kissed my fingers. "You have beautiful fingernails, too."

"Maybe I should just be an eyelash and fingernail model when I'm not working as a double-size stand-in for Drew Barrymore." I had to laugh at myself.

"You are fucking beautiful and I don't want to hear another word different. Now say what I say."

"Oh God."

"Do it…I am the hottest thing ever."

"Well, I can say that pretty easy. I am the hottest thing *ever*."

"And I love Barry Winchell."

"I love Barry Winchell." He laughed and crushed me into his chest. "Yeah, I knew it."

"'My beloved spake, and said unto me, Rise up, my love, my fair one, and come away. For, lo, the winter is past, the rain is over and gone.'"

"What's that?"

"It's from the Bible."

"You never know what you'll find in there." He held me tighter.

"'I do. But it doesn't change anything. I'm so…"

"Ah, what did I say?"

"Ok, then. I'm so lucky. I'm the luckiest ever."

"That's more like it." And I was. I couldn't have been more lucky.

21

Pageant

I hated the last minutes of a pageant, waiting in front as I had eleven times before with the stiff hand of the other girl held firmly in mine. This time her name was Epiphany, one of the up-and-comers of the black girl old school. For talent she had performed a solo dance routine to "Keep Pushin On," risky but well done. She and I alone waited for the crown after the runners-up were relegated to 'clap sister' status with a burdensome cluster of cheap flowers and sent to the back. Their only function now was to clap for whoever won. Girls who left a pageant without a prize 'rode the booger bus' home, and these ticket-holders impatiently awaited boarding and departure from an exhausting night. My eyes were unfocused, pupils constricted to pinpoints in the electric white spotlight, never really seeing the crowd before us clearly in a smoky black mass of silhouettes at my feet.

"Good luck." I whispered. Epiphany squeezed my hand and I felt her thick acrylic nails bite into my flesh. I knew she would endure the painful process of prying them off after the pageant, alone somewhere in a barely afforded apartment. I felt bad for the queens who had to go back to being boys in the daytime. Bianca was going on and on about something, drawing out the suspense as any good emcee would, but all I could think was, 'Good lord, shut up and get on with it.'

We waited for the announcement of first runner up, which would by default reveal the winner. Being first runner up was never rewarding, the announcement instantly overshadowed by the crowds realization that that girl next to her was the winner. She would be shunted aside as quickly as possible, tossed a little money to help compensate for the numerous expenses involved in competing, and forgotten. She was left with piles of unopened 'just-in-case' panty hose to pack away, half empty boxes of fingernails clicking as they went into her bag. Her dresser would say she was robbed and demand to see the score sheets, snatching down racks of clothing and hustling wigs into bags, displaying for her the anger and disappointment she could not let anyone see, lest she appear unprofessional. I always tried not to expect to win, never letting my hopes get high enough to cause a visible ripple if they crashed down. It had become clear to me that the nervous smile which surfaced whenever I was uncomfortable was more a baring of teeth than a placation, a feral involuntary response to threat and danger cultivated into politeness by Southern convention. I once read an anthropological theory that laughter was a derivation of barking, a noise to frighten away an attacker, a response to the unexpected. I saw this in the nervous laugh and smile that suffixed every joke at my expense, every cruel comment directed at me over the years. But after seven consecutive times as a first runner-up in pageants of varying importance, from a tiny affair held in the sleaziest bar in Nashville to state-level competitions, I had begun to tap into self-confidence, and I had begun to win. I had stood in front like this with some other girl three times in succession in the past two years, and each of those times I was crowned. This night was to be no different, except for the moment my life was changed forever.

Chyna's apartment the night before was full of people and music, preparing me for the pageant. Erica had produced some of her hoarded rhinestones and was hot-gluing rows of fiery pink ones along the seams of my talent gown. Chyna sat on the couch that had slept a thousand homeless queens and tended a row of wig heads, each bearing a different category's coiffure. Mismatched sets of thrift-store hot rollers were plugged in a daisy chain of extension cords at her feet, browned from years of use and stubborn Aquanet baked into every crevasse. Ebullient gospel music blasted from the stereo, declaring subservience to the all-encompassing love of Jesus Christ.

"Bitch, do you have everything you need?" Chyna's words were spoken like a stab in the kidney, but she somehow still sounded loving.

"I gotta get that outfit Austria's lending me and I'll have everything. She's lettin me borrow her red cape for presentation, and those red thigh-high boots."

"Can you walk in 'em?" Erica never looked up from her stoning.

"As good as you can!"

"Clumsy bitches." Chyna spoke aloud to herself and returned to breaking up the shiny barrel curls of my evening gown hair with an exaggerated primness. She then looked up to meet our unblinking stares with all the surprise of an 80's soap-opera villainess overheard at a cocktail party. "Oh, I'm sorry. Did you hear that? Ha HA!" That horrible, wonderful shrieking laugh.

In preparation for a pageant, a girl must have three basic things: a presentation, a talent and an evening gown. Some variants involve swimsuits or sportswear, different spreads of points for the categories, but those three things will get most girls through any system. I focused on the Entertainer of the Year, or EOY, system, which awarded the most points to the talent category and required that eveningwear be creative, as opposed to the basic beads-and-rhinestones theme. Never feeling particularly beautiful, I decided that a system rewarding talent and creativity was my best bet and concentrated on building a reputation amongst its community of judges, admirers, contestants and past winners.

My ability to play the violin was fairly unique in our wasteland of Whitney and Britney, sure to bring extra points in an EOY competition, so I centered my reputation on this skill. In the world of drag, the center of which was pop, dance and R&B music, I hadn't at first seen a place for my homegrown talent. My fiddle had been a friend since childhood, and I found it opened doors for me, started conversations I did not have the courage to initiate, and gave me the feeling that I was special in some way. That I possessed a talent others envied.

My first pageant successes came from playing my family's traditional bluegrass folk style, dressed in a red and white checked gingham square dancing dress. At the end of the live fiddling, I clogged to a dance mix of 'Cotton-Eyed Joe.' The vibrant, organic sound of live music spilling from the club speakers caused heads to snap around to the stage. When I handed off my gleaming instrument and the first strains of the newly popular dance song began, people stirred from their stunned paralysis and began to cheer. The crowd screamed and I clogged with all my heart, feeling the first flush of excitement expand in my chest. Then the stage went dark except for black light and strobe. My white crinolines glowed, expanding and contracting like a blue jellyfish, seeming to float in the light. I would hear for years afterward how people had never seen anything so bizarre in their lives, and the image proved an indelible one. From pigtails and gingham, clogging and playing the fiddle I managed to build the beginnings of a reputation.

For talent in this year's Tennessee EOY I planned to lip-synch Sinead O'Connor's ethereal recording of "Don't Cry for Me, Argentina," playing my violin as expressively and sweetly as possible over the instrumental portions that came throughout the song. This would be what was known as a "clean" talent: simple, elegant and with little room for mistakes.

My style had become smoother, more sophisticated, but still included as much mockery of convention as I could slip in. I sought a reminiscence of dark fairy tales and Disney witches gone glamorous. I was finally becoming incarnate the dark angel I had visualized inside for so many years.

"Why *dark angel?*" some talent night girl had asked once, when I shared this image in an unguarded moment. I could not explain to her what it was to fall from out of the fold to which I had once belonged, into this new role. To nonetheless claim some cutting shards of the broken belief in God, salvaged because I knew them to be true among the many lies. That person had a face, and a body, shaped in strength and perseverance. My face. My body. To my silence she said, "Is that why you always wear that cross?"

"This cross is a scar. I'll always wear it."

She backed away and left. I looked up from the mirror, done with applying mascara, and blessed the empty room.

At noon on the Sunday of the pageant, contestants began arriving, some from far outside Nashville and a few locals everyone knew. Some girls had an entourage consisting of sponsors and dancers and some kind of manager. Being creatures of the night, we all looked disheveled and grumpy, McDonald's coffee and bottled water was scattered on the round bar tables in the theater. I had worked in that very room every week for many years, but in the daylight it seemed unfamiliar, bleached out and skeletal, cracks and scuffs newly visible in a harsh mix of fluorescent light and sun filtered through the vents in the ceiling. We girls were similarly unflattered by the sun and time of day. Weave tracks showed through hair pulled back in messy ponytails. Exotic bodies were concealed in loose t-shirts and sweat pants. We knew that tonight our appearances would count for everything, so energy was not wasted on the morning. When the pageant owner arrived, we gathered around to receive instructions, turn in last-minute applications and fees, and finally to draw numbers for contestant order. "One" was the dreaded position for superstitious and practical reasons, and any girl arriving late for the meeting (there was always one) was immediately assigned this number, moving everyone back a space. Each draw from a turned up ball-cap was met with expressions of relief or comic dismay. Laughter and camaraderie prevailed among the relaxed group, lower numbers met with ahh's and oh's from supporters or joking detractors of the girls. There was immediate bargaining among the holders for preferred positioning. I pushed in to take my turn, and when I pulled a folded bit of torn-off notebook paper from the hat, I opened it to reveal lucky number seven. A good sign, I thought. Aside from its usual magical properties, seven guaranteed that I would have plenty of time to get ready for each category and relax, unlike the hapless number one, who would rush through the entire night. I ran across the stage and upstairs, two at a time as always, to lay out supplies in my dressing room and prepare for the evening. The out-of-town girls gathered in our guest room downstairs off the side of the stage, their crew stringing racks of clothing along pipes hung from exposed rafters. Each girl claimed her area at the long mirrored table along the wall by laying out an ancient towel stained with countless nights of base and powder, lipstick and glitter, patterns of stage makeup as individual as fingerprints. Most everyone bought their makeup mirrors at thrift stores, rotating ovals, rectangles and circles glowing with dusty fluorescence in this circumstance their owners of a previous era could never have predicted. Suitcases were unzipped to reveal glorious scintillations from heavily beaded silk gowns, light flashing from mirrored costumes and slick patent leather. Racks of foam heads crowned with wigs of every conceivable style and color were balanced on chairs, piles of shoes beneath. Drag slaves, as they were lovingly called, scurried everywhere polishing oversized rhinestone jewelry, sorting through cases of music. And the backstage manager, who had not yet given up or gotten too drunk, provided direction and gossip to anyone paying attention.

Upstairs, I had the unchallenged benefit of being an employee of the club with my own dressing room. The bar was rented that night by whoever owned the pageant, but its employees were still allowed to use their resources, and I was grateful for the relative sanctuary. Special guest entertainers were booked to fill time between contestant changes and categories, usually former winners and whoever was locally popular at the moment. These girls got ready upstairs, cast members opening their rooms to share space and enjoy socializing with old friends. The ubiquitous dressers and drag slaves ran in and out, fetching cocktails and delivering messages with a look of urgent purpose that contrasted with the easy, festive demeanor of their respective divas. The narrow scuffed halls rang with laughter and gleefully gossipy outbursts of 'Girl,

NO! and 'Bitch!' from rows of dressing room doors propped open spilling loud music and suitcases of drag. With close to eight hours until the start of the pageant, I put on a CD of Bluegrass gospel and began to clean my room, hanging gowns, capes, suits and unclassifiable costumes on the bar of clothing that filled one entire wall. On the opposite side I piled thigh-high boots in red, white, black, lavender and school bus yellow beneath a wall of spiky heels in leather and silk. I straightened leaning stacks of CD's and hung my seventeen wigs back on their nails beside the shoes. A table ran the length of the center wall, various large mismatched looking-glasses pushed back to allow room for my own yellowing plastic makeup mirror and array of cosmetics. Creamy foundation in "fair." Two Tupperware bowls resting on top of their airtight lids filled with fragrant Coty air spun powder in shades designed to high- and low-light my face. Ragged brushes in need of washing. Circular disks of pigment were grouped by use: sienna for contour, rose for blush, subtle pink and Egyptian gold for eyes. Large black eyelashes to be attached with rubbery weave glue waited next to pots of glitter, eyeliners in black, gold and white, mascara standing next to a palette of lipsticks dark red and blackish purple. Pencils in brown and black filled with color soft as butter waited to outline lips and brows, and over everything a thin layer of settled powder. I was ready.

Barry and I had discussed his coming down for the pageant again earlier that day, in a phone call.

"Hello? Barry?"

"Hey Babe, what are you doin?"

I was in bed, as I always was until two or three P.M. "Just awakening from my coma." I looked at the clock and winced. "Oooh, I shoulda been up at noon, I've still gotta go throw some more money away on this pageant."

"You want me to come? I can help you backstage or something."

"Well, it's the Fourth of July...I thought you had a carnival and keg and all that up there?"

"Yeah, but I wanted you to come to the carnival with me..."

I wasn't anywhere near comfortable enough with my look to attend a carnival on base, but I couldn't admit that to him. Anyway, we had just spent four of his days off in a row together the previous week, part of the weird schedule they had him on, and honestly, after being together that entire time I kind of wanted the next two days solo. It wasn't that I didn't want to see him, but there was so much to do. And during the pageant my dressing room would be crazy. I didn't want him sitting around backstage through the interminable hours of stress, including my own. Surely he would have more fun at a carnival and keg party with his friends.

"Mmm, I *know*. But I have to do this pageant or my spon-sters will withdraw the other half of my prize money from Miss Nashville." *Spon-ster* was my combination of the words *sponsor* and *monster*. "Honey, just stay up there and do your friends thing. We'll see each other next week, and if I win I'll wear the crown for you. *Heh heh.*"

"Ok...yeah, I have to take care of Nasty tonight anyway. Duty."

"That's the dog?"

"Our mascot. I wish we didn't have that damn hour drive between us." He sounded so cute.

"I know. Trust me, if we didn't we'd be having French toast in about ten minutes. But hey, I better get up and get crackin on this stuff or I'll end up in bed all day."

"You sleep too damn much."

"Twenty-four seven if I could."

"Quit your drag-assin then and get up. I gotta go, somebody's yelling at me."

"Are you at work? That's my tax money you're wastin, slacker."

"Bye Sarah. I'll call you tonight, see how you did."

"Ok. Wish me luck...Bye, Barry"

"I love you."

"I love you too."

Bianca strained to read the handwritten sheet with the pageant's outcome in the shifting vagaries of light on stage. Everyone was waiting. The girl next to me dropped my hand to smooth her gown and then reached for it again. Bianca found what she was looking for and moved the hand with the microphone and list up to her mouth. The other hand simultaneously held a cigarette and cocktail. Her trademark voice poured like gravel from the sound system, eliciting a chorus of imitators bleating "*Heyyy!*"

"*Heyyyyy* yourself, motherfuckers." There was a smile in her voice, an innocence in the raspy laugh she made as she took a quick sip from her cocktail. That little laugh had traveled intact over a long course of years and experiences. She tipped the plastic cup towards the audience and took another sip, a drag from her cigarette, and then smacked her lips with a wet sounding *Ahhh!* Aside from her voice, and obvious talent, she was famous for a close attachment to the physical vices.

"Do y'all want to know which one of these bitches won?" There was the expected uproar. I was excited to note that more voices were yelling my name than the other girl's. "Well..." Bianca looked at the page again. "Hey, have I told y'all about the time me and Stephanie Wells drove up to Fort Campbell?"

"Yeah, yeah," someone yelled out. "If Rita Ross had been with you, you could'a saved the Lincoln Continental!" The crowd was frenzied for results. Chaos boiled at her feet. Bianca laughed over the noise.

"Ok, Ok. The winner is...y'all give me a drum-roll..." Everyone banged on their tables.

It was killing me. *"SHUT UP AND SAY IT, WHORE! GET THIS OVER WITH!"* I thought.

"*...Contestant number seven, Calpernia Addams!*"

When my name was announced the first time I won a pageant, I jumped up and down and screamed like a game show contestant. That's what it was to me then, and the prize had been validation. With that first crown, I had physical claim to a bit of pride and the status of a professional showgirl. Now winning was more of a relief than anything. The money spent competing was ridiculous. I couldn't afford to lose it. And losing is more and more embarrassing the more established and 'famous' one becomes. So when I accepted the roses and knelt down to have the massive thirteen-inch rhinestone crown pinned to my head, my mood was light. I smiled and was excited and grateful, but mostly I was just relieved. Chelsey put on music for my crowning walk down the runway. Usually winners got Whitney Houston, but she knew me better. It was an ethereal, urgent performance of "Ave Maria" by Sinead O'Connor, from my talent cd. When I listened to it at home it was so beautiful it made me feel light, entranced, as if I were flying. They finished pinning and I stood. I walked. I floated down the runway. It felt nice to win, after such a long fight to even be there at all.

Sixty miles to the northwest, Barry lay sleeping on an Army cot beside the barracks mascot, a dog named Nasty. The keg party was over and they were both exhausted. The cot was on the landing outside his room because it was Barry's duty to watch the dog, but his room-mate Justin did not want the animal inside. As Barry slept and Nasty watched, a Private named Calvin Glover moved past him and into the room. There was talk, and then Justin gave him a baseball bat. The door was opened again. At about the same time a glittering crown was lowered onto my head, Calvin swung the bat at Barry's sleeping face, again and again, until the man I knew was no more.

When it was done, all I wanted was go home and wash my face. Stage makeup is so heavy. I posed for a few pictures. Took off the ridiculously huge crown. I signed some papers. Took a stack of twenties and counted them to make sure the full five hundred was there. This was solitary work, people's attentions directed elsewhere once the pageant was over. At the announcement of winner, there is a polite congratulation, and then everyone scatters to dissect whatever result through the prism of their own involvements. I changed from the heavy beaded gown into jeans and my Reese's Peanut Butter Cup t-shirt, skipping a bra. Alone in my dressing room I looked at the crown, tracing its fiery lines of rhinestones. It really was beautiful. And this time I had won a scepter, too. My first. I was more proud of these things than I had realized. I decided to take the crown home with me and sleep with it beside my bed, so that I could see it twinkle in the semi-dark. I wanted to show it to Barry tomorrow. I knew he would get a kick out of it.

Outside the night was humid and warm. Tennessee summers seemed to get hotter every year. I hefted my huge bag into the cab of my truck and then carefully nestled the crown into the paper trash in my floorboard. I laid the scepter beside me on the seat, so that I could play with it as I drove. It was tipped with a bright star of crystals and reminded me of a magic wand.

The Link was situated amongst factories and warehouses down by the Cumberland River. The area itself was safe, if a bit industrial looking, but the interstate home could only be reached through the edge of the projects. Here there were haggard streetwalkers and bums minding their outposts on poorly lit streets. Corpses of Happy Meals flapped in the wake of trucks entering and leaving the highway. As I prepared to merge onto the ramp towards home, I felt a lurch and looked with dismay at my gas-gauge fallen well below empty. I let out a frustrated moan, knowing my truck well enough to realize that I had about five blocks of mobility left. Why did I always *do* stuff like this? I made an instant decision to continue into the seedy neighborhood towards a gas station I remembered and passed under the interstate. Run-down homes and midnight wanderers passed by my anxious gaze, but I could see the gas station in the distance. It looked dark, and I remembered it was the Fourth of July. Perhaps there would be another one down a little further...

By now I didn't have enough gas to even consider going back to the club. My engine began to stutter and I was only able to continue forward by riding the clutch and barely pressing on the gas. I passed two more closed stations and just managed to coast my Chevy into a brightly lit Krystal's parking lot with the last wisps of fuel in my tank. It felt as if I had come to a stop on a darkened movie set, soundless and empty. Outside the restaurant's stark halogen lights, the neighborhood looked to be assembled entirely from shadows. An understanding of my situation coalesced like the gently materializing fog on my windows. My face was painted with exaggerated stage makeup sure to appear shocking to anyone I might ask for help. Sure to draw attention from people when I needed to go unnoticed in this place. Half an hour ago I had been the center of attention in a room of five hundred people. Now I was alone in what passed for Nashville's ghetto. In my pocket was a fat roll of twenty-dollar bills and beside me lay a piece of jewelry bigger than my head. The makeup was industrial, designed to withstand sweat and hours of exertion, so there was no way to get it off without making a smudged mess. The money could be hidden, and I slipped it under my seat. I covered over the crown and scepter with fast-food sacks and newspapers. Then I steeled myself for whatever might come and exited the safety of the cab. There was a phone booth a block away, and I walked with a tired expression that I hoped said, "I really don't wanna be bothered with kickin your ass." As if I could have. There was no one else on the street.

I reached the phone booth without incident and called the club, feeling foolish as I described my situation. I secured a promise of rescue as soon as the registers were counted down.

I passed another forty-five minutes in the truck, listening to 98.7 and being wryly amused at myself. The Krystal's was closed, so I couldn't even order a soggy little square burger. There was no one on the street and I relaxed enough to push aside the paper and look at my crown again. *Yay, I won!* I thought, in a gently self-mocking voice. I think I was embarrassed to allow myself the pleasure, but I grew more and more excited as I thought about the title. The money. *That was pretty nifty.*

I was rescued from these thoughts by the arrival of my manager with a can of gas. We laughed a little at how stupid I was, but we were both terribly tired and little was said. He made sure my truck would start and drove away into the dark. Home, I thought. I must get home.

The first step back towards myself was a long, hot shower. Being Calpernia fed some thing inside me, starved for so many years that it would never be completely full, but the exhaustion that followed could not be denied. The house was empty, quiet, and I let the water lay down my gel-stiffened curls and play over my face. I always peeked into the swing-out medicine cabinet mirror beside the shower after that, to see the immaculately painted face beaded with water. The only thing that ran was my mascara, in messy black rivulets down my cheeks. I imagined I looked like Ophelia, all wet and crying dark tears. I smiled into the mirror and leaned back into the shower. A handful of baby oil and my filthy drag-rag was all it took to scrub away the face, and then I washed my hair twice to get rid of the crunchiness. Then the body, then I brushed my teeth. The same ritual, same order, every night for years and years. I found myself wishing Barry was here, waiting for me in bed. My own fault, I thought. He had asked.

I dried off and went into my room, where the muted television was playing a rebroadcast of the ten-o'clock news. The remote was not in its usual place beside my bed and I spent an annoyed minute looking for it. I would rather look for the remote than walk over and turn the channel manually, and I finally gave up and just put on some panties so I could walk around the house. One never knew if a window shade might be open a crack or someone might knock at the door. "I suppose to some people, being caught in their panties would be devastating too, though…" I said aloud to no one in particular. The crown glittered on my bed. "I'm a winner." I laughed at myself.

In the kitchen I took one from a stack of 99-cent Kroger pizzas in the freezer and crammed it into my toaster oven. It didn't quite fit while frozen and was tilted up where one edge stuck out the mostly closed door, but as it softened in the heat the door curled it back into itself. A sweating phalanx of Dr Pepper cans filled the lower half of the refrigerator, and I relocated one to the freezer to chill further.

I hated the telephone and used it as seldom as possible. Because of this, I simply hit redial and the only number I had been calling recently began to ring. Barry had his phone turned on just for me, I thought. Just for me. It rang and rang and there was no answer. "Hey Barry, guess what? I won!" I said into the rings. Ha ha. I hung up.

With everything balanced on a tray, I went to my room and settled in. The cheap pizza smelled so good. I sat on the bed and the buried remote clicked on the volume.

"...Fort Campbell soldier dead..." Something reaching from far away crossed miles of gray nothing and hooked into delicate internal organs I hadn't known were there. It tugged, on the edge of tearing something out. I was afraid to move. I dug out the control and turned the TV all the way up. It couldn't be. A tingling numbness was beginning in my heart and stomach, around the hooks. No way. My brain had cleared, and its empty page buzzed to be filled with information. Barry is going to call me. I'm going to call him, right now. He's there waiting for me, and always will be there. Don't be stupid. This can't happen to us. Can't. The woman continued speaking in her flat, informative voice, and a photo of Barry Winchell appeared over her left shoulder. There was a dropping of pressure around my head, as if I had been rocketed to a great height, and then in one ripping withdrawal my entire insides were torn from me and carried away beyond the horizon, into the lightning and fire that had always lived there. Much much later I would remember the words I could not hear at that moment, from inside the storm. "This was never meant to be yours and never will be. Stupid. Never was. Never will be." I fell from the bed. Some sounds must have bled from the cracks in my skin, some moaning and tears. I can't remember very well. Those hours are lost to me.

I lived the next week on my best friend Oscar's couch. Other friends came and went, the best ones somehow knowing without my having to tell anyone. I wanted nothing but sleep and could not bear to be touched. When I could move, it was to make phone calls, to the base and the hospital looking for information. I knew from working at a hospital myself that they could tell me nothing over the phone. Family members only. A memorial service was to be held on base. I did not dare go. Calls began to come from work, the relaying of messages from the first wave of media seeking me out. My only real source for discovering what had happened was the television news, and I watched every broadcast for details. The phone kept ringing. I slept. Alone. Why hadn't I called him? Why hadn't I brought him down?

22

The Trial

The heat was so thick that summer. It fell onto me like molasses or tar and broke down whatever makeup I tried to wear into its powerless components of grease and pigment. I hadn't realized the inadequacy of my wardrobe until I tried to dress for court. I was expecting my ride in less than an hour and scrabbled through the clothes on my floor with trembling hands. Nothing was right. Low rise jeans, little T-shirts that said things like 'Meow' and 'Reese's Peanut Butter Cups—Two Great Tastes that Taste Great Together!" right across the breasts. I had to look right, so that they could understand. I wanted them to see me and know why Barry had liked me. I was going to see the people who had killed him. I had to see their faces, hear what they had to say for themselves.

'*That's* what he got killed for? Now that's a prime grade-A example of a faggot there.'

Don't look at me. I know. I already know what you're thinking. A crazy thought, Carrie's mother, popped into my head: "They're all gonna laugh at you. They're all gonna laugh at you." A laugh pushed up past the tension like a bubble surfacing in slime. I hated myself.

I finally settled on a navy suit with white piping that one of my talent-night girls had given me. It was a size too small and decades out of fashion, but I jammed it on anyway. I pulled on a pair of sheer stockings (was I supposed to wear these in the summer? I didn't know...) and dropped to my knees in front of the closet to dig for shoes. I quickly realized I had only stilettos from work and tennis shoes. Everyone was going to be looking at me. Alone. What Barry and I had was private, they had no right to stare and pry and ask and judge, but they would. 'It's not…' But I couldn't even allow myself to use the word 'fair.' The concept was a joke. A huge balloon of emotion began to expand inside me, humming as if filled with bees, and I knew I could not let it explode, or whatever was inside would destroy me. I leaned forward, knuckles white around some fabric at hand, and I could feel my face clench in silent rictus. A hot, damp exhalation escaped against the cigarette-scented jeans beneath my face and I realized I was lying down in the pile of clothing. My open eyes rimmed with moisture but no tear gathered and ran. "You're gonna make this suit look worse than it already does." I said aloud. My voice wavered. "Get up and get ready, you stupid idiot."

In the bathroom I rinsed my face with cold water and retrieved a boutique's worth of cosmetics. My hands trembled slightly and a sticky film of sweat reappeared at my lip and hairline. I desperately wanted to get in the shower and scrub myself, but there was no time. I began dabbing on concealer, my face getting closer and closer to the mirror as I looked for any flaw that might be covered, until my nose bumped the cold glass. I jerked back in frustration. "Stupid!" The sweat was diluting the makeup and blotting only left a mottled, ineffective patch of color. "You look like a man. Everybody's gonna throw up when they see you. A man in a dress. A stupid freak." I was talking out loud, whispering, hissing the words. I stared into the mirror, hypnotized, moving more and more slowly till my whole body tingled, bloodless. "Dammit." I shook it off and got my fan from the bedroom to set it up beside the bathroom mirror. The light breeze it provided seemed to help. I would remain in control. Precious seconds melted away in the heat.

I finished with powder and mascara, then struggled with whether or not to wear lipstick. Finally I settled for plain old Cherry Chapstick. 'You're worried about your stupid face and he's layin there dead.' I raked my hair back into a chignon, secured it with chopsticks and resolutely took out the lowest heels I had in my closet, which were unfortunately clear Lucite open-toes. It was either that or four inch black pumps. They looked impossibly frivolous to me then. Humiliating. As I slipped them on, over my hose, I closed my eyes and whispered, "Dammit dammit dammit. Fuck." I packed the makeup into my purse and a washrag for sweating, and when I was done I went back towards the bathroom.

I paused at the door. I wanted to look in the mirror again. 'You look like a man. You may as well know it for sure than go around stupid.'

'No, I look as good as I can, and there's no use starin at myself and makin it worse.' But still I wanted to go. All my armaments were ready for hating what I would see and only needed to sight the target. I almost started forward again and put out a hand to catch the doorway. The need was a physical force, invisible as magnetism but completely real. I laughed a little at myself, feeling crazy. "I am not gonna do it. I'm not."

I went into the kitchen and poured a glass of water, of which I had exactly one sip before the honking of my ride called me out into the blinding sunlight.

The trial was held in prefabricated structures like school portables or trailers, easily lost among hundreds of other similar buildings if not for the reporters and their attendant crews in satellite vans and rental cars. Many of these were faces I had watched for years covering local trage-dies and scandals, now incarnate outside the glowing screen and look-ing at me. Everyone had an attitude of routine seriousness. The military personnel all in green camouflage, the newspeople and gay groups in suits. A serious Army spokeswoman named Pamela wore a different kind of detachable bun every day, which I dispassionately noted and catalogued without mention to anyone.

I watched the trial on a large projection screen with the media and activist groups in a building across the street from the one serving as courtroom. Correspondents were seated at a horseshoe table directly in front, and I watched uncomfortably among other people in rows of chairs behind them. It felt like church somehow, with the pews and formality and horror. The military personnel must have been well schooled on dealing with my presence, because not one person in uniform looked at me or spoke to me directly during the entire trial. I was a ghost.

"Do you know which person is Calpernia Addams?" It was the first day of the trial and a woman I recognized from the local news stood beside me. She held a donut wrapped in a napkin and a cup of coffee.

"Yes...That's me." So here it starts, I thought. I told her our story, part there, part outside in front of a camera. We waited for the trial to begin, for the screen to light up and show me faces, friendly and deadly and impartial as every person involved took his turn in the chair. I sat in my chair cold as stone and learned of things I had not known. Barry had never told me. I had never asked. Weeks of harassment and cruelty, mocking and hateful words Barry had endured every day when he left my soft rooms of light and air to return here to his death. Face after face filled the screen, uncomfortable, sad, guilty, telling of particular taunts they had overheard, moments of humiliation. 'But he was your top gun,' I said to myself. 'He was your brother. Why didn't you stop this? Why?' Day after day passed, and at the end of each one I learned another way to hate myself for sleeping through the ringing of my phone, forever letting him go.

Cardboard trays of fat yellow donuts and government issued coffee became my sole diet, something to fill my sick stomach. I watched the screen, unrolling digest of a stolen life, desperate for details, details of his daily life and last day alive. I wanted to see Fisher. Glover. I had to hear them speak. I wanted to know why, and how, and how could they. When they finally came, it explained nothing, and I only wanted to leave.

In between sessions I went outside, walking up and down the lot in the mesmerizing pneumatic drone of industrial air-conditioners. People left me alone, in my suits and heels and patched up face. I didn't care anymore. This very white sky, hot and centered by the burning yellow sun, had been his sky. He had walked or driven these very roads, maybe thinking of me and counting the hours until he could leave and come back to my pale arms, my soft kisses. They had called him "faggot," and other names almost too stupid to be offensive to my mind, with its hard-won catalogue of endured insults. I wished I had known. I could have helped him, defended him. I played in my mind again and again a fantasy: my hand catching the bat, as light as foam against my fingers, and plucking it from the boy who would be a killer. 'Wake up, Barry. Wake up. Let's go.' I would have taken him from there. I had wished I were dead so often anyway, I would have taken the blow if I could have. Easy to think, impossible to know, but I imagined it. The force against my flesh, the wood striking and taking away life. If I could lay down there in his place, I believe I still would. It was my fault it ever happened anyway, I told myself, and the tears came finally. It's all my fault.

"Calpernia?" It was a reporter. "Have you been watching all this? What do you think? Could I get a statement from you?"

"It's…horrible. Too horrible. I can't right now, I'm sorry. I'll be back." I turned and walked away, into the heat and the sun. No one could follow me now. It seemed easier to cry in the light.

23

Epilogue

It's the Fourth of July, 2001, and I'm in my old Chevy truck on the way to Clarksville, Tennessee. Earlier in the day I was sweating under its hood to replace a worn-out alternator, the fairly simple task interrupted by offers of help in the parking lot of Nashville's Mexican Auto-Zone. Now, at 10:15pm, I pray that nothing else will go wrong with the put-upon engine as I prepare to cross forty-odd miles of nothing from city to city.

Deciding to go back was an impulse. I spent the day mostly alone, eating, walking, wordless. The Tennessee humidity was like a hot, damp cloth pressed against my face, and looking any kind of decent was just about impossible. I usually kicked around town in jeans and some little top, purple tennis shoes and my hair a medusa-like mass of curls. After an hour of scraping sweat-glued bangs from my eyes, I decided I had to get into some air-conditioning more effective than the diffuse whisper leaking out of my truck's open dash. I passed a theater in my wandering and spun the steering wheel a hard right into its shimmering asphalt lot. Perfect.

"Two?" he asked, after I requested a seat. The ticket sellers always seem surprised I'm alone. I guess most girls don't go by themselves. I wasn't there to be with anyone, though. In the darkness of a theater the throbbing tentacles of worry could detach and slip away into blackness for a little while. There was only the bright image of another world filling my vision.

I felt drugged after the movie. I'd hardly spoken to anyone all day, and the passage of hours made words harder to grasp, like melting ice-cubes slipping from my fingers. In two years the experience of Barry's murder had coalesced into a heavy stone, a stack of memories preserved in the acrid atmosphere of a just-missed gunshot or strike of lightning. But on the Fourth of July I call up the ghosts of possibility and guilt, wonder what might have been. I try to look across from this line of events to alternate realities, where the lives have not been entangled and then broken by clumsy hands unable to figure the knots. Driving the emptying streets, I had no plan but to listen to the familiar thoughts play themselves out. Then a voice from the radio announced a carnival to be held tonight, in Clarksville. On base. To celebrate the Fourth of July.

The sky is already darkening with an infusion of night and stars. I pull into a gas station and walk back out with containers of oil and gasoline additives and a candy bar. An indeterminate perimeter of scrubby grass and weeds reaches out from the backdrop of woods towards the station's lot, advance scouts already penetrating cracks throughout the blacktop. As I pop my hood, a thick clerk pushes open the door to ask if I need any help. I can't fault Southern manners, so I only smile and say no thanks. A moment's work and my poor engine is as lubricated and optimized as ten dollars of chemical science can make it. I wipe my hands on the dark denim of my jeans, swipe at my rebellious hair, and I am on the road.

The drive from Nashville to Clarksville is not a terribly long one, in physical miles. Close to forty of them, a passage that cuts through limestone hills like a cross-section through layer cake fossilized and iced with verdant deciduous forest. In Tennessee every horizon is shaped by the roll of a hill covered in trees, something I appreciated more after traveling flatter and more urban landscapes. I can see the occasional light of a house or yes, even trailer, out in the woods. Otherwise it is a storybook scene of green and mist and ever deepening sky. Silent fireworks appear at random intervals, launched from some humble country porch to coruscate and twinkle a moment before spent dust and sticks fall invisibly back to earth. Any sound is lost in the rumble of my truck, hypnotic drone for the miles to unroll in with changeless regularity.

Alone, I give myself dispensation for self-pity. With no one to see, I conjure scenarios and ideas marked as off-limits for public viewing. The tears come. Not only for what could have been with Barry, but also for other new sorrows laid up in waiting for these moments of release. I suppress my cynical ego just long enough to ask, "Will I ever be loved?" It is a gentle cry, easily hidden if some observer should enter the scene. What if I had called? What if they hadn't known my secret? What flaw in me allowed this possibility to solidify into a burning moment of anger and death? Selfish of me, to take the blame, but that is the luxury of private thought.

As I come nearer to my exit, the lights on either side of the interstate are brighter. From here it all looks like a waterlogged Polaroid, colors bleeding out into gray from blurred outlines. Small-town pit stops sprawl, nothing taller than a story or two, everything seeming long resigned to a modest existence. When the off-ramp finally comes, I feel unexpectedly cavalier about the possible dangers this town holds for me. I slide into the first gas station, a huge truck-stop combination, and pop out of my truck with a flourish of hair and arching back. In a way I almost wish someone *would* figure me out, that the sheer stunning insolence of my existence would punch a button marked "destroy" deep inside them and I'd be done in with a flare of quick liberating violence. But these thoughts are without substance, and besides, my walk across the immense lot to the cashier is unremarkable to anyone. When I catch a glance from a cute boy pumping gas, I know I'm glad to be alive. There is so much more to see. Dying can be had any day.

I remember the route to the base because I drove it so many times to the improvised courthouse during the trial. I had dropped Barry off once a long time ago, at some obscure back entrance, but the main gate had been a new experience. Now past eleven at night, the landmarks are cast in reflected neon from dark-hour haunts. Streetlamps divide the lots into dissipating circles of electric white while other buildings hide invisibly in their absence. I follow the signs to Fort Campbell Army Base, past the lamprey pawn-stores and loan-shark shacks that always ride alongside military bases. Gate Four is stark in its halogen glare, venous flow of red taillights queuing in and white headlights streaming out. Tonight is the carnival, everyone is welcome, and the sentries give me a stiff-handed salute as I pass.

Fort Campbell is laid out in an intentionally bewildering manner. I heard somewhere that bases were designed to be difficult targets for invasion, so being a ways off the interstate and hard to navigate were protective measures, I suppose. I remember the summer when I rode in past media vehicles encrusted with antennae and satellite dishes, past the following eyes of anyone who understood what our Army escort meant. It was so hot that summer; I will always remember that feeling. My face was melting, cracking off in front of everyone's judging eyes. Tonight I hardly need any makeup, and the air has cooled to a tolerable degree. I am free in the comfort of favorite jeans and cotton. During the trial a soldier had recognized me resting during lunch break and shouted a question across the walk as he held the paper with Barry's murder in his hands. "HEY! *You* wanna be in the papers?!" Then he and his friends were laughing. No one is looking at me tonight. Maybe now, two years later, he is at home asleep next to his wife, his girlfriend…his boyfriend, for all I know. I begin to doubt there is any kind of carnival left at this late hour, but I follow the signs around the dark base and finally come to what I am looking for.

There is always a sense of majesty in the sight of a Ferris wheel. It is simply a matter of size. However complex a video game, or however exciting a movie, they cannot loom so bright and graceful in the vegetable-scented air of a limitless country night. Spotty lines of leftover cars sprawl out in patterns like a partially filled-in crossword, and families roam among them looking for their own. I park immediately, despite the sure availability of spaces closer, because I know I will need the walk to calm increasing nervousness that buzzes just below my heart. A moment away is the luminous, simple carnival. Crowds of young people move through and around its attractions, none of them aware of who I am, what it means to me to be here on this night. My shoes whisper through the cool grass, voices come close and pass by. Music blares from a large open tent, rowdy and coarse, unsettling to me despite its happy intent. The last night Barry was alive he was supposed to go to this carnival. He went to bed instead.

"No charge for a pretty girl!" A heavy man with black mustache and beard looks disturbingly like my Dad. He offers a handful of darts from inside the little stall, slow, uninterested. "No charge, you pop five balloons I give you a big one." The stuffed animals, I assume. I remember them from childhood. Only available at fairs and carnivals, they were full of pinhead-sized Styrofoam granules that leaked from the clumsy seams after a few hours of play. I wearily hold out my hand for the darts, wondering at the same time when everything had become so cynical, so post-modern ironic. Neither of us wanted to be, at that particular second, in a rickety balloon-stall, but what the hell…I throw a dart, aware that I am young and shapely and probably attractive to this dirty, sweating man. My awareness shows in the way my arm moves, my back turned at the waist, the way I smile. I know I am doing it, don't even care what it means, and pop two of five balloons. "Three more tries for the big one, two dollars."

"No, no, just give me what I earned with those two."

"That's just a little one, you don't want that…"

"Hand it over." I smile, hand out, flirting for no reason by being demanding. He wants to argue, I can tell, but some animation in his face goes out and he digs a minuscule Chihuahua doll from a battered cardboard box-full. A knockoff of the Taco Bell dog, and just about a year late at that. "Thanks!" I walk away feeling accomplished. In a tragic, perverse way it means something to me that someone finds me attractive here, in the very place where my guy was murdered for doing the same thing. I know it is pathetic, but tonight's my night. I allow it.

After a few circles of the carnival and a corn-dog I am ready to go. I had been watching with melancholy desperation for signs that someone had figured me out, that I am something more exotic than they might have guessed at first glance. I wanted to walk away feeling I had passed completely, and the only way I could do so was if I detected no negative attention. Always realistic to the point of self-punishment, I was completely ready to be discovered and chased out like Frankenstein with torches and pitchforks. But nothing had happened, for whatever reason. I feel like I have stolen something rare, and thus follows the urge to flee. My earlier attitude had evaporated and now I am only bored and uncomfortable in a crowd of people I don't know. I begin to make my way towards the path leading back to the cars. As I leave, I pass a group of young soldiers, who yell for me to come over. I smile and continue walking, but one detaches and runs after me to nervously offer his phone number. "You don't wanna date me...I'm *poison*." I wink, trying to be mysterious, the worldly older woman to this nineteen-year-old boy. When he insists, I take him by the shoulders and place a maternal kiss on his cheek before gently turning him around and back towards his group with a little shove. How could he not *know?* I ask myself. On some level it still surprises me. I walk on with his buddies cheering at my back.

A bit further down another group calls out to me. As I get closer to my truck my desire to be inside it and leaving here grows more intense, and I do not even turn around. The voice comes again, mean this time. "We don't want your ho' ass anyway!" I keep my pace but break off the path, across the grass and back to my truck and safety. Never forget, I tell myself, you are always a stranger here, always carry a smoldering deadly secret. Never fully relax, never completely let go.

The ride back to Nashville is as quiet as the one coming. No one even knew that I'd left. No one to worry, to call or ask questions. I am tired with the thrill of danger departed, and unsure of what I am coming away with. I do know now that I could have gone there and not been hated. And if so, if I hadn't sparked the fire, then it wasn't my fault. I will try to believe this, I tell myself, starting the engine.

In spite of the hour, I still feel hot, and crank down the window to let in some of the night air that rushes by. It is steeped with the scent of damp woods, and cold at this great speed. Above is only stars. I sail up and down the rolling hills like dark waves in a whispering sea, completely alone. But I have my memories. And I know what it feels like to be loved.